PRAISE FOR
A YEAR WITH G. K. CHESTERTON

"*A Year with G. K. Chesterton* will be a treasure, both for those who are coming to his wit and wisdom as a fresh discovery and for those who have known and loved his work for years. I am among the latter but Kevin Belmonte's reading is so wide, his eye for a gem so acute, and his principles of selection so original, that I have been as much surprised by previously undiscovered treasures as I have been pleased with familiar friends.

Chesterton's talent for paradox and his ability to embody profound truth in simple images makes him as compelling now as he was a hundred years ago. Though Kevin Belmonte's selection is full of Chesterton's whimsy and humour, he has also brought out perhaps the most important side of GKC—that he was a prophet in his own time and a prophet for ours, speaking out against insidious evils and kindling us all again to a common love of the common good."

> — The Reverend Dr. Malcolm Guite, chaplain of Girton College, Cambridge University

"Kevin Belmonte writes in the preface to this excellent book that his editing of it has been a gift. As an author who has written regularly on Chesterton I can understand his sense of gratitude at having been able to spend so much time with a genius as genial as the great GKC. Thanks to Belmonte's labor of love we can all spend a few moments of every day of the year in Chesterton's inimitable company. All admirers of Chesterton and the Christian truth he explicates so sublimely will be grateful to Kevin Belmonte for this gem of a gift."

> — Joseph Pearce, author of *Wisdom and Innocence: A Life of G. K. Chesterton*

A YEAR WITH
G. K. CHESTERTON

365 Days of Wisdom, Wit, and Wonder

Kevin Belmonte, Editor

THOMAS NELSON
Since 1798

NASHVILLE   DALLAS   MEXICO CITY   RIO DE JANEIRO

Published in Nashville, Tennessee, by Thomas Nelson. Thomas Nelson is a registered trademark of Thomas Nelson, Inc.

Thomas Nelson, Inc., titles may be purchased in bulk for educational, business, fund-raising, or sales promotional use. For information, please e-mail SpecialMarkets@ThomasNelson.com.

Library of Congress Cataloging-in-Publication Data

Chesterton, G. K. (Gilbert Keith), 1874–1936.
    A year with G.K. Chesterton : 365 days of wisdom, wit, and wonder / Kevin Belmonte, editor.
      p. cm.
    Includes bibliographical references (p.).
    ISBN 978-1-59555-493-2
    1. Chesterton, G. K. (Gilbert Keith), 1874–1936—Quotations. 2. Christianity—Quotations, maxims, etc. I. Belmonte, Kevin Charles. II. Title.
PR4453.C4A6 2012
828'.91209—dc23
                                                2012019231

Printed in the United States of America

12 13 14 15 16 QG 6 5 4 3 2 1

To Joel Miller, for the privilege of traveling in Chesterton's company . . . and to the memory of Chuck Colson, a great friend to me, and my books. Requiescat in pace.

*[Chesterton] has a marvellous sense of transfiguration...
The whole visible universe is full of magic and mystery.
It burgeons into symbolic colours and shapes, and passes
like a pageant before him. There is hardly a living writer
who can so quicken our appreciation of the dignity and
fantasy underlying common things.*

—ERNEST WILLING

CONTENTS

PREFACE

I was brought back ... by the strong influence of two writers, the Presbyterian, George MacDonald, and the Roman Catholic, G. K. Chesterton.

—C. S. Lewis

The opportunity to craft a book called *A Year with G. K. Chesterton* has been a gift. It is as though one has been welcomed to an inn where a fire blazes in the hearth and a hearty meal awaits. Chesterton bids you enter—amid a host of guests already seated at the table.

And like Samuel Johnson, whom he much admired, it is not too much to say that Chesterton was a host unto himself. Scarcely anything worthy of comment seems to have escaped his notice, and his reflections on all manner of subjects—faith, literature, the visual arts, or philosophy—are as trenchant and moving as they are wise.

One wonders where he ever found the time to read as much, and retain as much, as he did. But then, both he and his questing intellect moved about his beloved London in a hansom cab. People walked to places in his day, and took their time over things in ways that reveal what we have lost in our constant rush to get to who-knows-where with ever-increasing speed. Chesterton reminds us that it is well worth consulting a map of the cosmos before a swift departure from the station.

I believe those who take up the daily readings in the collection that follows will be glad of the chance to keep company with so thoughtful a friend.

I know I have been.

The recurring themes of his writing are so many boon companions—travellers well met as we journey to the far country—the place where things we now see in twilight will become reality in the swift sunrise of God's making.

Kevin Belmonte
Woodholme
December 2011

JANUARY 1

Therefore, if anyone is in Christ, he is a new creation; old things have passed away; behold, all things have become new.
—2 CORINTHIANS 5:17 NKJV

The object of a New Year is not that we should have a new year. It is that we should have a new soul and a new nose; new feet, a new backbone, new ears, and new eyes. Unless a particular man made New Year resolutions, he would make no resolutions. Unless a man starts afresh about things, he will certainly do nothing effective. Unless a man starts on the strange assumption that he has never existed before, it is quite certain that he will never exist afterwards. Unless a man be born again, he shall by no means enter into the Kingdom of Heaven.

A PASSAGE FROM *THE LIVING AGE* MAGAZINE (1905)

Liberty is altogether a mystical thing. All attempts to justify it rationally have always failed. Ruskin tried to attack it by pointing out that the stars had it not and the universe had it not. So good a mystic ought to have known that it is just because man has it and the universe has it not, that man is called the Image of God and the universe merely His masterpiece.

ON THIS DAY

- In 1920, GKC and his wife, Frances, visited the Forum and Colosseum in Rome.

DURING THIS MONTH

- In 1887, twelve-year-old GKC graduated to St. Paul's day school.
- And in 1914, GKC's novel *The Flying Inn* was published.

JANUARY 2

> *For God so loved the world that He gave His only*
> *begotten Son, that whoever believes in Him should not*
> *perish but have everlasting life.*
>
> —JOHN 3:16 NKJV

Every one on this earth should believe, amid whatever madness or moral failure, that his life and temperament have some object on the earth. Every one on the earth should believe that he has something to give to the world which cannot otherwise be given. Every one should, for the good of men and the saving of his own soul, believe that it is possible, even if we are the enemies of the human race, to be the friends of God.

A PASSAGE FROM *THE LIVING AGE* MAGAZINE (1905)

This forgetfulness of what we have is the real Fall of Man and the Fall of All Things. The evil which infects the immense goodness of existence does not embody itself in the fact that men are weary of woes and oppressions. It embodies itself in the shameful fact that they are often weary of joys and weary of generosities. Poetry, the highest form of literature, has here its immortal function; it is engaged continually in a desperate and divine battle against things being taken for granted. A fierce sense of the value of things lies at the heart [of literature].

ON THIS DAY ————————————————————

- In 1932, GKC's article "How Gray Wrote 'The Elegy'" was published in the *Illustrated London News*.

JANUARY 3

*But now in Christ Jesus you who once were far off have
been brought near by the blood of Christ.*

—EPHESIANS 2:13 NKJV

Red is the most joyful and dreadful thing in the physical
universe; it is the fiercest note, it is the highest light, it is the
place where the walls of this world of ours wear thinnest and
something beyond burns through. It glows in the blood which
sustains and in the fire which destroys us, in the roses of our
romance and in the awful cup of our religion. It stands for all
passionate happiness, as in faith or in first love.

A PASSAGE FROM *THE LIVING AGE* MAGAZINE (1905)

*If a man were to say that science stands for barbarism and religion
for civilization, he would in these days be accused of a mere trick
of topsy-turveydom. Yet there is one sense, at least, in which this is
unquestionably true. The generalizations which science makes true
or false are of necessity limitations of human hope. The laws which
science deduces, fairly or unfairly, are necessarily, like all laws, a
restraint of liberty. The nearer a man is to an ordered and classi-
fied being, the nearer he is to an automaton. The nearer he is to an
automaton, the nearer he is to a beast. The lowest part of man is
that which he does in accordance with law, such as eating, drinking, growing a beard, or falling over a precipice. The highest part of
him is that which is most lawless: spiritual movements, passionate
attachment, art.*

- In 1920, GKC and his wife, Frances, set sail for the Holy Land.
- And in 1931, GKC's article "The Breakdown of the Materialist System" was published in the *Illustrated London News*.

JANUARY 4

I will praise You, for I am fearfully and wonderfully made; marvellous are Your works, and that my soul knows very well.

—PSALM 139:14 NKJV

This world and all our powers in it are far more awful and beautiful than we ever know until some accident reminds us. If you wish to perceive that limitless felicity, limit yourself if only for a moment. If you wish to realize how fearfully and wonderfully God's image is made, stand upon one leg. If you want to realize the splendid vision of all visible things—wink the other eye.

A PASSAGE FROM *THE LIVING AGE* MAGAZINE (1905)

The universe is of necessity the perfectly lonely thing. You may state the eternal problem in the form of saying: "Why is there a Cosmos?" But you can state it just as well by saying: "Why is there an omnibus?" You can say: "Why is there everything?" You can say instead: "Why is there anything?" For that law and sequence and harmony and inevitability on which science so proudly insists are in their nature only true of the relations of the parts to each other. The whole, the nature of things itself, is not legal, is not consecutive, is not harmonious, and not inevitable. It is wild, like a poem; arbitrary, like a poem; unique, like a poem.

ON THIS DAY

- In 1908, GKC's article "Why I Am Not a Socialist" was published in *The New Age.*
- And in 1930, GKC's article "The Complexity of Liberty" was published in the *Illustrated London News.*

JANUARY 5

So, as much as is in me, I am ready to preach the gospel.
—ROMANS 1:15 NKJV

I am not prepared to admit that there is, or can be, properly speaking, in the world anything that is too sacred to be known. That spiritual beauty and spiritual truth are in their nature communicable and that they should be communicated, is a principle which lies at the root of every conceivable religion. Christ was crucified upon a hill, and not in a cavern, and the word Gospel itself involves the same idea as the ordinary name of a daily paper. Whenever, therefore, a poet or any similar type of man can, or conceives that he can, make all men partakers in some splendid secret of his own heart, I can imagine nothing saner and nothing manlier than his course in doing so. Thus it was that Dante made a new heaven and a new hell out of a girl's nod in the streets of Florence.

A PASSAGE FROM *THE LIVING AGE* MAGAZINE (1905)

It is the function, then, of literature to liberate a subject, or a spirit, or an incident, or a personality, from those irrelevancies which

prevent it, first from being itself, and, secondly, from becoming per-
fectly allegorical of the essence of things. Everything about the cow
in our daily experience of it which accidentally prevents us from
realizing its deeper magic, such, for instance, as our happening
to be an old lady and afraid of cows, or our being an impecunious
farmer and obliged to sell the cow, or even (though this is less likely)
an ox and obliged to regard the cow with more specialized and per-
haps more passionate sentiment . . . We must, if necessary, put the
cow in greener fields of fairy land, and under a sun that is strange
to men. We must set her dark against an impossible sunset, like the
end of the gods—or breast deep amid flowers of Paradise; if only
so we can make her seem more utterly cowish, and therefore more
utterly mysterious. We must put her in Eden; we must put her in
Elysium; we must put her in Topsy-turveydom. To sum it all up in a
word, we must put her in a book, in a book where her rounded cow-
ishness will be safe from impertinences and side issues, from bulls
who regard her as a female, and farmers who regard her as a prop-
erty—and old ladies who regard her as the devil. Similar methods,
I need hardly say, are needed to preserve the rounded humanity of
the Cabinet Minister.

ON THIS DAY ──────────────────────────────

- In 1929, GKC's article "The Guild Idea" was published in
  the *Illustrated London News*.

JANUARY 6

And the nations of them which are saved shall walk in the light of it: and the kings of the earth do bring their glory and honour into it.

—REVELATION 21:24

If our faith had been a mere fad of the fading empire, fad would have followed fad in the twilight, and if the civilization ever re-emerged (and many such have never re-emerged) it would have been under some new barbaric flag. But the Christian Church was the last life of the old society and was also the first life of the new. She took the people who were forgetting how to make an arch, and she taught them to invent the Gothic arch. In a word, the most absurd thing that could be said of the Church is the thing we have all heard said of it. How can we say that the Church wishes to bring us back into the Dark Ages? The Church was the only thing that ever brought us out of them.

A PASSAGE FROM *THE LIVING AGE* MAGAZINE (1905)

Literature at its best, then, is essentially a liberation of types, persons, and things; a permission to them to be themselves in safety and to the glory of God. It offers a fuller consideration of a man's case than the world can give him; it offers, to all, noble possibilities of fuller growth than is practicable upon earth; it offers to the meanest soul whom it studies the divine emptiness of an uncreated world. It gives a man what he often longs for more than houses or gardens—deserts.

A PASSAGE FROM *A MISCELLANY OF MEN* (1912)

But travelling in the great level lands has a curiously still and lonely quality; lonely even when there are plenty of people on the road and in the market-place. One's voice seems to break an almost elvish silence.

ON THIS DAY

- In 1901, GKC's first review for the *Daily News* was published.

JANUARY 7

For the message of the cross is foolishness to those who are perishing, but to us who are being saved it is the power of God.

—I CORINTHIANS 1:18 NKJV

His soul will never starve for exploits or excitements who is wise enough to be made a fool of. He will make himself happy in the traps that have been laid for him; he will roll in their nets and sleep. All doors will fly open to him who has a mildness more defiant than mere courage. The whole is unerringly expressed in one fortunate phrase—he will be always taken in. To be taken in everywhere is to see the inside of everything. It is the hospitality of circumstance. With torches and trumpets, like a guest, the greenhorn is taken in by Life. And the sceptic is cast out by it.

A PASSAGE FROM *A MISCELLANY OF MEN* (1912)

I came along a lean, pale road south of the fens, and found myself in a large, quiet, and seemingly forgotten village. It was one of those places that instantly produce a frame of mind which, it may be, one afterwards decks out with unreal details. I dare say that grass did not really grow in the streets, but I came away with a curious impression that it did. I daresay the marketplace was not literally lonely and without sign of life, but it left the vague impression of being so. The place was large and even loose in design, yet it had the air of something hidden away and always overlooked. It seemed shy, like a big yokel; the low roofs seemed to be ducking behind the hedges and railings; and the chimneys holding their breath. I came into it in that dead hour of the afternoon which is neither after lunch nor before tea, nor anything else even on a half-holiday; and I had a fantastic feeling that I had strayed into a lost and extra hour that is not numbered in the twenty-four.

ON THIS DAY

- In 1914, GKC presided over an evening event in the King's Hall, King Street, Covent Garden, as judge at the mock trial of John Jasper for the murder of Edwin Drood—all in celebration of Charles Dickens' unfinished novel *The Mystery of Edwin Drood*.

JANUARY 8

O Lord, our Lord, how excellent is Your name in all the earth, who have set Your glory above the heavens!

—PSALM 8:1 NKJV

The fact is that purification and austerity are even more necessary for the appreciation of life and laughter than for anything else. To let no bird fly past unnoticed, to spell patiently the stones and weeds, to have the mind a storehouse of sunsets, requires a discipline in pleasure and an education in gratitude.

A PASSAGE FROM *A MISCELLANY OF MEN* (1912)

I entered an inn which stood openly in the market-place yet was almost as private as a private house . . . In the front window a stout old lady in black with an elaborate cap sat doing a large piece of needlework. She had a kind of comfortable Puritanism about her; and might have been (perhaps she was) the original Mrs. Grundy. A little more withdrawn into the parlour sat a tall, strong, and serious girl, with a face of beautiful honesty and a pair of scissors stuck in her belt, doing a small piece of needlework. Two feet behind them sat a hulking labourer with a humorous face like wood painted scarlet, with a huge mug of mild beer which he had not touched, and probably would not touch for hours. On the hearthrug there was an equally motionless cat; and on the table a copy of Household Words. *I was conscious of some atmosphere, still and yet bracing, that I had met somewhere in literature.*

ON THIS DAY ———————————————————————

- In 1920, GKC and his wife, Frances, arrived in Cairo, Egypt, a stage of their journey to the Holy Land.

JANUARY 9

But from the beginning of the creation God made them male and female. For this cause shall a man leave his father and mother, and cleave to his wife; and they twain shall be one flesh: so then they are no more twain, but one flesh.

—MARK 10:6–8

When I say that religion and marriage and local loyalty are permanent in humanity, I mean that they recur when humanity is most human; and only comparatively decline when society is comparatively inhuman.

A PASSAGE FROM *A MISCELLANY OF MEN* (1912)

Then I remembered that it was the atmosphere in some of Wordsworth's rural poems; which are full of genuine freshness and wonder, and yet are in some incurable way commonplace. This was curious; for Wordsworth's men were of the rocks and fells, and not of the fenlands or flats. But perhaps it is the clearness of still water and the mirrored skies of meres and pools that produces this crystalline virtue. Perhaps that is why Wordsworth is called a Lake Poet instead of a mountain poet. Perhaps it is the water that does it. Certainly the whole of that town [where I found myself] was like a cup of water given at morning.

ON THIS DAY

- In 1932, GKC's article "A Detective Story with Twelve Authors" was published in the *Illustrated London News*.

JANUARY 10

And so it was, when Jesus had ended these sayings, that the people were astonished at His teaching, for He taught them as one having authority.
—MATTHEW 7:28–29 NKJV

A man's soul is as full of voices as a forest; there are ten thousand tongues there like all the tongues of the trees: fancies, follies, memories, madnesses, mysterious fears, and more mysterious hopes. All the settlement and sane government of life consists in coming to the conclusion that some of those voices have authority and others not.

A PASSAGE FROM *A MISCELLANY OF MEN* (1912)

After a few sentences exchanged at long intervals in the manner of rustic courtesy, I inquired casually what was the name of the town. The old lady answered that its name was Stilton, and composedly continued her needlework. But I had paused with my mug in air, and was gazing at her with a suddenly arrested concern. "I suppose," I said, "that it has nothing to do with the cheese of that name."

"Oh, yes," she answered, with a staggering indifference, "they used to make it here."

I put down my mug with a gravity far greater than her own. "But this place is a Shrine!" I said. "Pilgrims should be pouring into it from wherever the English legend has endured alive. There ought to be a colossal statue in the market-place of the man who invented Stilton cheese. There ought to be another colossal statue of the first cow who provided the foundations of it. There should be a burnished tablet let into the ground on the spot where some courageous man first ate Stilton cheese, and survived."

JANUARY 11

> And so we have the prophetic word confirmed, which you
> do well to heed as a light that shines in a dark place, until
> the day dawns and the morning star rises in your hearts.
> —2 PETER 1:19 NKJV

The idea of a crowd of human strangers turned into comrades for a journey is full of the oldest pathos and piety of human life.

That profound feeling of moral fraternity and frailty, which tells us we are indeed all in the same boat, is not the less true if expressed in the formula that we are all in the same bus. As for the idea of the lamp-post, the idea of the fixed beacon of the branching thoroughfares, the terrestrial star of the terrestrial traveller, it could only be, but actually is, the subject of countless songs.

A PASSAGE FROM *A MISCELLANY OF MEN* (1912)

The wind awoke last night with so noble a violence that it was like the war in heaven; and I thought for a moment that the Thing had broken free. For wind never seems like empty air. Wind always sounds full and physical, like the big body of something; and I fancied that the Thing itself was walking gigantic along the great roads between the forests of beech.

ON THIS DAY

- In 1908, GKC's article "The Survival of Christmas" was published in the *Illustrated London News*.
- And in 1920, while in Cairo, Egypt, GKC and his wife, Frances, "went to church at St. Mary's," the chapel of the English bishop of Jerusalem, who was then in attendance.

JANUARY 12

But sanctify the Lord God in your hearts, and always be ready to give a defense to everyone who asks you a reason for the hope that is in you . . .

—1 PETER 3:15 NKJV

As an old-fashioned person, who still believes that Reason is a gift of God and a guide to truth, I must confine myself to saying that I do not want a God whom I have made, but a God who has made me.

A WORD OF THE DAY

Once abolish the God, and the government becomes the God.

A PASSAGE FROM *A MISCELLANY OF MEN* (1912)

The man who thinks backwards is a very powerful person to-day: indeed, if he is not omnipotent, he is at least omnipresent. It is he who writes nearly all the learned books and articles, especially of the scientific or sceptical sort; all the articles on Eugenics and Social Evolution.

ON THIS DAY

- In 1920, GKC and his wife, Frances, set out to see the pyramids at Giza.
- And in 1929, GKC's article "Spiritualism and Agnosticism" was published in the *Illustrated London News*.

JANUARY 13

For godly sorrow produces repentance leading to salvation.
                               —2 CORINTHIANS 7:10 NKJV

There is something more peculiar and provocative in the Christian idea, and it was expressed in the words *repentance* and *humility*. Or, to put it in more topical terms, it means that when we face the facts of the age, the first facts we face should be the faults of ourselves; and that we should at least consider, concerning any fact, the possibility that it is our fault.

A PASSAGE FROM *A MISCELLANY OF MEN* (1912)

I mean [here] the red flower called Fire. Fire, the most magic and startling of all material things, is a thing known only to man and the expression of his sublime externalism. It embodies all that is human in his hearths and all that is divine on his altars. It is the most human thing in the world; seen across wastes of marsh or medleys of forest, it is veritably the purple and golden flag of the sons of Eve.

A PASSAGE FROM *ALL I SURVEY* (1933)

All that dark and yet exuberant imagery belongs to a tradition that can be seen in the art and ornament of Spain. It can be seen in the special Spanish love of black; the black which is not the negation of colour, but rather the accumulation of colour. It can be seen in the rich darkness of Spanish churches, fretted with the golden fire of countless candles.

JANUARY 14

For the word of God is living and powerful . . . and is a discerner of the thoughts and intents of the heart.
—HEBREWS 4:12 NKJV

We need something like a test. It is necessary to have in hand a truth to judge modern philosophies.

A PASSAGE FROM *A MISCELLANY OF MEN* (1912)

A modern intellectual comes in and sees a poker. He is a positivist; he will not begin with any dogmas about the nature of man, or any daydreams about the mystery of fire. He will begin with what he can see, the poker; and the first thing he sees about the poker is that it is crooked.

He says, "Poor poker; it's crooked." Then he asks how it came to be crooked; and is told that there is a thing in the world (with which his temperament has hitherto left him unacquainted)—a thing called fire. He points out, very kindly and clearly, how silly it is of people, if they want a straight poker, to put it into a chemical combustion which will very probably heat and warp it.

"Let us abolish fire," he says, "and then we shall have perfectly straight pokers. Why should you want a fire at all?" They explain to him that a creature called Man wants a fire, because he has no fur or feathers. He gazes dreamily at the embers for a few seconds, and then shakes his head.

"I doubt if such an animal is worth preserving," he says. "He must eventually go under in the cosmic struggle when pitted against well-armoured and warmly protected species, who have wings and trunks and spires and scales and horns and shaggy hair. If Man cannot live without these luxuries, you had better abolish Man."

At this point, as a rule, the crowd is convinced; it heaves up all its clubs and axes, and abolishes him. At least, one of him.

JANUARY 15

The Lord is my light and my salvation.
—PSALM 27:1 NKJV

The visible clue to the Middle Ages is colour. The mediæval man could paint before he could draw. In the almost startling inspiration which we call stained glass, he discovered something that is almost more coloured than colour; something that bears the same relation to mere colour that golden flame does to golden sand. He did not, like other artists, try in his pictures to paint the sun; he made the sun paint his pictures. He mixed the aboriginal light with the paints upon his palette.

LINES FROM THE POEM, "GLENCOE"

The star-crowned cliffs seem hinged upon the sky,
The clouds are floating rags across them curled,
They open to us like the gates of God
Cloven in the last great wall of all the world.
But you have clothed with mercy like a moss
The barren violence of its primal wars,
Sterile although they be and void of rule,
You know my shapeless crags have loved the stars.
How shall I thank you, O courageous heart,
That of this wasteful world you had no fear;
But bade it blossom in clear faith and sent
Your fair flower-feeding rivers: even as here
The peat burns brimming from their cups of stone
Glow brown and blood-red down the vast decline
As if Christ stood on yonder clouded peak
And turned its thousand waters into wine.

JANUARY 16

I thank God, whom I serve . . . as my forefathers did.
                              —2 TIMOTHY 1:3 NKJV

A man looking at the round arches of the old Roman and Norman architecture could not possibly have calculated from them that, a hundred years afterwards, the delicate energy of the Gothic would be piercing the sky with spires and pointed arches as if with spears and arrows. That was an act of free imagination and, properly understood, an act of free will. . . .

We may guess some of the fulfilments of a later generation; but we cannot share in any of its surprises. We may know a little about the heritage of our grandchildren, but nothing about their windfalls or their wilder adventures. If we want windfalls and wild adventures, we must consider the ways of our grandfathers and not our grandchildren. If we want the wildest emotions of novelty and astonishment, we can only find them in mouldering stones and fading tapestries, in the museum of antiquities or the place of tombs.

A PASSAGE FROM *A MISCELLANY OF MEN* (1912)

Newspaper editors and proprietors are more despotic and dangerous by what they do not utter than by what they do. We have all heard the expression "golden silence." The expression "brazen silence" is the only adequate phrase for our editors. If we wake out of this throttled, gaping, and wordless nightmare, we must awake with a yell. The Revolution that releases England from the fixed falsity of its present position will be not less noisy than other revolutions. It will contain, I fear, a great deal of that rude accomplishment described among little boys as "calling names"; but that will not matter much so long as they are the right names.

ON THIS DAY ─────────────────────────────

- In 1920, GKC gave a lecture at the general headquarters in Cairo, Egypt, for the military personnel stationed there on the whimsically titled topic, "Sightseeing for the Blind."
- And in 1932, GKC's article "Dead Dragons, Then and Now" was published in the *Illustrated London News*.

JANUARY 17

*For you shall go out with joy, and be led out with peace;
the mountains and the hills shall break forth into singing
before you, and all the trees of the field shall clap their
hands.*

—ISAIAH 55:12 NKJV

Grown-up people are not strong enough to exult in monotony. But perhaps God is strong enough to exult in monotony. It is possible that God says every morning, "Do it again" to the sun; and every evening, "Do it again" to the moon. It may not be automatic necessity that makes all daisies alike; it may be that God makes every daisy separately, but has never got tired of making them. It may be that He has the eternal appetite of infancy; for we have sinned and grown old, and our Father is younger than we.

LINES FROM THE POEM "THE WISE MEN"

Step softly, under snow or rain,
To find the place where men can pray;
The way is all so very plain
That we may lose the way.
Oh, we have learnt to peer and pore
On tortured puzzles from our youth,
We know all labyrinthine lore,
We are the three wise men of yore,
And we know all things but the truth.

JANUARY 18

Jesus said to him, "I am the way, the truth, and the life.
No one comes to the Father except through Me."

—JOHN 14:6 NKJV

The Romans were quite willing to admit that Christ was a God. What they denied was that He was the God—the highest truth of the cosmos. And this is the only point worth discussing about Christianity.

LINES FROM THE POEM, "A SONG OF GIFTS TO GOD"

When the first Christmas presents came, the straw where
  Christ was rolled
Smelt sweeter than their frankincense, burnt brighter
  than their gold,
And a wise man said, "We will not give; the thanks would
  be but cold."

*"Nay," said the next, "To all new gifts, to this gift or
    another,
Bends the high gratitude of God; even as He now, my
    brother,
Who had a Father for all time, yet thanks Him for a
    Mother."
"Yet scarce for Him this yellow stone or prickly smells
    and sparse,
Who holds the gold heart of the sun that fed these timber
    bars,
Nor any scentless lily lives for One that smells the stars."
Then spake the third of the Wise Men; the wisest of the
    three:
"We may not with the widest lives enlarge His liberty,
Whose wings are wider than the world . . ."*

ON THIS DAY

- In 1904, GKC and his wife, Frances, had "an amusing lunch" with their friend, the noted essayist and caricaturist Max Beerbohm.
- In 1920, GKC gave an address in the Anglican Bishop's Chapel of Cairo, Egypt.
- In 1921, the Chestertons left New York for Northampton, Massachusetts, where GKC lectured at Smith College.
- And in 1930, GKC's article "The Truth of Medieval Times" was published in the *Illustrated London News*.

JANUARY 19

> *Knowest thou the ordinances of heaven? Canst thou set*
> *the dominion thereof in the earth?*
>
> —JOB 38:33

There is one central conception of the book of Job, which literally makes it immortal, which will make it survive our modern time and our modern philosophies as it has survived many better times and many better philosophies. That is the conception that the universe, if it is to be admired, is to be admired for its strangeness and not for its rationality, for its splendid unreason and not for its reason. Job's friends attempt to comfort him with philosophical optimism, like the intellectuals of the eighteenth century. Job tries to comfort himself with philosophical pessimism like the intellectuals of the nineteenth century. But God comforts Job with indecipherable mystery, and for the first time Job is comforted. Eliphaz gives one answer. Job gives another answer, and the question still remains an open wound. God simply refuses to answer, and somehow the question is answered. Job flings at God one riddle, God flings back at Job a hundred riddles, and Job is at peace. He is comforted with conundrums. For the grand and enduring idea in the poem, as suggested above, is that if we are to be reconciled to this great cosmic experience it must be as something divinely strange and divinely violent, a quest, or a conspiracy, or some sacred joke.

A PASSAGE FROM *A MISCELLANY OF MEN* (1912)

Going mad is the slowest and dullest business in the world. I have very nearly done it more than once in my boyhood, and so have nearly all my friends, born under the general doom of mortals, but especially

*of moderns; I mean the doom that makes a man come almost to the
end of thinking before he comes to the first chance of living.*

ON THIS DAY ———————————————————————————————

- In 1920, GKC lectured at a military barracks in Cairo,
  Egypt.
- And in 1929, GKC's article "If I Were A Preacher" was
  published in the *Illustrated London News.*

JANUARY 20

*Who coverest thyself with light as with a garment: who
stretchest out the heavens like a curtain.*

—Psalm 104:2

Matthew Arnold was a fine critic, but, like many modern critics, he sometimes allowed the dislike of mysticism to lead him
merely into mystification. And he never said a sillier thing, I
may respectfully remark, than when he said that Wordsworth
was fanciful in recalling the love of Nature in childhood,
because a man's best appreciation of Nature comes when he is
about thirty. This may be true of him considered as a landscape
painter or a landscape gardener, but Wordsworth was thinking of something much deeper and more divine than any such
technical judgments. It was something expressed even better
than by Wordsworth, I think, in a very marvellous poem by
Traherne about the white light shining on all things in infancy.

A PASSAGE FROM *A MISCELLANY OF MEN* (1912)

When I arrived to see the performance of the Buckinghamshire Players, who acted Miss Gertrude Robins's Pot Luck at Naphill a short time ago, it is the distressing, if scarcely surprising, truth that I entered very late . . .

[It was a] strange journey that was the cause of my coming in late . . . And the truth is that I had one eye on an ancient and timeless clock, hung uselessly in heaven; whose very name has passed into a figure for such bemused folly. In the true sense of an ancient phrase, I was moonstruck. A lunar landscape a scene of winter moonlight had inexplicably got in between me and all other scenes. If any one had asked me I could not have said what it was; I cannot say now. Nothing had occurred to me; except the breakdown of a hired motor on the ridge of a hill. It was not an adventure; it was a vision.

ON THIS DAY ────────────────────────────

- In 1920, GKC and his wife, Frances, set out from Cairo, Egypt, for Jerusalem.

JANUARY 21

One thing I have desired of the Lord, that will I seek: that I may dwell in the house of the Lord all the days of my life, to behold the beauty of the Lord, and to inquire in His temple.

—PSALM 27:4 NKJV

The Eden of the Middle Ages was really a garden, where each of God's flowers—truth and beauty and reason—flourished for its own sake, and with its own name.

A PASSAGE FROM *A MISCELLANY OF MEN* (1912)

One cannot find anything more infinite than a finite horizon, free and lonely and innocent. The Dutch veldt may be a little more desolate than Birmingham. But I am sure it is not so desolate as that English hill was, almost within a cannon-shot of High Wycombe.

I looked across a vast and voiceless valley straight at the moon, as if at a round mirror. It may have been the blue moon of the proverb; for on that freezing night the very moon seemed blue with cold. A deathly frost fastened every branch and blade to its place. The sinking and softening forests, powdered with a grey frost, fell away underneath me into an abyss which seemed unfathomable. One fancied the world was soundless only because it was bottomless: it seemed as if all songs and cries had been swallowed in some un-resisting stillness under the roots of the hills.

JANUARY 22

Then shall be brought to pass the saying that is written:
"Death is swallowed up in victory. O Death, where is
your sting? O Hades, where is your victory?"
—1 CORINTHIANS 15:54–55 NKJV

Under the white fog of snow high up in the heaven the whole atmosphere of the city was turned to a very queer kind of green twilight, as of men under the sea. The scaled and sullen sunset behind the dark dome of St. Paul's had in it smoky and sinister colours—colours of sickly green, dead red or decaying bronze, that were just bright enough to emphasise the solid whiteness of the snow. But right up against these dreary colours rose the black bulk of the cathedral; and upon the top of the cathedral was a random splash and great stain of snow, still clinging as to an Alpine peak. It had fallen accidentally, but just so fallen as to half drape the dome from its very topmost point, and to pick out in perfect silver the great orb and the cross. When Syme saw it he suddenly straightened himself, and made with his sword-stick an involuntary salute.

He knew that that evil figure, his shadow, was creeping quickly or slowly behind him, and he did not care. It seemed a symbol of human faith and valour that while the skies were darkening that high place of the earth was bright. The devils might have captured heaven, but they had not yet captured the cross.

A PASSAGE FROM *THE BALL AND THE CROSS* (1909)

The vessel took one long and sweeping curve across the sky and came nearer and nearer to MacIan, like a steam-engine coming round a bend. It was of pure white steel, and in the moon it gleamed like the armour of Sir Galahad. The simile of such virginity is not inappropriate; for, as it grew larger and larger and lower and lower, Evan saw that the only figure in it was robed in white from head to foot and crowned with snow-white hair, on which the moonshine lay like a benediction. The figure stood so still that he could easily have supposed it to be a statue. Indeed, he thought it was until it spoke.

"Evan," said the voice, and it spoke with the simple authority of some forgotten father revisiting his children, "you have remained here long enough, and your sword is wanted elsewhere."

Blessed is the man You choose, and cause to approach You,
that he may dwell in Your courts. We shall be satisfied with
the goodness of Your house, of Your holy temple.

—PSALM 65:4 NKJV

A man never knows what tiny thing will startle him to such ancestral and impersonal tears. Piles of superb masonry will often pass like a common panorama; and on this grey and silver morning the ruined towers of the cathedral stood about me somewhat vaguely like grey clouds. But down in a hollow where the local antiquaries are making a fruitful excavation, a magnificent old ruffian with a pickaxe (whom I believe to have been St. Joseph of Arimathea) showed me a fragment of the old vaulted roof which he had found in the earth; and on the whitish grey stone there was just a faint brush of gold. There seemed a piercing and swordlike pathos, an unexpected fragrance of all forgotten or desecrated things, in the bare survival of that poor little pigment upon the imperishable rock. . . . It was as if men had been able to preserve a fragment of the sunset.

A PASSAGE FROM *THE BALL AND THE CROSS* (1909)

The evening sky, a dome of solid gold, unflaked even by a single sunset cloud, steeped the meanest sights of London in a strange and mellow light. It made a little greasy street off St. Martin's Lane look as if it were paved with gold. It made the pawnbroker's half-way down it shine as if it were really that Mountain of Piety that the French poetic instinct has named it; it made the mean pseudo-French bookshop, next but one to it, a shop packed with dreary indecency, show for a moment a kind of Parisian colour.

And the shop that stood between the pawnshop and the shop of dreary indecency, showed with quite a blaze of old world beauty, for it was, by accident, a shop not unbeautiful in itself. The front window had a glimmer of bronze and blue steel, lit, as by a few stars, by the sparks of what were alleged to be jewels; for it was in brief, a shop of bric-a-brac and old curiosities. A row of half bur-nished seventeenth century swords ran like an ornate railing along the front of the window; behind was a darker glimmer of old oak and old armour.

ON THIS DAY ────────────────────────────────

- In 1932, GKC's article "On Making Good" was published in the *Illustrated London News*.

JANUARY 24

The entrance of thy words giveth light . . .
—PSALM 119:130

Telling the truth about the terrible struggle of the human soul is surely a very elementary part of the ethics of hon-esty. . . . This older and firmer conception of right as existing outside human weakness and without reference to human error, can be felt in the very lightest and loosest of the works of old English literature. It is commonly unmeaning enough to call Shakspere a great moralist; but in this particular way Shakspere is a very typical moralist. Whenever he alludes to right and wrong it is always with this old implication. Right is right, even if nobody does it. Wrong is wrong, even if every-body is wrong about it.

A PASSAGE FROM *THE LIVING AGE* MAGAZINE (1909)

In the current number of an excellent weekly paper there appeared a letter on the subject of Meredith and Dickens, which is very typical of all that we must throw off in the modern world or perish.

Why anybody should want to compare Meredith and Dickens any more than Hesiod and Thackeray, I do not know. But the letter was to this effect; that Dickens could not really be a great artist, because in his books one could divide men into good and bad; and with Meredith, it was alleged (very unjustly) one could not do this. There could be no stronger case of that strange fanaticism which fills our time; the fanatical hatred of morality, especially of Christian morality. The writer did not contend that the men of Dickens were incredibly good or incredibly bad; he admitted that many of the villains had virtues and that nearly all of the virtuous men had weaknesses. He objected to the books simply because they recognized a rough essential division between villains and virtuous people. It did not seem to strike him that everybody does recognize this in daily life. It did not occur to him to go and ask workmen whether there is such a thing as a bad master; or women whether there is such a thing as a bad husband; or tradesmen whether there is such a thing as a bad debt. Still less did it occur to him to ask the experience of all mankind, and all the books that have been written on the earth, whether there is not such a thing as a bad man . . .

Vice and virtue do shade into each other in every character; tallness and shortness are only a matter of degree. But to blame Dickens for describing Boythorne as good and Quilp as bad is to complain of him for stating that Boythorne was tall and Quilp rather short.

JANUARY 25

Before the mountains were brought forth, or ever You had formed the earth and the world, even from everlasting to everlasting, You are God.

—PSALM 90:2 NKJV

Verbally speaking the enigmas of Jehovah seem darker and more desolate than the enigmas of Job; yet Job was comfortless before the speech of Jehovah and is comforted after it. He has been told nothing, but he feels the terrible and tingling atmosphere of something which is too good to be told. The refusal of God to explain His design is itself a burning hint of His design. The riddles of God are more satisfying than the solutions of man.

A PASSAGE FROM *THE LIVING AGE* MAGAZINE (1909)

[George] Meredith, like Browning, must be rescued from his admirers. And there could hardly be a better end to begin at than this simple matter of the allegation about ethics. It is an atrocious libel upon Meredith to say that he was scientific or purely psychological or even purely aesthetic. It is a black slander to say that he did not preach, or that his characters are not properly placarded as good and bad. They are; just as much and just as little as in Dickens or any other writer whose books it is endurable to read.

Books without morality in them are books that send one to sleep standing up. Meredith at least was not of that sort; he was complex, but quite the reverse of colourless. His convictions may have been right or wrong; but they were very burning convictions.

- In 1908, GKC's article "Aristocrats as Mystagogues" was published in the *Illustrated London News*.

JANUARY 26

Assuredly, I say to you, whoever does not receive the
kingdom of God as a little child will by no means enter it.
—LUKE 18:17 NKJV

The devil can quote Scripture for his purpose; and the text of Scripture which he now most commonly quotes is, "The kingdom of heaven is within you." That text has been the stay and support of more Pharisees and prigs and self-righteous spiritual bullies than all the dogmas in creation; it has served to identify self-satisfaction with the peace that passes all understanding. And the text to be quoted in answer to it is that which declares that no man can receive the kingdom except as a little child. What we are to have inside is the childlike spirit; but the childlike spirit is not entirely concerned about what is inside. It is the first mark of possessing it that one is interested in what is outside. The most childlike thing about a child is his curiosity and his appetite and his power of wonder at the world. We might almost say that the whole advantage of having the kingdom within is that we look for it somewhere else.

A PASSAGE FROM *THE BALL AND THE CROSS* (1909)

Across the great plains and uplands to the right and left of the lane,
a long tide of sunset light rolled like a sea of ruby, lighting up the

long terraces of the hills and picking out the few windows of the scattered hamlets in startling blood-red sparks. But the lane was cut deep in the hill and remained in an abrupt shadow. The two men running in it had an impression not uncommonly experienced between those wild green English walls; a sense of being led between the walls of a maze.

ON THIS DAY

- In 1921, GKC and his wife, Frances, departed New York for New Haven, Connecticut, where Chesterton gave a lecture to "a very enthusiastic audience"—after which "hundreds of Yale boys stormed the platform for handshakes and autographs."
- And in 1929, GKC's article "Myths and Metaphors" was published in the *Illustrated London News*.

JANUARY 27

The earth is the Lord's, and all its fullness, the world and those who dwell therein.

—PSALM 24:1 NKJV

When I had looked at the lights of Broadway by night, I made to my American friends an innocent remark that seemed for some reason to amuse them. I had looked, not without joy, at that long kaleidoscope of coloured lights arranged in large letters and sprawling trade-marks, advertising everything, from pork to pianos, through the agency of the two most vivid and most mystical of the gifts of God; colour and fire. I said to them, in my simplicity, "What a glorious garden of wonders this would be, to any one who was lucky enough to be unable to read."

A PASSAGE FROM *THE LIVING AGE* MAGAZINE (1909)

Meredith did what Dickens never did. He wrote a Morality; a pure and stern satiric allegory for the lashing of one special vice. The Egoist is not a man; he is a sin. And, as in all the old and wholesome Moralities of the ages of faith, the object of fixing the vice on one man is really to fix it upon all men.

We have all posed with the Egoist, just as we have all fallen with Adam. There is no character in Dickens which is symbolic and moral in that extreme sense and degree. Micawber is not Improvidence, Sikes is not Brutality in the utterly naked and abstract sense in which Sir Willoughby Patterne is Selfishness.

JANUARY 28

And the ransomed of the Lord shall return, and come to Zion with singing, with everlasting joy on their heads. They shall obtain joy and gladness, and sorrow and sighing shall flee away.

—ISAIAH 35:10 NKJV

The central idea of the great part of the Old Testament may be called the idea of the loneliness of God. God is not the only chief character of the Old Testament; God is properly the only character in the Old Testament.

A PASSAGE FROM *THE LIVING AGE* MAGAZINE (1909)

But [George] Meredith, though in no way orthodox, is the very antithesis of all this. That impersonal deity which is Hardy's villain is Meredith's hero and champion. Nature betrays all the heroines of Hardy. Nature enters to save all the heroines of Meredith.

The argument of Hardy is that human beings with their brief joy and brittle ideals might get on very well if the general wave of the world did not overturn them or smash them into sticks. The argument of Meredith is that our little lives always stagnate into hypocrisy or morbidity, unless the general wave of the world continually refreshes and recreates us.

A PASSAGE FROM *THE BALL AND THE CROSS* (1909)

On that fantastic fringe of the Gaelic land where he walked as a boy, the cliffs were as fantastic as the clouds. Heaven seemed to humble itself and come closer to the earth. The common paths of his little village began to climb quite suddenly and seemed resolved to go to heaven. The sky seemed to fall down towards the hills; the hills took hold upon the sky. In the sumptuous sunset of gold and purple and peacock green cloudlets and islets were the same. Evan lived like a man walking on a borderland, the borderland between this world and another.

ON THIS DAY

- In 1920, GKC and his wife, Frances, newly arrived in Jerusalem, walked to the Zion Gate "near the house of Caiaphas and the scene of the Last Supper."

Thus says the Lord: "Stand in the ways and see, and ask
for the old paths, where the good way is, and walk in it;
then you will find rest for your souls."

—JEREMIAH 6:16 NKJV

The pale leaf falls in pallor, but the green leaf turns to
gold;
We that have found it good to be young shall find it good
to be old;
Life that bringeth the marriage-bell, the cradle and the
grave.
Life that is mean to the mean of heart, and only brave to
the brave.

A THOUGHT TO PONDER

Since Christianity broke the heart of the world and mended it, one
cannot really be a Pagan; one can only be an anti-Christian.

A PASSAGE FROM *THE LIVING AGE* MAGAZINE (1909)

Swinburne was not a Pagan in the least; he was a pseudo-Parisian
pessimist. Thomas Hardy is not a Pagan; he is a Nonconformist
gone sour. It is not Pagan to revile the gods nor is it Pagan to exalt a
street-walker into a symbol of all possible pleasure.

The Pagan felt that there was a sort of easy and equable force pressing upon us from Nature; that this force was breezy and beneficent, though not specially just or loving; in other words, that there was, as the strength in wine or trees or the ocean, the energy of kindly but careless gods.

This Paganism is now impossible, either to the Christian or the sceptic. We believe so much less than that—and we desire so much more. But no man in our time ever came quite so near to this clean and well-poised Paganism as Meredith. He took the mystery of the universe lightly; and waited for the gods to show themselves in the forest.

ON THIS DAY

- In 1920, GKC and his wife, Frances, visited the Holy Sepulchre and the Christian quarter of Jerusalem.

JANUARY 30

The Lord is my strength and song, and He has become my salvation; He is my God, and I will praise Him; my father's God, and I will exalt Him.

—Exodus 15:2 NKJV

Between us, by the peace of God, such truth can
     now be told;
Yea, there is strength in striking root and good in
     growing old.

A PASSAGE FROM *THE LIVING AGE* MAGAZINE (1909)

We talk of the curiosity of the Greeks; but there is also something almost eerie about their lack of curiosity. There is a wide gulf between the [showy] unanswered questions of Socrates and the parched and passionate questions of Job.

A PASSAGE FROM *THE BALL AND THE CROSS* (1909)

Then after a silence he cried with a rending sincerity: "Are you really there, Evan? Have you ever been really there? Am I simply dreaming?"

MacIan had been listening with a living silence to every word, and now his face flamed with one of his rare revelations of life.

"No, you good atheist," he cried; "no, you clean, courteous, reverent, pious old blasphemer. No, you are not dreaming—you are waking up."

"What do you mean?"

"There are two states where one meets so many old friends," said MacIan; "one is a dream, the other is the end of the world."

"And you say—"

"I say this is not a dream," said Evan in a ringing voice.

"You really mean to suggest—" began Turnbull.

"Be silent! or I shall say it all wrong," said MacIan, breathing hard. "It's hard to explain, anyhow. An apocalypse is the opposite of a dream. A dream is falser than the outer life. But the end of the world is more actual than the world it ends. I don't say this is really the end of the world, but it's something like that—it's the end of something. All the people are crowding into one corner. Everything is coming to a point."

JANUARY 31

> *He shall receive blessing from the Lord, and righteousness*
> *from the God of his salvation.*
>
> —PSALM 24:5 NKJV

But the power of hoping through everything, the knowledge that the soul survives its adventures, that great inspiration comes to the middle-aged; God has kept that good wine until now. It is from the backs of the elderly gentlemen that the wings of the butterfly should burst.

A PASSAGE FROM *THE LIVING AGE* MAGAZINE (1909)

I have heard modern people talk of the heedlessness of all the old rituals and reliquaries and the need for a simple religion of the heart. But their demand is rather dangerous, especially to themselves.

If we really had a simple religion of the heart we should all be loaded with relics, and rituals would be going on all day long. If our creed were only of the higher emotions, it would talk of nothing else but special shrines, sacred spots, indispensable gestures, and adorable rags and bones.

In short, a religion of pure good feeling would be a positive orgy of superstition. This seems to me excessive; I prefer a little clean theology to keep the thing within bounds.

ON THIS DAY

- In 1931, GKC's article "The Modern Joy in Doubt" was published in the *Illustrated London News*.

FEBRUARY 1

> *For there is no authority except from God, and the*
> *authorities that exist are appointed by God.*
> —ROMANS 13:1 NKJV

America is the only nation in the world that is founded on a creed. That creed is set forth . . . in the Declaration of Independence; perhaps the only piece of practical politics that is . . . also great literature. It enunciates that all men are equal in their claim to justice, that governments exist to give them that justice, and that their authority is for that reason just. . . . It clearly names the Creator as the ultimate authority from whom these equal rights are derived.

A PASSAGE FROM *THE LIVING AGE* MAGAZINE (1909)

In all [George Meredith's] work there is the smell and taste of things: it is grass and not the ghost of grass; fire and not the shadow of fire; beer and not the chemical analysis of beer. Nothing is so fine in Meredith as the satisfying solidity of everything. The wind in which Clara Middleton walked is a real wind; the reader can feel it in his hair. The wine which Dr. Middleton drank is a real wine; the reader can get drunk on it.

It is true that Meredith, when one does not understand him, appears like a bewildering filigree or a blinding spider's web; but this is a question of the difficulty of finding his meaning, not of what it is like when found.

DURING THIS MONTH

- In 1908, GKC's novel *The Man Who Was Thursday* was published. Some early copies were, however, printed in 1907.

- In 1910, GKC's novel *The Ball and the Cross* was published.
- In 1911, GKC's study *Appreciations and Criticisms of Charles Dickens* was published.
- In 1912, GKC's novel *Manalive* was published.
- And in 1913, GKC's study *The Victorian Age in Literature* was published.

FEBRUARY 2

For now we see in a mirror, dimly, but then face to face. Now I know in part, but then I shall know just as I also am known.

—1 CORINTHIANS 13:12 NKJV

So, with the wan waste grasses on my spear,
I ride for ever, seeking after God.
My hair grows whiter than my thistle plume,
And all my limbs are loose; but in my eyes
The star of an unconquerable praise:
For in my soul one hope for ever sings,
That at the next white corner of a road
My eyes may look on Him.

A PASSAGE FROM *THE LIVING AGE* MAGAZINE (1909)

Mr. Henry James has all Meredith's power of taking one's breath away with a sort of light, flashing and flying psychology, as of a sage suddenly dowered with wings. He also can stun the reader with one small but unexpected truth.

Mr. Henry James has all Meredith's intellectualism and nearly all his intellect. Exactly what he lacks is his materialism. Therefore it comes that he lacks his mysticism also; so that one could not say of Mr. Henry James that he was a pious Pagan, worthy at any moment to worship Apollo. Meredith is best at gods; Mr. Henry James is best at ghosts.

ON THIS DAY

- In 1920, on a day "like a glorious June day in England," GKC and his wife, Frances, walked to where they could see the Mount of Olives and the Garden of Gethsemane in Jerusalem.

FEBRUARY 3

Go therefore and make disciples of all the nations, baptizing them in the name of the Father and of the Son and of the Holy Spirit, teaching them to observe all things that I have commanded you; and lo, I am with you always.
—MATTHEW 28:19–20 NKJV

For to us Trinitarians (if I may say it with reverence)—to us God Himself is a society. It is indeed a fathomless mystery of theology. . . . Suffice it to say here that this triple enigma is as comforting as wine and open as an English fireside. . . . This thing that bewilders the intellect utterly quiets the heart.

A PASSAGE FROM *THE LIVING AGE* MAGAZINE (1909)

[George] Meredith made us feel the bodily presence of people as well as their spiritual presence; and even delighted in the very bodily, as in schoolboys. And all this is, I think, ultimately

connected with his conception of the universe, vague or pantheist as many may call it.

But Meredith was not a pantheist; he was a Pagan. The difference consists in this tremendous fact; that a Pagan always has sacraments, while a pantheist has none. Meredith always sought for special and solid symbols to which to cling; as in that fine poem called, "A Faith on Trial," in which all his agonies are answered, not by a synthesis or a cosmology, but suddenly by a white cherry-branch in bloom.

FEBRUARY 4

Is not God in the height of heaven? And see the highest stars, how lofty they are!

—JOB 22:12 NKJV

For every tiny town or place
God made the stars especially;
Babies look up with owlish face
And see them tangled in a tree.

A PASSAGE FROM *THE LIVING AGE* MAGAZINE (1909)

There is a thing which is often called progress, but which only occurs in dull and stale conditions; it is indeed, not progress, but a sort of galloping plagiarism. To carry the same fashion further and further is not a mark of energy, but a mark of fatigue.

One can fancy that in the fantastic decline of some Chinese civilization one might find things automatically increasing, simply because everybody had forgotten what the things were meant for. Hats might be bigger than umbrellas, because every one had forgotten to wear them. Walking sticks might be taller than lances, because nobody ever thought of taking them out on a walk. The human mind never goes so fast as that except when it has got into a groove.

The converse is also true. All really honest and courageous thought has a tendency to look like truism. For strong thought about a thing is always thought about its original nature; while weak thought is always thought about its most recent developments. The really bold thinker is never afraid of platitude; because platitudes are the great primeval foundations.

FEBRUARY 5

You in Your mercy have led forth the people whom You have redeemed; You have guided them in Your strength to Your holy habitation.

—Exodus 15:13 nkjv

No one . . . can ever forget the impression of that awful chapter [in Bunyan's autobiography] *Grace Abounding,* in which the sinner takes refuge in place after place only to expect that roof after roof will crash down upon him, and that he is safe nowhere if the very Universe that he inherits belongs to one who is his enemy. Nor will anyone forget the chapter in which the sinner is reconciled to the Universe, and walks about the fields and cannot forbear from talking to the birds about the great mercy of God.

A PASSAGE FROM *THE LIVING AGE* MAGAZINE (1909)

All tame and trivial thought is concerned with following a fashion onward to its logical extremity. All clear and courageous thought is concerned with following it back to its logical root. A man may make hats larger and larger and be only as mad as a hatter. But if he can quite perfectly explain what a hat is he must have the great sanity of Aristotle.

A PASSAGE FROM *ALL I SURVEY* (1933)

But Swift was not a man gifted with the particular grace with which this literary legend would distinguish him. He was not a man who specially saw a spiritual significance in common things, or learned great lessons from small objects, or had anything about him of the poet who finds poetry in prose.

He was a religious man in an irreligious age; but only because he was really too intellectual a man to be merely an irreligious man. He had nothing about him of the mystic, who sees divine symbols everywhere, who turns a stone and starts a wing.

FEBRUARY 6

> *The fear of the Lord is the instruction of wisdom, and before honor is humility.*
>
> —PROVERBS 15:33 NKJV

This humility, as I say, was with Arnold a mental need. He was not naturally a humble man; he might even be called a supercilious one. But he was driven to preaching humility merely as a thing to clear the head. He found the virtue which was just then being flung in the mire as fit only for nuns and slaves: and he saw that it was essential to philosophers. The most unpractical merit of ancient piety became the most practical merit of modern investigation.

I repeat, he did not understand that headlong and happy humility which belongs to the more beautiful souls of the simpler ages. He did not appreciate the force (nor perhaps the humour) of St. Francis of Assisi when he called his own body "my brother the donkey." That is to say, he did not realise a certain feeling deep in all mystics in the face of the dual destiny. He did not realise their feeling (full both of fear and laughter) that the body is an animal and a very comic animal.

Matthew Arnold could never have felt any part of himself to be purely comic—not even his singular whiskers. He would never, like Father Juniper, have "played see-saw to abase himself." In a word, he had little sympathy with the old ecstasies of self-effacement. But for this very reason it is all the more important that his main work was an attempt to preach some kind of self-effacement even to his own self-assertive age. He realised that the saints had even understated the case for humility. They had always said that without humility we should never see the better world to come. He realised that without humility we could not even see this world.

ON THIS DAY

- In 1921, GKC gave a lecture in New York City at the Times Square Theatre. Afterward, he was asked if there was any psychological significance in his frequent use of paradoxes. Trying to look as solemn as he could, he answered gravely: "I never use paradox. The statements I make are wearisome and obvious common sense. I have even been driven to the tedium of reading through my own books, and have been unable to find any paradox. In fact, the thing is quite tragic, and some day I hope to write an epic called 'Paradox Lost.'" On this occasion, he was also asked about the special relationship between Britain and America. In reply, he stated: "The best way to achieve union is for someone to do well what I have done feebly, and that is to discuss the common heritage between the literature and the culture we both claim."

FEBRUARY 7

Acquaint now thyself with him, and be at peace: thereby
good shall come unto thee.

—JOB 22:21

In the bald catalogue of biography with which I began [this essay], I purposely omitted the deathbed in the old bachelor house in Bolt Court in 1784. That was no part of the sociable and literary [Samuel] Johnson but of the solitary and immortal one.

I will not say that he died alone with God, for each of us will do that; but he did in a doubtful and changing world what in securer civilizations the saints have done, he detached himself from time as in an ecstasy of impartiality; and saw the ages with an equal eye. He was not merely alone with God; he even shared the loneliness of God, which is love.

A PASSAGE FROM *THE LIVING AGE* MAGAZINE (1909)

But in a plain and happy society the Public House is the Parish Council. The townsmen argue in the tavern about the politics of the town, invoking abstract principles which cannot be proved, and rules of debate which do not in the least matter; their wives teach the children to say their prayers and wish politics at the bottom of the sea. That is the happiest condition of humanity.

ON THIS DAY ————————————————————

- In 1920, GKC and his wife, Frances, went to the Holy Sepulchre in Jerusalem.

*"And God will wipe away every tear from their eyes; there
shall be no more death, nor sorrow, nor crying. There
shall be no more pain, for the former things have passed
away." Then He who sat on the throne said, "Behold, I
make all things new."*

—REVELATION 21:4–5 NKJV

[In *The Book of Job,*] when God is speaking of snow and hail in
the mere catalogue of the physical cosmos, He speaks of them as
a treasury that He has laid up against the day of battle—a hint
of some huge Armageddon in which evil shall be at last over-
thrown. Nothing could be better, artistically speaking, than
this optimism breaking through agnosticism like fiery gold
round the edges of a black cloud.

ON THIS DAY

- In 1930, Frances Chesterton wrote a letter to Father Charles
  O'Donnell, president of the University of Notre Dame, con-
  taining a dedicatory poem, "The Arena," for the university.
  It reads, in part:

    *I have seen, where a strange country
    Opened its secret plains about me,
    One great golden dome . . .
    Like a sun-burst on the mountains*

FEBRUARY 9

But we speak the wisdom of God in a mystery, the hidden
wisdom which God ordained before the ages.

—1 CORINTHIANS 2:7 NKJV

[God] unrolls before Job a long panorama of created things, the horse, the eagle, the raven, the wild ass, the peacock, the ostrich, the crocodile. He so describes each of them that it sounds like a monster walking in the sun. The whole is a sort of psalm or rhapsody of the sense of wonder. The maker of all things is astonished at the things He has Himself made.

This we may call the third point. Job puts forward a note of interrogation; God answers with a note of exclamation. Instead of proving to Job that it is an explicable world, He insists that it is a much stranger world than Job ever thought it was. Lastly, the poet has achieved in this speech, with that unconscious artistic accuracy found in so many of the simpler epics, another and much more delicate thing. Without once relaxing; the rigid impenetrability of Jehovah in His deliberate declaration, he has contrived to let fall here and therein the metaphors, in the parenthetical imagery, sudden and splendid suggestions that the secret of God is a bright and not a sad one—semi-accidental suggestions, like light seen for an instant through the cracks of a closed door.

ON THIS DAY

- In 1920, GKC and his wife, Frances, awoke to find it snowing in Jerusalem. The snowing continued into the next day—the first time a "deep snow" had taken place in ten years.
- And in 1929, GKC's article "England and Dogmatic Christianity" was published in the *Illustrated London News.*

FEBRUARY 10

Indeed heaven and the highest heavens belong to the
Lord your God.

—DEUTERONOMY 10:14 NKJV

It is one of the splendid strokes [in *The Book of Job*] that God rebukes alike the man who accused, and the men who defended Him; that He knocks down pessimists and optimists with the same hammer.

And it is in connection with the mechanical and supercilious comforters of Job that there occurs the still deeper and liner inversion of which I have spoken. The mechanical optimist endeavours to justify the universe avowedly upon the ground that it is a rational and consecutive pattern. He points out that the fine thing about the world is that it can all be explained. That is the one point, if I may put it so, on which God in return, is explicit to the point of violence. God says, in effect, that if there is one fine thing about the world, as far as men are concerned, it is that it cannot be explained. He insists on the inexplicableness of everything; "Hath the rain a father? . . . Out of whose womb came the ice?" He goes farther, and insists on the positive and palpable unreason of things; "Hast thou sent the rain upon the desert where no man is, and upon the wilderness wherein there is no man?" God will make man see things, if it is only against the black background of nonentity. God will make Job see a startling universe.

A PASSAGE FROM *THE LIVING AGE* MAGAZINE (1917)

There is no taking refuge in relativism or the modern picture of progress as a walk along a road. If shutting all the windows was right, opening them all was wrong; and you cannot even walk along a road if you run alternately north and south.

A PASSAGE FROM *ALL I SURVEY* (1933)

It is an eternal truth that the fathers stone the prophets and the sons build their sepulchres; often out of the same stones. For the reasons originally given for execution are often the same as the reasons given later for canonization. But it might be added that there is often a third phase, in which the grandsons wreck and reduce to ruins the sepulchres that the sons have made. The process of the acceptation or rejection of prophets, true and false, is not quite so simple a progress as it appeared to the progressive philosophy of the nineteenth century. It is full of ups and downs; even for a dead prophet, who is not generally allowed to remain dead in peace.

FEBRUARY 11

For the Spirit searches all things, yes, the deep things of God.

—1 CORINTHIANS 2:10 NKJV

The Book of Job stands definitely alone because the Book of Job definitely asks, "But what is the purpose of God? Is it worth the sacrifice even of our miserable humanity? Of course it is easy enough to wipe out our own paltry wills for the sake of a will that is grander and kinder. But is it grander and kinder? Let God use His tools; let God break His tools. But what is He doing and what are they being broken for?" It is because of this question that we have to attack as a philosophical riddle the riddle of the Book of Job.

The present importance of the Book of Job cannot be expressed adequately even by saying that it is the most interesting of ancient books. We may almost say of the Book of Job that it is the most interesting of modern books. In truth, of course, neither of the two phrases covers the matter, because fundamental human religion and fundamental human irreligion are both at once old and new; philosophy is either eternal or it is not philosophy. The modern habit of saying, "This is my opinion, but I may be wrong," is entirely irrational. If I say that it may be wrong I say that is not my opinion. The modern habit of saying "Every man has a different philosophy; this is my philosophy and it suits me"; the habit of saying this is mere weak-mindedness. A cosmic philosophy is not constructed to fit a man; a cosmic philosophy is constructed to fit a cosmos. A man can no more possess a private religion than he can possess a private sun and moon.

PASSAGES FROM THE ESSAY, "FALLACIES OF THE FUTURISTS"

There are running about England today some thousands of a certain sort of people ... They are in revolt against something they have forgotten in favour of something else which (by their own account) they have not yet found.

If I think a man honest, and it is answered that he had been in prison, then it is rational for me to reply that St. Paul or Cervantes was in prison. But it is not rational of me to say that all the people in prison must be like Cervantes or St. Paul. There must be a prima facie *case for the new thing; otherwise it is obvious that nothing is being asked of it but newness.*

FEBRUARY 12

> *You are my hiding place; You shall preserve me from*
> *trouble; You shall surround me with songs of deliverance.*
> —PSALM 32:7 NKJV

That the prose poem, which is so much nobler than most poetical poems after the Elizabethan age, should be used to help our sailors is more suitable than it seems. Bunyan was a Midland man, if ever there was one; and there is not, I think, in his wonderful fairy tale so much as a whisper of the sea. Yet he was of the sort that might have been a sailor as he was a soldier; and there is in his book a sort of knarled goodness such as sailors know.

Or again, it might be counted an irony that the Puritan's tale should be turned into a stage play, and even a Miracle play; and adorned, as it is here, with all the medieval delight of the eye and dignity of the body, of which the Puritans despoiled themselves. Yet again, Bunyan was a dramatist if ever there was one: he could not have been long kept from what is called going on the stage. None were more full of Puritan purpose than the Scotch: but I number almost among my nursery traditions that a great Scotch mystic, the late George Macdonald, appeared as Great-heart. It is something of a tribute to him, both physically and spiritually, that it seemed natural to me even when I was a boy.

For Bunyan the Midlander was right. When we send forth our sailors, we do not fear the wide seas, but only the narrow river. Mere distances are not appalling; rather they are pleasing; productive of welcomes and of travellers' tales. The tenderness felt for sailors, by all that humanity that can be called human, is due to their daily proximity to that dark rivulet which Bunyan found flowing through Bedfordshire, and which flows through every land and sea. We love these men because they are always threatened; and we like any institution which may enable such threatened men to live long.

GKC IN THE *NEW YORK TIMES* (1921)

As it happened, I travelled about America with two sticks, like a Japanese nobleman with his two swords. I fear the simile is too stately. I bore more resemblance to a [man] with two crutches or a highly ineffectual version of the devil on two sticks. I carried them both because I valued them both and did not wish to risk losing either of them in my erratic travels. One is a very plain grey stick from the woods of Buckinghamshire, but as I took it with me to Palestine it partakes of the character of a pilgrim's staff. When I can say that I have taken the same stick to Jerusalem and to Chicago, I think the stick and I may both have a rest. The other, which I value even more, was given me by the Knights of Columbus at Yale, and I wish I could think that their chivalric title allowed me to regard it as a sword.

FEBRUARY 13

You are the salt of the earth.
—MATTHEW 5:13 NKJV

John Bunyan was born in 1628, probably in the November of the year, since his baptism followed in that month. His birthplace was the village of Elstow, just outside Bedford. His family was a good example of a thing of which there are many examples, and of which there cannot be too many—a sort of aristocracy, plain and insignificant in name and handicraft, but rooted in the land like a royal dukedom.

GKC IN THE *NEW YORK TIMES* (1921)

I am not certain that brevity is the soul of wit, but brevity is an excellent substitute for wit.

The answer to our Anglo-American friendship, I believe, is imagination—imaginative art. Think of England in the terms of Sam Weller. That is what Dickens tried to present. Dickens may have had his quarrel with America, but nevertheless he made England human. What cannot be achieved by politics or diplomacy can be done through literature—seeing a nation a real mass of humanity.

There are three things to be desired on earth—life, happiness and liberty.

ON THIS DAY

- In 1932, GKC's article "The Age of Suggestion" was published in the *Illustrated London News*.

FEBRUARY 14

You meant evil against me; but God meant it for good.
—GENESIS 50:20 NKJV

In the year of the Restoration [Bunyan] was arrested for having preached to unlawful assemblies, and was imprisoned in Bedford Gaol for twelve years. In this sudden isolation, shut out from effective acting or speaking, it occurred to him systematically to write, and he opened the first window on the dark and amazing drama which had been going on within his seemingly dull personality while he ran about the fields to be away from his stepmother or leaned on his pike by the watch fires of the great war.

GKC IN THE *NEW YORK TIMES* (1921)

It seemed to me it would have been too absurd never to have come to America, if only for a day. I have come to see this country and to talk, to give inadequate after-dinner speeches known as lectures. I do not know what I shall say until the time comes. I am a journalist and am so vastly ignorant of many things, but because I am a journalist, I write and talk about them all.

English humour is casual and often finds vent in comic songs. A typical example was told me by a Glasgow Scotsman in mid-Atlantic.

Here, Mr. Chesterton quoted four lines of an English comic song, which ran something like this:

> *Father's got the sack from the waterworks*
> *For smoking of his old cherry briar;*
> *Father's got the sack from the waterworks,*
> *Because he might set the works on fire.*

ON THIS DAY ─────────────────────────────

- In 1931, GKC's article "The Conflict of Romance and Realism" was published in the *Illustrated London News*.

FEBRUARY 15

You number my wanderings; put my tears into Your bottle;
are they not in Your book?

—PSALM 56:8 NKJV

Before the Puritans were swept off the scene for ever, they had done two extraordinary things. They had broken to pieces in plain battle on an English meadow the chivalry of a great nation, bred from its youth to arms. And they had brought forth from their agony a small book, called *The Pilgrim's Progress*, which was greater literature than the whole contemporary culture of the great Renaissance, founded on three generations of the worship of learning and art.

GKC IN THE *NEW YORK TIMES* (1921)

On January 21, 1921, GKC spoke in the Times Square Theatre in answer to the question, "Shall We Abolish the Inevitable?" The following are some of his remarks.

If we are going to discuss a moral, social or political matter, let us in God's name ask whether the thing we propose to abolish or to foster is good or bad in itself, and examine every question upon its own merits. Then our minds will be cleared of this fog of fatality which hangs upon our civilisation. Whatever man is, he is not in that sense a part of nature. He has committed crimes and performed heroisms which no animal ever tried to do. Let us hold ourselves free from the boundary of the material order of things, for so shall we have a chance in the future to do things far too historic for prophecy.

- In 1920, GKC gave a lecture at the English College in Jerusalem. He received thanks in five languages from the students who attended.

FEBRUARY 16

But I will sing of Your power; yes, I will sing aloud of
Your mercy in the morning; for You have been my defense
and refuge in the day of my trouble.

—PSALM 59:16 NKJV

The Pilgrim's Progress certainly exhibits all the marks of such a revival of primitive power and mystery. Its resemblance to the Bible is not mere imitation of style; it is also a coincidence of mood. Bunyan, who was a soldier in Cromwell's army, had himself been thrown into a world almost as ferocious and obscure as that of Gideon, or the Maccabees, and he was really under the influence of the same kind of emotion. This was simply because, as I have said, Puritanism was a thing barbaric, and therefore eternal.

Nowhere, perhaps, except in Homer, is there such a perfect description conveyed by the use of merely plain words. The description in Bunyan of how Moses came like a wind up the road, and was but a word and a blow; or how Apollyon straddled quite over the breadth of the way and swore by his infernal den— these are things which can only be paralleled in sudden and splendid phrases out of Homer or the Bible, such as the phrase about the monstrous and man-killing hands of Achilles, or the war-horse who laughs at the shaking of the spear.

GKC IN THE *NEW YORK TIMES* (1921)

Belief in the inevitable always presupposes a sort of vacuum in which forces are working. The moves in a game of chess are mathematical facts, but suppose you prophesy that one player in a certain game will checkmate his opponent in a number of moves. He may go crazy, or kick over the board in a rage, or in a spirit of compassion make all his moves the wrong ones. All predictions are like that. They presuppose that the rules will be kept to, but suppose they are not?

ON THIS DAY

- In 1929, GKC's article "On the Essay" was published in the *Illustrated London News*.

FEBRUARY 17

And in the night His song shall be with me—A prayer to the God of my life.

—PSALM 42:8 NKJV

There may be some—I do not know if there are—who will be so much alienated by the seventeenth century apparatus of the great story, so much out of sympathy with endless arguments about the Atonement, so unresponsive to the significance of the Scriptural names and titles, so weary of old texts, so scornful of old doctrines, that they will fancy that this ancient Puritan poetry of danger [in *The Pilgrim's Progress*] is interesting only from a literary and not at all from a philosophical or religious point of view. For such people there is, I suppose, still waiting untried that inevitable mood in which a man may stand amid a field of flowers in the quiet sunlight and realise suddenly that of all conceivable things the most acutely dangerous thing is to be alive.

GKC IN THE *NEW YORK TIMES* (1921)

Intangible falsehood, based upon no authority, is of all things the most difficult to fight.

Like the man who did not believe in ghosts because he had seen so many, I do not believe in inevitable fates.

A PASSAGE FROM *THE BALL AND THE CROSS* (1909)

A fierce inspiration fell on him suddenly; he would strike them where they stood with the love of God. They should not move till they saw their own sweet and startling existence. They should not go from that place till they went home embracing like brothers and shouting like men delivered. From the Cross from which he had fallen fell the shadow of its fantastic mercy.

FEBRUARY 18

For You are my lamp, O Lord; the Lord shall enlighten my darkness.

—2 SAMUEL 22:29 NKJV

A legend has run round the newspapers that Bernard Shaw offered himself as a better writer than Shakespeare. This is false and quite unjust; Bernard Shaw never said anything of the kind. The writer whom he did say was better than Shakespeare was not himself, but Bunyan. And he justified it by attributing to Bunyan a virile acceptance of life as a high and harsh adventure, while in Shakespeare he saw nothing but profligate pessimism, the *vanitas vanitatum* of a disappointed voluptuary. According to this view Shakespeare was always saying, "Out, out, brief candle," because his was only a ballroom candle; while Bunyan was seeking to light such a candle as by God's grace should never be put out.

GKC IN THE *NEW YORK TIMES* (1921)

At the opening of a lecture Chesterton gave on January 23 at the Times Square Theatre in New York City, he was introduced as "the Prince of Paradoxes." So followed a memorable evening, during which he offered the following remarks, some whimsical, others eloquent and moving.

In response to being called "the Prince of Paradoxes," Chesterton said that "as a fantastic statement flying in the face of common sense, it could not be applied to himself, an ardent defender of common sense."

One is constantly told that it is morbid to think about illness. But to me it seems perfectly healthy to think about disease and morbid to think about health. A man is only wasting his time when he thinks about the absence of disease when it is absent.

No decent man desires that there shall be an instrument of torture too powerful for his courage.

God also bearing witness both with signs and wonders,
[and] with various miracles . . .

—Hebrews 2:4 nkjv

The most incredible thing about miracles is that they happen.
A few clouds in heaven do come together into the staring shape
of one human eye. A tree does stand up in the landscape of a
doubtful journey in the exact and elaborate shape of a note of
interrogation. . . . In short, there is in life an element of elfin
coincidence which people reckoning on the prosaic may perpetually miss. As it has been well expressed in the paradox of
Poe, wisdom should reckon on the unforeseen.

PASSAGES FROM *THE NEW JERUSALEM* (1920)

I have heard that there is a low doorway at the entrance to a famous
shrine which is called the Gate of Humility; but indeed in this sense
all gates are gates of humility, and especially gates of this kind.

Any one who has ever looked at a landscape under an archway
will know what I mean, when I say that it sharpens a pleasure with
a strange sentiment of privilege. It adds to the grace of distance
something that makes it not only a grace, but a gift. Such are the
visions of remote places that appear in the low gateways of a Gothic
town; as if each gateway led into a separate world.

It was in the season of Christmas that I came out of my little gar-
den in that " field of the beeches" between the Chilterns and the
Thames, and began to walk backwards through history to the place
from which Christmas came. For it is often necessary to walk back-
wards, as a man on the wrong road goes back to a sign-post to find

the right road. The modern man is more like a traveller who has forgotten the name of his destination, and has to go back whence he came, even to find out where he is going. That the world has lost its way few will now deny; and it did seem to me that I found at last a sort of sign-post.

FEBRUARY 20

This is the message which we have heard from Him and declare to you.

—1 JOHN 1:5 NKJV

"You're an astounding card," he said, staring. "I shall come and hear your sermons if they're as amusing as your manners." His voice changed a little, and he leaned back in his chair.

"Oh, there are sermons in a cruet-stand, too," said Father Brown, quite gravely. "Have you heard of faith like a grain of mustard-seed; or charity that anoints with oil? And as for vinegar, can any soldiers forget that solitary soldier, who, when the sun was darkened—"

A PASSAGE FROM *THE NEW JERUSALEM* (1920)

A friend of mine described his book, The Path to Rome, *as a journey through all Europe that the Faith had saved; and I might very well describe my own journey as one through all Europe that the War has saved. The trail of the actual fighting, of course, was awfully apparent everywhere; the plantations of pale crosses seemed to crop up on every side like growing things; and the first French villages through which I passed had heard in the distance, day and night, the guns of the long battle-line, like the breaking of an endless exterior sea of night upon the very borderland of the world. I felt it most as we passed the noble towers of Amiens . . .*

Whatever else the war was, it was like the resistance of something as solid as land, and sometimes as patient and inert as land, against something as unstable as water, as weak as water; but also as strong as water, as strong as water is in a cataract or a flood. It was the resistance of form to formlessness.

ON THIS DAY

• In 1920, GKC and his wife, Frances, walked together to the Garden of Gethsemane in Jerusalem.

FEBRUARY 21

He alone spreads out the heavens, and treads on the waves of the sea.

—JOB 9:8 NKJV

For the edge of the sea is like the edge of a sword; it is sharp, military, and decisive; it really looks like a bolt or bar, and not like a mere expansion. It hangs in heaven, grey, or green, or blue, changing in colour, but changeless in form, behind all the slippery contours of the land and all the savage softness of the forests, like the scales of God held even.

A PASSAGE FROM *THE NEW JERUSALEM* (1920)

I descended from the desert train at Ludd, which had all the look of a large camp in the desert; appropriately enough perhaps, for it is the traditional birthplace of the soldier St. George . . . A motor car sent by friends had halted beside the platform; I got into it with a not unusual vagueness about where I was going; and it wound its way up miry paths to a more rolling stretch of country with patches of cactus here and there. And then with a curious abruptness I became conscious that the whole huge desert had vanished, and I was in a new land. The dark red plains had rolled away like an enormous nightmare; and I found myself in a fresh and exceedingly pleasant dream.

I know it will seem fanciful; but for a moment I really felt as if I had come home; or rather to that home behind home for which we are all homesick. The lost memory of it is the life at once of faith and of fairytale. Groves glowing with oranges rose behind hedges of grotesque cactus or prickly pear; which really looked like green dragons guarding the golden apples of the Hesperides. On each side of the road were such flowers as I had never seen before under the sun; for indeed they seemed to have the sun in them rather than the sun on them.

FEBRUARY 22

> *These all died in faith, not having received the promises,*
> *but having seen them afar off were assured of them,*
> *embraced them and confessed that they were strangers*
> *and pilgrims on the earth.*
>
> —HEBREWS 11:13 NKJV

The Christian optimism is based on the fact that we do not fit in to the world. I had tried to be happy by telling myself that man is an animal, like any other which sought its meat from God. But now I really was happy, for I had learnt that man is a monstrosity. I had been right in feeling all things as odd, for I myself was at once worse and better than all things. The optimist's pleasure was prosaic, for it dwelt on the naturalness of everything; the Christian pleasure was poetic, for it dwelt on the unnaturalness of everything in the light of the supernatural. The modern philosopher had told me again and again that I was in the right place, and I had still felt depressed even in acquiescence. But I had heard that I was in the wrong place, and my soul sang for joy, like a bird in spring. The knowledge found out and illuminated forgotten chambers in the dark house of infancy. I knew now why grass had always seemed to me as queer as the green beard of a giant, and why I could feel homesick at home.

A PASSAGE FROM *THE NEW JERUSALEM* (1920)

Only in a wild Eastern tale could one picture a pilgrim or traveller finding such a garden in the desert [as I found there in Ludd]; and I thought of the oldest tale of all, and the garden from which we came.

But there was something in it yet more subtle; which there must be in the impression of any earthly paradise. It is vital to such a dream that things familiar should be mixed with things fantastic; as when an actual dream is filled with the faces of old friends. Sparrows, which seem to be the same all over the world, were darting hither and thither among the flowers; and I had the fancy that they were the souls of the town-sparrows of London and the smoky cities, and now gone wherever the good sparrows go.

ON THIS DAY ———————————————————

- In 1920, GKC and his wife, Frances, attended a service at St. George's Anglican Cathedral in Jerusalem.

FEBRUARY 23

> *I would have lost heart, unless I had believed that I would*
> *see the goodness of the Lord in the land of the living.*
> —PSALM 27:13 NKJV

And my haunting instinct that somehow good was not merely a tool to be used, but a relic to be guarded, like the goods from Crusoe's ship—even that had been the wild whisper of something originally wise, for, according to Christianity, we were indeed the survivors of a wreck, the crew of a golden ship that had gone down before the beginning of the world.

A PASSAGE FROM *TREMENDOUS TRIFLES* (1909)

That is what makes life at once so splendid and so strange. We are in the wrong world. When I thought that was the right town, it bored me; when I knew it was wrong, I was happy. So the false optimism, the modern happiness, tires us because it tells us we fit into this world. The true happiness is that we don't fit. We come from somewhere else. We have lost our way.

ON THIS DAY ─────────────────────────────

- In 1920, GKC and his wife, Frances, attended a party in the Holy City where "all Jerusalem must have been present." The large group of dignitaries included "the Grand Mufti, the Greek Patriarch, Armenian Patriarch, Syrian Patriarch, Coptic Christians, Greek Orthodox priests, Jews, Arabs, Muslims, British officers and their wives."

FEBRUARY 24

To each according to his own ability . . .
—MATTHEW 25:15 NKJV

Now if we take this house or home as a test, we may very generally lay the simple spiritual foundations of the idea. God is that which can make something out of nothing. Man (it may truly be said) is that which can make something out of anything. In other words, while the joy of God [may] be unlimited creation, the special joy of man is limited creation, the combination of creation with limits.

Man's pleasure, therefore, is to possess conditions, but also to be partly possessed by them; to be half-controlled by the flute he plays or by the field he digs. The excitement is to get the utmost out of given conditions.

VERSE FROM *TREMENDOUS TRIFLES* (1909)

Happy is he and more than wise
Who sees with wondering eyes and clean
This world through all the grey disguise
Of sleep and custom in between.

ON THIS DAY ────────────────────────────

- In 1906, GKC's article "On Long Speeches and Truth" was published in the *Illustrated London News*.

FEBRUARY 25

Assuredly, I say to you, unless you are converted and
become as little children, you will by no means enter the
kingdom of heaven.

—MATTHEW 18:3 NKJV

But if you want to see what a vast and bewildering array of valuable things you can get at a halfpenny each you should do as I was doing last night. I was gluing my nose against the glass of a very small and dimly lit toy shop in one of the greyest and leanest of the streets of Battersea. But dim as was that square of light, it was filled (as a child once said to me) with all the colours God ever made. Those toys of the poor were like the children who buy them; they were all dirty; but they were all bright. For my part, I think brightness more important than cleanliness; since the first is of the soul, and the second of the body. You must excuse me; I am a democrat; I know I am out of fashion in the modern world.

As I looked at that palace of pigmy wonders, at small green omnibuses, at small blue elephants, at small black dolls, and small red Noah's arks . . . that lit shop-window became like the brilliantly lit stage when one is watching some highly coloured comedy. I forgot the grey houses and the grimy people behind me as one forgets the dark galleries and the dim crowds at a theatre. It seemed as if the little objects behind the glass were small, not because they were toys, but because they were objects far away. The green omnibus was really a green omnibus, a green Bayswater omnibus, passing across some huge desert on its ordinary way to Bayswater. The blue elephant was no longer blue with paint; he was blue with distance. . . . The red Noah's ark was really the enormous ship of earthly salvation riding on the rain-swollen sea, red in the first morning of hope.

A PASSAGE FROM *THE BALL AND THE CROSS* (1909)

Turnbull looked up . . . He had seen the blue but gloomy eyes of the western Highlander troubled by as many tempests as his own west Highland seas, but there had always been a fixed star of faith behind the storms.

FEBRUARY 26

And the Ancient of Days was seated; His garment was white as snow.

—DANIEL 7:9 NKJV

And one of the two or three defiant verities of the best religious morality, of real Christianity, for example, is exactly this same thing; the chief assertion of religious morality is that white is a colour. Virtue is not the absence of vices or the avoidance of moral dangers; virtue is a vivid and separate thing, like pain or a particular smell. Mercy does not mean not being cruel or sparing people revenge or punishment; it means a plain and positive thing like the sun, which one has either seen or not seen.

Chastity does not mean abstention from sexual wrong; it means something flaming, like Joan of Arc. In a word, God paints in many colours; but He never paints so gorgeously, I had almost said so gaudily, as when He paints in white. In a sense our age has realised this fact, and expressed it in our sullen costume.

PASSAGES FROM *VARIED TYPES* (1903)

Shakespeare's Much Ado About Nothing *is a great comedy, because behind it is the whole pressure of that love of love which is the youth of the world, which is common to all the young, especially to those who swear they will die bachelors and old maids.*

Cyrano de Bergerac came to us as the new decoration of an old truth, that merriment was one of the world's natural flowers, and not one of its exotics. The gigantesque levity, the flamboyant eloquence, the Rabelaisian puns and digressions were seen to be once more what they had been in Rabelais, the mere outbursts of a human sympathy and bravado as old and solid as the stars.

FEBRUARY 27

If you seek her as silver, and search for her as for hidden treasures; then you will understand the fear of the Lord, and find the knowledge of God.

—PROVERBS 2:4–5 NKJV

And then followed an experience impossible to describe. It was as if I had been blundering about since my birth with two huge and unmanageable machines, of different shapes and without apparent connection—the world and the Christian tradition. I had found this hole in the world: the fact that one must somehow find a way of loving the world without trusting it; somehow one must love the world without being worldly. I found this projecting feature of Christian theology, like a sort of hard spike, the dogmatic insistence that God was personal, and had made a world separate from Himself. The spike of dogma fitted exactly into the hole in the world—it had evidently been meant to go there—and then the strange thing began to happen. When once these two parts of the two machines had come together, one after another, all the other parts fitted and fell in with an eerie exactitude. I could hear bolt after bolt over all the machinery falling into its place with a kind of click of relief. Having got one part right, all the other parts were repeating that rectitude, as clock after clock strikes noon.

A PASSAGE FROM *ALL I SURVEY* (1933)

The Humanists are human beings; that, at least, may be tentatively conceded to them; and human beings are allowed to think, even while they do not carve, paint, build, or play the fiddle. But when we consider Creation with a significance a little deeper, we find it a little more difficult. It is much too difficult to dogmatize about; nor am I dogmatizing: I am only asking questions, like Socrates, of people whom I suspect of not knowing what their own dogmas are.

ON THIS DAY

- In 1932, GKC's article "More on Making Good" was published in the *Illustrated London News*.

FEBRUARY 28

And where the Spirit of the Lord is, there is liberty.
—2 CORINTHIANS 3:17 NKJV

I suppose Mr. Blatchford would say that in his [determinist] Utopia nobody would be in prison. What do I care whether I am in prison or no, if I have to drag chains everywhere. A man in his Utopia may have, for all I know, free food, free meadows, his own estate, his own palace. What does it matter? he may not have his own soul. Every thought that comes into his head he must regard as the click of a machine. [If this is true,] what is the good of sunrises and palaces? Was ever slavery like unto this slavery? Was ever man before so much a slave?

I know that this will never be. Mr. Blatchford's philosophy will never be endured among sane men. But if ever it is I will easily predict what will happen. Man, the machine, will stand up in these flowery meadows and cry aloud, "Was there not once a thing, a church, that taught us we were free in our souls?"

A PASSAGE FROM *VARIED TYPES* (1903)

But the vast practical work of Francis is assuredly not to be ignored, for this amazingly unworldly and almost maddeningly simple-minded infant was one of the most consistently successful men that ever fought with this bitter world. It is the custom to say that the secret of such men is their profound belief in themselves, and this is true, but not all the truth. Workhouses and lunatic asylums are thronged with men who believe in themselves.

Of Francis it is far truer to say that the secret of his success was his profound belief in other people, and it is the lack of this that has commonly been the curse of these obscure Napoleons.

Francis always assumed that every one must be just as anxious about their common relative, the water-rat, as he was. He planned a visit to the Emperor to draw his attention to the needs of "his little sisters, the larks." He used to talk to any thieves and robbers he met about their misfortune in being unable to give rein to their desire for holiness.

It was an innocent habit, and doubtless the robbers often "got round him," as the phrase goes. Quite as often, however, they discovered that he had "got round" them, and discovered the other side, the side of secret nobility.

The Lord looks down from heaven upon the children of
men, to see if there are any who understand, who seek
God. They have all turned aside, they have together
become corrupt; there is none who does good, no, not one.

—PSALM 14:2–3 NKJV

If only Mr. Blatchford would ask the real question. It is not,
"Why is Christianity so bad when it claims to be so good?"
The real question is, "Why are all human beings so bad when
they claim to be so good?" Why is not the most noble scheme
a guarantee against corruption? If [Mr. Blatchford] will boldly
pursue this question, will really leave delusions behind and
walk across the godless waste, alone, he will come at last to a
strange place. His sceptical pilgrimage will end at a place where
Christianity begins.

A PASSAGE FROM *WILLIAM BLAKE* (1910)

[Blake] truly seemed to wait for the opening of the door of death
as a child waits for the opening of the cupboard on his birthday . . .
He was in his last moments in that wonderful world of whiteness in
which white is still a colour. He would have clapped his hands at a
white snowflake, and sung as at the white wings of an angel at the
moment when he himself turned suddenly white with death.

ON THIS DAY

- In 1908, GKC's article "The Ethics of Fairy-Tales" was
  published in the *Illustrated London News*.

MARCH 1

I am not mad, most noble Festus, but speak the words of truth and reason.

—ACTS 26:25 NKJV

It was Huxley and Herbert Spencer and Bradlaugh who brought me back to orthodox theology. They sowed in my mind my first wild doubts of doubt. Our grandmothers were quite right when they said that Tom Paine and the free-thinkers unsettled the mind. They do. They unsettled mine horribly. The rationalist made me question whether reason was of any use whatever; and when I had finished Herbert Spencer I had got as far as doubting (for the first time) whether evolution had occurred at all. As I laid down the last of Colonel Ingersoll's atheistic lectures the dreadful thought broke across my mind, "Almost thou persuadest me to be a Christian." I was in a desperate way.

This odd effect of the great agnostics in arousing doubts deeper than their own might be illustrated in many ways. I take only one. As I read and re-read all the non-Christian or anti-Christian accounts of the faith, from Huxley to Bradlaugh, a slow and awful impression grew gradually but graphically upon my mind—the impression that Christianity must be a most extraordinary thing. For not only (as I understood) had Christianity the most flaming vices, but it had apparently a mystical talent for combining vices which seemed inconsistent with each other. It was attacked on all sides and for all contradictory reasons. No sooner had one rationalist demonstrated that it was too far to the east than another demonstrated with equal clearness that it was much too far to the west. No sooner had my indignation died down at its angular and aggressive squareness than I was called up again to notice and condemn its enervating and sensual roundness.

- In 1908, George Bernard Shaw wrote to GKC: "What about that play? I shall repeat my public challenge to you; vaunt my superiority; insult your corpulence; torture Belloc; if necessary, call on you and steal your wife's affections by intellectual and athletic displays, until you contribute something to the British drama."

- In 1904, GKC's novel *The Napoleon of Notting Hill* was published. Also in 1904, GKC's book-length study of the artist *G. F. Watts* was published.
- And in 1935, GKC's collection of mystery stories, *The Scandal of Father Brown*, was published.

MARCH 2

And the earth brought forth grass, the herb that yields seed according to its kind, and the tree that yields fruit, whose seed is in itself according to its kind. And God saw that it was good.

—Genesis 1:12 nkjv

What Christianity says is merely this. That this repetition in Nature has its origin not in a thing resembling a law but a thing resembling a will. . . . Christianity holds that the world and its repetition came by will or Love as children are begotten by a father, and therefore that other and different things might come by it. Briefly, it believes that a God who could do anything so extraordinary as making pumpkins go on being pumpkins, is like the prophet, Habbakuk, *Capable de tout* [capable of anything]. If you do not think it extraordinary that a pumpkin is always a pumpkin, think again. You have not yet even begun philosophy. You have not even seen a pumpkin.

A PASSAGE FROM *WILLIAM BLAKE* (1910)

All [Blake's images of] animals are as absolute as the animals on a shield of heraldry. His lambs are of unsullied silver, his lions are of flaming gold. His lion may lie down with his lamb, but he will never really mix with him . . .

Go back and read Blake's poems about animals, as, for instance, about the lamb and about the tiger. You will see quite clearly that he is talking of an eternal tiger, who rages and rejoices for ever in the sight of God. You will see that he is talking of an eternal and supernatural lamb, who can only feed happily in the fields of heaven.

ON THIS DAY

- In 1929, GKC's article "Buddhism and Christianity" was published in the *Illustrated London News*.

MARCH 3

For we do not have [in Christ] a High Priest who cannot sympathize with our weaknesses, but was in all points tempted as we are, yet without sin. Let us therefore come boldly to the throne of grace, that we may obtain mercy and find grace to help in time of need.

—HEBREWS 4:15–16 NKJV

Now when Christianity came, the ancient world had just reached this dilemma. It heard the Voice of Nature-Worship crying, "All natural things are good. War is as healthy as the flowers. Lust is as clean as the stars." And it heard also the cry of the hopeless Stoics and Idealists: "The flowers are at war: the stars are unclean: nothing but man's conscience is right and that is utterly defeated."

Both views were consistent, philosophical and exalted: their only disadvantage was that the first leads logically to murder and the second to suicide. After an agony of thought the world saw the sane path between the two. It was the Christian God. He made Nature but He was Man.

PASSAGES FROM *WHAT'S WRONG WITH THE WORLD* (1910)

It is man, says Aristotle, who is the measure. It is the Son of Man, says Scripture, who shall judge the quick and the dead.

The future is a blank wall on which every man can write his own name as large as he likes; the past I find already covered with illegible scribbles, such as Plato, Isaiah, Shakespeare, Michael Angelo, Napoleon. I can make the future as narrow as myself; the past is obliged to be as broad and turbulent as humanity.

And the upshot of this modern attitude is really this: that men invent new ideals because they dare not attempt old ideals. They look forward with enthusiasm, because they are afraid to look back.

MARCH 4

> *But where can wisdom be found? And where is the place*
> *of understanding?*
>
> —JOB 28:12 NKJV

Here is the failure of Agnosticism. That our every-day view of
the things we do (in the common sense) know, actually depends
upon our view of the things we do not (in the common sense)
know. It is all very well to tell a man, as the Agnostics do, to "cul-
tivate his garden." But suppose a man ignores everything outside
his garden, and among them ignores the sun and the rain?

This is the real fact. You cannot live without dogmas about these
things. You cannot act for twenty-four hours without deciding
either to hold people responsible or not to hold them responsible.
Theology is a product far more practical than chemistry.

A PASSAGE FROM *WHAT'S WRONG WITH THE WORLD* (1910)

If it be really true that men sickened of sacred words and wearied of
theology, if this largely unreasoning irritation against "dogma" did
arise out of some ridiculous excess of such things among priests in
the past, then I fancy we must be laying up a fine crop of cant for our
descendants to grow tired of.

A PASSAGE FROM *IRISH IMPRESSIONS* (1919)

Wherever men are still theological, there is still some chance of their
being logical.

A PASSAGE FROM *THE NEW JERUSALEM* (1920)

I do not admit that theological points are small points. Theology is only thought applied to religion; and those who prefer a thoughtless religion need not be so very disdainful of others with a more rationalistic taste. The old joke that the Greek sects only differed about a single letter is about the lamest and most illogical joke in the world. An atheist and a theist only differ by a single letter; yet theologians are so subtle as to distinguish definitely between the two.

MARCH 5

How much better to get wisdom than gold!
—PROVERBS 16:16 NKJV

I will try and explain why I think a religious philosophy necessary and why I think Christianity the best religious philosophy. But before I do so I want you to bear in mind two historical facts. I do not ask you to draw my deduction from them or any deduction from them. I ask you to remember them as mere facts throughout the discussion.

1. Christianity arose and spread in a very cultured and very cynical world in a very modern world. Lucretius was as much a materialist as Haeckel, and a much more persuasive writer. . . .
2. Christianity, which is a very mystical religion, has nevertheless been the religion of the most practical section of mankind. It has far more paradoxes than the Eastern philosophies, but it also builds far better roads.

A PASSAGE FROM *THE NEW JERUSALEM* (1920)

The Christianity of Jerusalem is highly historic, and cannot be understood without historical imagination. And this is not the strong point perhaps of those among us who generally record their impressions of the place.

As the educated Englishman does not know the history of England, it would be unreasonable to expect him to know the history of Moab or of Mesopotamia. He receives the impression, in visiting the shrines of Jerusalem, of a number of small sects squabbling about small things. In short, he has before him a tangle of trivialities, which include the Roman Empire in the West and in the East, the Catholic Church in its two great divisions, the Jewish race, the memories of Greece and Egypt, and the whole Mahometan world in Asia and Africa.

It may be that he regards these as small things; but I should be glad if he would cast his eye over human history, and tell me what are the large things. The truth is that the things that meet to-day in Jerusalem are by far the greatest things that the world has yet seen. If they are not important nothing on this earth is important.

MARCH 6

Inquire, please, of the former age, and consider the things discovered by their fathers; for we were born yesterday, and know nothing, because our days on earth are a shadow.

—JOB 8:8–9 NKJV

If the Christian God really made the human race, would not the human race tend to rumours and perversions of the Christian God? If the centre of our life is a certain fact, would not people far from the centre have a muddled version of that fact?

A PASSAGE FROM *ORTHODOXY* (1908)

[Some] people professed that the universe was one coherent thing; but they were not fond of the universe. But I was frightfully fond of the universe and wanted to address it by a diminutive. I often did so; and it never seemed to mind.

Actually and in truth I did feel that these dim dogmas of vitality were better expressed by calling the world small than by calling it large. For about infinity there was a sort of carelessness which was the reverse of the fierce and pious care which I felt touching the pricelessness and the peril of life. They showed only a dreary waste; but I felt a sort of sacred thrift.

For economy is far more romantic than extravagance. To them stars were an unending income of half-pence; but I felt about the golden sun and the silver moon as a schoolboy feels if he has one sovereign and one shilling. These subconscious convictions are best hit off by the colour and tone of certain tales. Thus I have said that stories of magic alone can express my sense that life is not only a pleasure, but a kind of eccentric privilege.

I may express this other feeling of cosmic cosiness by allusion to another book always read in boyhood, Robinson Crusoe, which I read about this time, and which owes its eternal vivacity to the fact that it celebrates the poetry of limits, nay, even the wild romance of prudence. Crusoe is a man on a small rock with a few comforts just snatched from the sea: the best thing in the book is simply the list of things saved from the wreck.

MARCH 7

> *We spend our years as a tale that is told.*
> —Psalm 90:9

A story is the highest mark,
For the world is a story and every part of it.
And there is nothing that can touch the world,
or any part of it,
That is not a story.

PASSAGES FROM *ORTHODOXY* (1908)

Life (according to the faith) is very like a serial story in a magazine: life ends with the promise (or menace) "to be continued in our next."

But a man can expect any number of adventures if he goes travelling in the land of authority. One can find no meanings in a jungle of scepticism; but the man will find more and more meanings who walks through a forest of doctrine and design. Here everything has a story tied to its tail, like the tools or pictures in my father's house; for it is my father's house. I end where I began—at the right end. I have entered at least the gate of all good philosophy. I have come into my second childhood.

ON THIS DAY

- In 1908, GKC's article "The Anomalies of English Politics" was published in the *Illustrated London News*.

Where were you when I laid the foundations of the earth?
Tell Me, if you have understanding.

—JOB 38:4 NKJV

A cosmos one day being rebuked by a pessimist replied, "How can you who revile me consent to speak by my machinery? Permit me to reduce you to nothingness and then we will discuss the matter."

Moral. You should not look a gift universe in the mouth.

PASSAGES FROM *ORTHODOXY* (1908)

For the universe is a single jewel, and while it is a natural cant to talk of a jewel as peerless and priceless, of this jewel it is literally true. This cosmos is indeed without peer and without price: for there cannot be another one.

To vary the metaphor, I was like one who had advanced into a hostile country to take one high fortress. And when that fort had fallen the whole country surrendered and turned solid behind me. The whole land was lit up, as it were, back to the first fields of my childhood.

All those blind fancies of boyhood . . . became suddenly transparent and sane. I was right when I felt that roses were red by some sort of choice: it was the divine choice . . . Even those dim and shapeless monsters of notions which I have not been able to describe, much less defend, stepped quietly into their places like colossal caryatides of the creed. The fancy that the cosmos was not vast and void, but small and cosy, had a fulfilled significance now, for anything that is a work of art must be small in the sight of the artist; to God the stars might be only small and dear, like diamonds.

MARCH 9

You will show me the path of life; in Your presence is
fullness of joy.

—PSALM 16:11 NKJV

It is absurd indeed that Christians should be called the enemies of life because they wish life to last for ever; it is more absurd still to call the old comic writers dull because they wished their unchanging characters to last for ever.

Both popular religion with its endless joys, and the old comic story, with its endless jokes, have in our time faded together. We are too weak to desire that undying vigour. We believe that you can have too much of a good thing—a blasphemous belief, which at one blow wrecks all the heavens that men have hoped for. The grand old defiers of God were not afraid of an eternity of torment. We have come to be afraid of an eternity of joy.

PASSAGES FROM *HERETICS* (1905)

Great joy does not gather the rosebuds while it may; its eyes are fixed on the immortal rose which Dante saw. Great joy has in it the sense of immortality; the very splendour of youth is the sense that it has all space to stretch its legs in.

About the whole cosmos there is a tense and secret festivity—like preparations for Guy Fawkes' day. Eternity is the eve of something. I never look up at the stars without feeling that they are the fires of a schoolboy's rocket, fixed in their everlasting fall.

ON THIS DAY ────────────────────

- In 1929, GKC's article "The New Generations and Morality" was published in the *Illustrated London News.*

MARCH 10

*"But who do you say that I am?" Simon Peter answered
and said, "You are the Christ, the Son of the living God."
Jesus answered and said to him, "Blessed are you, Simon
Bar-Jonah, for flesh and blood has not revealed this to
you, but My Father who is in heaven."*

—MATTHEW 16:15–17 NKJV

*Man is a spark flying upwards, God is everlasting.
Who are we, to whom this cup of human life has
been given, to ask for more? Let us love mercy
and walk humbly. What is man, that thou regardest him?
Man is a star unquenchable. God is in him incarnate.
His life is planned upon a scale colossal, of which
he sees glimpses. Let him dare all things,
claim all things: he is the son of Man, who
shall come in the clouds of glory,
saw these two strands mingling to make the religion of man.*

A PASSAGE FROM *ALL I SURVEY* (1933)

*Swift, as I have said, was a man who could write what nobody else
could have written, and often at a time when nobody else would
have dared to write it. He could write the truth about a time in
which perhaps more lies were told, and about which perhaps more
lies have since been taught, than any other episode in English history. He could say the right thing, and say it exactly rightly; with a
deadly detachment or a stunning understatement unmatched in the
satires of mankind.*

MARCH 11

Whoever receives this little child in My name receives
Me; and whoever receives Me receives Him who sent Me.
For he who is least among you all will be great.

—LUKE 9:48 NKJV

We must certainly be in a novel;
What I like about this novelist is that he takes
such trouble about his minor characters.

PASSAGES FROM *THE EVERLASTING MAN* (1925)

As soon as I had clearly in my mind this conception of something solid in the solitary and unique character of the divine story, it struck me that there was exactly the same strange and yet solid character in the human story that had led up to it; because that human story also had a root that was divine.

It is still a strange story, though an old one, how [the wise men] came out of orient lands, crowned with the majesty of kings and clothed with something of the mystery of magicians. That truth that is tradition has wisely remembered them almost as unknown quantities, as mysterious as their mysterious and melodious names; Melchior, Caspar, Balthazar.

But there came with them all that world of wisdom that had watched the stars in Chaldea and the sun in Persia; and we shall not be wrong if we see in them the same curiosity that moves all the sages. They would stand for the same human ideal if their names had really been Confucius or Pythagoras or Plato. They were those who sought not tales but the truth of things, and since their thirst for truth was itself a thirst for God.

MARCH 12

And of His fullness we have all received, and grace for grace.
—JOHN 1:16 NKJV

Praised be God for all sides of life, for friends, lovers, art, literature, knowledge, humour, politics, and for the little red cloud away there in the west—

PASSAGES FROM GKC'S SERMONS AT ST. PAUL'S CHURCH, COVENT GARDEN (1904)

Now the basis of Christianity as well as of Democracy is, that a man is sacred.

I began at any early age, like everybody else who has gone through the ordinary curriculum of a public school education, by doubting the existence of God, and being a Materialist. I have ended by doubting the existence of Materialism.

ON THIS DAY

- In 1910, the *Chicago Tribune* praised GKC's novel *The Ball and the Cross*, saying, "The flight in search of a duelling ground; the pursuit by the police; the friendly intervention of the anarchist wineshop-keeper . . . the renewed flight of the fighters, seconds, physicians, reporters, and the anarchist over the back fences—all these and other incidents are essentially Chestertonian."
- And in 1932, GKC's article "The Relics of Mediævalism" was published in the *Illustrated London News*.

MARCH 13

> *The goodness of God leads you to repentance.*
> —ROMANS 2:4 NKJV

> *Here dies another day*
> *During which I have had eyes, ears, hands*
> *And the great world round me;*
> *And with tomorrow begins another.*
> *Why am I allowed two?*

PASSAGES FROM *THE EVERLASTING MAN* (1925)

Here it is the important point that the Magi, who stand for mysticism and philosophy, are truly conceived as seeking something new and even as finding something unexpected. That tense sense of crisis which still tingles in the Christmas story, and even in every Christmas celebration, accentuates the idea of a search and a discovery.

Christmas for us in Christendom has become one thing, and in one sense even a simple thing. But like all the truths of that tradition, it is in another sense a very complex thing. Its unique note is the simultaneous striking of many notes; of humility, of gaiety, of gratitude, of mystical fear, but also of vigilance and of drama.

MARCH 14

The Lord is good to those who wait for Him, to the soul
who seeks Him.

—LAMENTATIONS 3:25 NKJV

Stevenson's enormous capacity for joy flowed directly out of his profoundly religious temperament. He conceived himself as an unimportant guest at one eternal and uproarious banquet.

A PASSAGE FROM *THE EVERLASTING MAN* (1925)

All this indescribable thing that we call the Christmas atmosphere only hangs in the air as something like a lingering fragrance or fading vapour from the exultant explosion of that one hour in the Judean hills nearly two thousand years ago. But the savour is still unmistakable, and it is something too subtle or too solitary to be covered by our use of the word peace. By the very nature of the story the rejoicings in the cavern were rejoicings in a fortress or an outlaw's den . . . There is in that image a true idea of an outpost, of a piercing through the rock and an entrance into an enemy territory. There is in this buried divinity an idea of undermining the world; of shaking the towers and palaces from below.

ON THIS DAY

- In 1905, GKC met the future prime minister Herbert Asquith at a dinner party.
- And in 1931, GKC's article "Rediscovering the Old Truths" was published in the *Illustrated London News*.

MARCH 15

*I have come that they may have life, and that they may
have it more abundantly.*

—JOHN 10:10 NKJV

*You say grace before meals
All right.
But I say grace before the play and the opera,
And grace before the concert and the pantomime,
And grace before I open a book,
And grace before sketching, painting,
Swimming, fencing, boxing, walking, playing, dancing;
And grace before I dip the pen in the ink.*

A PASSAGE FROM *THE EVERLASTING MAN* (1925)

Now compared to these wanderers the life of Jesus went as swift and
straight as a thunderbolt. It was above all things dramatic; it did
above all things consist in doing something that had to be done. It
emphatically would not have been done, if Jesus had walked about
the world for ever doing nothing except tell the truth. And even the
external movement of it must not be described as a wandering in
the sense of forgetting that it was a journey. This is where it was a
fulfilment of the myths rather than of the philosophies; it is a journey with a goal and an object, like Jason going to find the Golden
Fleece, or Hercules the golden apples of the Hesperides. The gold
that he was seeking was death. The primary thing that he was going
to do was to die . . .

No two things could possibly be more different than the death
of Socrates and the death of Christ. We are meant to feel that the
death of Socrates was, from the point of view of his friends at least,

a stupid muddle and miscarriage of justice interfering with the flow of a humane and lucid, I had almost said a light philosophy. We are meant to feel that Death was the bride of Christ as Poverty was the bride of St. Francis. We are meant to feel that his life was in that sense a sort of love-affair with death, a romance of the pursuit of the ultimate sacrifice. From the moment when the star goes up like a birthday rocket, to the moment when the sun is extinguished like a funeral torch, the whole story moves on wings with the speed and direction of a drama, ending in an act beyond words.

MARCH 16

He will swallow up death forever, and the Lord God will wipe away tears from all faces.

—ISAIAH 25:8 NKJV

Faith is always at a disadvantage; it is a perpetually defeated thing which survives all its conquerors. The desperate modern talk about dark days and reeling altars, and the end of Gods and angels, is the oldest talk in the world: lamentations over the growth of agnosticism can be found in the monkish sermons of the dark ages; horror at youthful impiety can be found in the *Iliad*. This is the thing that never deserts men and yet always, with daring diplomacy, threatens to desert them.

A PASSAGE FROM *THE BOOKMAN* (1903)

To most readers Mr. Chesterton is known as a literary critic with a distinctive style and a riotous gift of paradox. He could readily prove, they think, that black is white. His arresting ingenuity conceals the meaning underlying the adoption of this method.

Mr. Chesterton in his extravagance has never essayed to prove that black is white. But most men assert that grey is either black or white. He reveals the neglected element.

The real world is grey. All things are made up of the transitory union of contradiction; not permanent and isolated, but perpetually in motion: the momentary fusion of opposite forces. The accepted view sees only one of these. Mr. Chesterton disentangles the other, and hurls it at his astonished readers. Byron thus becomes the eager optimist, St. Francis the Apostle of Pleasure . . .

The method is adopted for a purpose. [Chesterton] designs to startle the average man, settling down acquiescent in a normal world, with the sudden realisation of the magical Universe in which we live.

ON THIS DAY

- In 1904, Frances Chesterton wrote in her diary: "One of the proudest days of my life. Gilbert preached at St. Paul's, Covent Garden, for the Christian Social Union." His two sermons were later published under the title, *Preachers from the Pew*.

- In 1929, GKC's article "Is Change Improvement?" was published in the *Illustrated London News*.

MARCH 17

*You shall love the Lord your God with all your heart,
with all your soul, with all your strength, and with all
your mind.*

—LUKE 10:27 NKJV

There is in modern discussions of religion and philosophy an absurd assumption that a man is in some way just and well-poised because he has come to no conclusion; and that a man is in some way knocked off the list of fair judges because he has come to a conclusion. It is assumed that the sceptic has no bias; whereas he has a very obvious bias in favour of scepticism.

I remember once arguing with an honest young atheist, who was very much shocked at my disputing some of the assumptions which were absolute sanctities to him (such as the quite unproved proposition of the independence of matter and the quite improbable proposition of its power to originate mind), and he at length fell back upon this question, which he delivered with an honourable heat of defiance and indignation:

"Well, can you tell me any man of intellect, great in science or philosophy, who accepted the miraculous?"

I said, "With pleasure. Descartes, Dr. Johnson, Newton, Faraday, Newman, Gladstone, Pasteur, Browning, Brunetière— as many more as you please."

To which that quite admirable and idealistic young man made this astonishing reply—"Oh, but of course they had to say that; they were Christians."

First he challenged me to find a black swan, and then he ruled out all my swans because they were black. The fact that all these great intellects had come to the Christian view was somehow or other a proof either that they were not great intellects or that they had not really come to that view. The argument thus stood in a charmingly convenient form: "All men that count have come to my conclusion; for if they come to your conclusion they do not count."

MARCH 18

> *The humble shall see this and be glad; and you who seek God, your hearts shall live.*
>
> —PSALM 69:32 NKJV

The pagans insisted upon self-assertion because it was the essence of their creed that the gods, though strong and just, were mystic, capricious, and even indifferent.

But the essence of Christianity was in a literal sense the New Testament—a covenant with God which opened to men a clear deliverance. They thought themselves secure . . . they believed themselves rich with an irrevocable benediction which set them above the stars; and immediately they discovered humility.

A PASSAGE FROM *THE BOOKMAN* (1903)

The function of imagination is not to make strange things settled so much as to make settled things strange; not to make wonders facts, but facts wonders.

LINES FROM *THE WILD KNIGHT* (1900)

I think that if they gave me leave
Within that world to stand,
I would be good through all the day
I spent in fairyland.

MARCH 19

Rejoice in the Lord always. Again I will say, rejoice!
—PHILIPPIANS 4:4 NKJV

Joy, which was the small publicity of the Pagan, is the gigantic secret of the Christian.

A PASSAGE FROM *THE BOOKMAN* (1903)

[Chesterton] crashes in upon the orderly scheme and the accepted wisdom and scatters them to the winds. Men are startled into attention and compelled to think. The attitude of the child is restored: wonderland returns to the earth and the age of perpetual marvel. We are shown as still living in the atmosphere of miracle, in the visible presence of God.

A PASSAGE FROM *THE BALL AND THE CROSS* (1909)

All this time MacIan had been in a sort of monstrous delirium, like some fabulous hero snatched up into the moon. The difference between this experience and common experiences was analogous to that between waking life and a dream. Yet he did not feel in the

least as if he were dreaming; rather the other way; as waking was
more actual than dreaming, so this seemed by another degree more
actual than waking itself. But it was another life altogether, like a
cosmos with a new dimension.

He felt he had been hurled into some new incarnation: into the
midst of new relations, wrongs and rights, with towering responsibilities and almost tragic joys which he had as yet had no time
to examine. Heaven had not merely sent him a message; Heaven
itself had opened around him and given him an hour of its own
ancient and star-shattering energy. He had never felt so much
alive before.

ON THIS DAY

- In 1932, GKC's article "The Spanish Magic in Chudel and
  Lindsay" was published in the *Illustrated London News*.

MARCH 20

*Do not think that I came to bring peace on earth. I did not
come to bring peace but a sword.*

—MATTHEW 10:34 NKJV

All modern philosophies are chains which connect and fetter;
Christianity is a sword which separates and sets free. No other
philosophy makes God actually rejoice in the separation of the
universe into living souls.

But according to orthodox Christianity this separation
between God and man is sacred, because this is eternal. That a
man may love God it is necessary that there should be not only
a God to be loved, but a man to love him. All those vague theo-
sophical minds for whom the universe is an immense melting-pot

are exactly the minds which shrink instinctively from that earthquake saying of our Gospels, which declare that the Son of God came not with peace but with a sundering sword.

PASSAGES FROM *THE BOOKMAN* (1903)

[Chesterton] is ever astonished at "the towering and tropical vision of things as they really are; the great Odyssey of strange-coloured oceans and strange-shaped trees, of dust like the wreck of temples and thistledown like the ruin of stars." In the twentieth century God still walks in the garden in the cool of the day, and every bush is aflame with His presence. No scientific discovery can lessen the exultant wonder with which he regards the ever-recurring miracle of the sunrise or the birth of a little child.

At present [Chesterton] is one of the few interesting writers in contemporary literature, with something to say . . . and the power of compelling a jaded and tired age to listen to his voice.

MARCH 21

> *Oh, the depth of the riches both of the wisdom and knowledge of God! How unsearchable are His judgments and His ways past finding out!*
> —ROMANS 11:33 NKJV

Now, this is exactly the claim which I have since come to propound for Christianity. Not merely that it deduces logical truths, but that when it suddenly becomes illogical, it has found, so to speak, an illogical truth. It not only goes right about things, but it goes wrong (if one may say so) exactly where the things go wrong. Its plan suits the secret irregularities, and expects the unexpected. It is simple about the simple truth; but it is stubborn about the subtle truth.

A PASSAGE FROM *A MISCELLANY OF MEN* (1912)

It was one of those wonderful evenings in which the sky was warm and radiant while the earth was still comparatively cold and wet. But it is of the essence of Spring to be unexpected; as in that heroic and hackneyed line about coming "before the swallow dares." Spring never is Spring unless it comes too soon. And on a day like that one might pray, without any profanity, that Spring might come on earth as it was in heaven.

A PASSAGE FROM *ROBERT LOUIS STEVENSON* (1928)

I believe that the lesson of [Stevenson's] life will only be seen after time has revealed the full meaning of all our present tendencies; I believe it will be seen from afar off like a vast plan or maze traced out on a hillside; perhaps traced by one who did not even see the plan while he was making the tracks. I believe that his travels and doublings and returns reveal an idea.

MARCH 22

Then one of the criminals who were hanged blasphemed Him, saying, "If You are the Christ, save Yourself and us." But the other, answering, rebuked him, saying, "Do you not even fear God, seeing you are under the same condemnation? And we indeed justly, for we receive the due reward of our deeds; but this Man has done nothing wrong." Then he said

to Jesus, "Lord, remember me when You come into Your
kingdom." And Jesus said to him, "Assuredly, I say to you,
today you will be with Me in Paradise."

—LUKE 23:39–43 NKJV

Diogenes looked for his honest man inside every crypt and
cavern, but he never thought of looking for it inside the thief.
And that is where the Founder of Christianity found the honest man; He found him on a gibbet and promised him Paradise.
Just as Christianity looked for the honest man inside the thief,
democracy looked for the wise man inside the fool.

A PASSAGE FROM *THE BOOKMAN* (1903)

*In personal appearance Mr. Chesterton is of gigantic stature . . . and
presents a formidable appearance when swaggering down Fleet
Street in the small hours of the morning, or in the midst of the crowd
which surges around him, and to which he is entirely oblivious.*

*Wearing a huge slouch hat, which is the despair of his friends,
he is generally taken for a returned Yeoman, or an escaped Boer
prisoner. He is accustomed to pursue long solitary walks through
London, often penetrating right through the great town, from north
to south or east to west. When over-wearied with journalism, he
will suddenly start on a country ramble, taking the train to some
station, the name of which pleases him, on the time-table, and striking thence in any direction to any destination. Here he wanders till
his friends organise relief parties, or till he strikes another railway
line, when he contentedly journeys homeward.*

ON THIS DAY ————————————————————————

- In 1930, GKC's article "T. S. Eliot on Dante" was published
  in the *Illustrated London News.*

MARCH 23

> ... *and by Him to reconcile all things to Himself, by*
> *Him, whether things on earth or things in heaven, having*
> *made peace through the blood of His cross.*
>
> —COLOSSIANS 1:20 NKJV

As we have taken the circle as the symbol of reason and madness, we may very well take the cross as the symbol at once of mystery and of health. Buddhism is centripetal, but Christianity is centrifugal: it breaks out. For the circle is perfect and infinite in its nature; but it is fixed for ever in its size; it can never be larger or smaller. But the cross, though it has at its heart a collision and contradiction, can extend its four arms for ever without altering its shape. Because it has a paradox in its centre it can grow without changing. The circle returns upon itself and is bound. The cross opens its arms to the four winds; it is a sign-post for free travellers.

PASSAGES FROM *THE BOOKMAN* (1903)

[Chesterton's] friends assert that he is writing too much; it is doubtful if any man with ideas can write too much—the ephemeral perishes, the permanent survives.

[Chesterton tells a man to] open his eyes, and outside he will find a region of magic, riotous, irrational, mysterious, opening around him like a gigantic flower. No age was ever more wonderful than the despised modern world. The suburbs of cities are the scenes of the Arabian Nights; gas lamps are fairy bubbles, machinery the efforts of a Cyclops, the Post Office the wings of a Mercury.

If Mr. Chesterton can inoculate the shifting and unimportant crowds of modern cities with this experience, he thinks strange results would follow; men would embrace in the streets, the priests would cut capers and the kings gather flowers, the heart of a child be restored with the child's awe and wonder and exultation in the greatness and the goodness of God.

ON THIS DAY

• In 1929, GKC's article "The Modern Censor" was published in the *Illustrated London News*.

MARCH 24

He who has received His testimony has certified that God is true.

—JOHN 3:33 NKJV

He does not understand Christianity because he will not understand the paradox of Christianity; that we can only really understand all myths when we know that one of them is true.

A PASSAGE FROM *LEO TOLSTOY* (1903)

The truth is that Tolstoy, with his immense genius, with his colossal faith, with his vast fearlessness and vast knowledge of life, is deficient in one faculty and one faculty alone. He is not a mystic: and therefore he has a tendency to go mad. Men talk of the extravagances and frenzies that have been produced by mysticism: they are a mere drop in the bucket.

In the main, and from the beginning of time, mysticism has kept men sane. The thing that has driven them mad was logic. It is significant that, with all that has been said about the excitability of poets, only one English poet ever went mad, and he went mad from a logical system of theology. He was Cowper, and his poetry retarded his insanity for many years. So poetry, in which Tolstoy is deficient, has always been a tonic and sanative thing. The only thing that has kept the race of men from the mad extremes of the convent and the pirate-galley, the night-club and the lethal chamber, has been mysticism—the belief that logic is misleading, and that things are not what they seem.

A PASSAGE FROM *ROBERT LOUIS STEVENSON* (1928)

Man is born with hope and courage indeed, but born outside that which he was meant to attain; that there is a quest, a test, a trial by combat or pilgrimage of discovery; or, in other words, that whatever else man is he is not sufficient to himself, either through peace or through despair. The very movement of the sentence is the movement of a man going somewhere and generally fighting something; and that is where optimism and pessimism are alike opposed to that ultimate or potential peace, which the violent take by storm.

MARCH 25

> *In Him was life, and the life was the light of men.*
> —JOHN 1:4 NKJV

The art of coloured glass can truly be called the most typically Christian of all arts or artifices. The art of coloured lights is as essentially Confucian as the art of coloured windows is Christian. Aesthetically, they produce somewhat the same impression on the fancy; the impression of something glowing and magical; something at once mysterious and transparent. But the difference between their substance and structure is the whole difference between the great western faith and the great eastern agnosticism. The Christian windows are solid and human, made of heavy lead, of hearty and characteristic colours; but behind them is the light. The colours of the fireworks are as festive and as varied; but behind them is the darkness. They themselves are their only illumination; even as in that stern philosophy, man is his own star. The rockets of ruby and sapphire fade away slowly upon the dome of hollowness and darkness. But the kings and saints in the old Gothic windows, dusky and opaque in this hour of midnight, still contain all their power of full flamboyance, and await the rising of the sun.

A PASSAGE FROM *THE OUTLOOK* MAGAZINE (1902)

Mr. Chesterton is the defendant of many supposedly "bad" things, among others of penny-dreadfuls, of rash vows, of skeletons, publicity, slang, and detective stories. These subjects, with many others, he discusses with a restful tolerance which apparently never degenerates into indifference, and with a certain caustic yet kindly manner peculiarly pleasant in this Philistine day. When worldlings despise the world, a defendant is required. Mr. Chesterton is such a man; and his clever book has been written to show how unfair it is to call those things bad which have been good enough to make other things better.

MARCH 26

In the greatness of his folly he shall go astray.
—PROVERBS 5:23 NKJV

The modern world is not evil; in some ways the modern world is far too good. It is full of wild and wasted virtues. When a religious scheme is shattered (as Christianity was shattered at the

Reformation), it is not merely the vices that are let loose. The vices are, indeed, let loose, and they wander and do damage. But the virtues are let loose also; and the virtues wander more wildly, and the virtues do more terrible damage.

The modern world is full of the old Christian virtues gone mad. The virtues have gone mad because they have been isolated from each other and are wandering alone. Thus some scientists care for truth; and their truth is pitiless. Thus some humanitarians only care for pity; and their pity (I am sorry to say) is often untruthful.

GKC, AS QUOTED IN *THE OUTLOOK* MAGAZINE (1905)

"Not only did I and do I believe these utterances to be true, but I never will be happy until they are vulgar . . . The truly spiritual democrat feels a certain exhilaration in uttering a paradox." Mr. Chesterton is so certain that truth has an obverse, forgotten side that he plans to present this so often in the form of paradox as to make what is hidden plain.

ON THIS DAY

- In 1932, GKC's article "Lawrence Hyde on the Modern Mind" was published in the *Illustrated London News*.

MARCH 27

His truth endures to all generations.
—PSALM 100:5 NKJV

It is always easy to let the age have its head; the difficult thing is to keep one's own. It is always easy to be a modernist; as it is easy to be a snob. To have fallen into any of those open traps of error and exaggeration which fashion after fashion and sect after sect set along the historic path of Christendom—that would indeed have been simple.

It is always simple to fall; there are an infinity of angles at which one falls, only one at which one stands. To have fallen into any one of the fads from Gnosticism to Christian Science would indeed have been obvious and tame. But to have avoided them all has been one whirling adventure; and in my vision the heavenly chariot flies thundering through the ages, the dull heresies sprawling and prostrate, the wild truth reeling but erect.

A PASSAGE FROM *THE OUTLOOK* MAGAZINE (1905)

[Chesterton] is a practical philosopher, but he speaks in paradox, revels in the abnormal, and lets a virile imagination have full play. In the garb of a warrior he is at heart a lover. In a day of seemingly triumphant materialism he is an idealist. Science having grown impudent and scornful, he comes to the defence of Religion.

His intellectual fertility first compels attention. The range of his comment on life is from British municipal or colonial politics to Greek art, from yellow journalism to current agnosticism and perennial mysticism, from a defence of slang to polemics against the "art for art's sake" theory of art.

One has scarcely grown accustomed to the flare and splutter of his arc light of paradox, with its effects of intense light and shade and the unnatural shadows stalking by the side of prosaic facts, when he is asked to wander serenely under the mellow light of the sun of wisdom. One has hardly recovered from the sense of moral exhilaration at seeing some entrenched evil hit square between the eyes with a caustic bit of candour, when one begins to hear the pious strains of a religionist who extols the supernatural and revels in the mysterious and the mystical.

MARCH 28

For as many as are led by the Spirit of God, these are sons of God.

—ROMANS 8:14 NKJV

Savonarola address himself to the hardest of all earthly tasks, that of making men turn back and wonder at the simplicities they had learnt to ignore. It is strange that the most unpopular of all doctrines is the doctrine which declares the common life divine. Democracy, of which Savonarola was so fiery an exponent, is the hardest of gospels; there is nothing that so terrifies men as the decree that they are all kings. Christianity, in Savonarola's mind, identical with democracy, is the hardest of gospels; there is nothing that so strikes men with fear as the saying that they are all the sons of God.

PASSAGES FROM *THE OUTLOOK* MAGAZINE (1905)

It has been wittily said of [Chesterton] that,

> *He gravely argues No means Yes,*
> *He shows that joy is deep distress,*
> *He tells you soap is made from cheese,*
> *And any well-known truth you please*
> *He proves with most consummate ease*
> *Confoundedly confutable.*

To lovers of literature in the essay form, or to lovers of biography, Chesterton comes as a piquant, iconoclastic, authentic personality. The conventions are disturbed, but when you have done reading you are awake, not asleep, invigorated, not somnolent. Browning's son may protest and the Athenaeum's reviewer curse and point out errors in fact, but when you have turned the last page of Chesterton's [study of] Browning, you know Browning better than if the task of interpretation had been done by an academic don.

MARCH 29

> *Then God saw everything that He had made, and indeed it was very good.*
>
> —GENESIS 1:31 NKJV

And the root phrase for all Christian theism was this, that God was a creator, as an artist is a creator.

PASSAGES FROM *THE OUTLOOK* MAGAZINE (1905)

Present-day hedonism has in Mr. Chesterton one of its most vigorous and consistent opponents, a hedonism that, as he says, "is more sick of happiness than an invalid is sick of pain, an art sense that seeks the assistance of crime, since it has exhausted nature." Hence, as an art critic, he fights lustily against the "art for art's sake" school; as a Christian of the "Catholic" Anglican type, he fights against Robert Blatchford and all who would make popular in England the secular, materialistic Socialism which grows apace on the Continent.

Mr. Chesterton lives at a time when there is much in contemporary politics, literature, and art for the trenchant satirist to convert into polemical literature, ephemeral and permanent. While we smart under the lash of his satire and cringe under the blows of his irony, we know that at heart he is a believer in his kind, and a humorist who also is a moralist.

Indeed, he is something more than a moralist, he is a religionist; and his point of view as a critic of contemporary life is only to be explained by recognition of the fact that he believes much of contemporary art, literature, and politics defective because religion has ceased to be a vital thing in life. "Once poetry and politics were equally religious and were great," *he says.* "Now they have been lopped from the tree only to rot on the ground or wither in the air. For the tree from which these fruits and flowers have been cut is that which our Northern forefathers worship, the Life-tree, Ygdrasil, whose branches take hold on heaven and whose fruit is the stars."

MARCH 30

Now faith is the substance of things hoped for, the evidence of things not seen.

—Hebrews 11:1 nkjv

As the word "unreasonable" is open to misunderstanding, the matter may be more accurately put by saying that each one of these Christian or mystical virtues involves a paradox in its own nature, and that this is not true of any of the typically pagan or rationalist virtues. Justice consists in finding out a certain thing due to a certain man and giving it to him. Temperance consists in finding out the proper limit of a particular indulgence and adhering to that. But charity means pardoning what is unpardonable, or it is no virtue at all. Hope means hoping when things are hopeless, or it is no virtue at all. And faith means believing the incredible, or it is no virtue at all.

GKC, AS QUOTED IN *THE OUTLOOK* MAGAZINE (1905)

Some modern eulogists of the "strong man" have set up misrepresentations of history so considerable that they can only be described as large and semi-learned lies. The viking and northern warrior, whose face was of stone and his eyes of steel, is, for example, a lie. The real vikings cried and kissed each other . . .

Exactly the same is true of that other historic figure who is generally, by the same people, similarly praised and similarly misrepresented—I mean the English Puritan. In modern romance the Puritan is always exhibited as a man of rock. He never shows his feelings. The real Puritan, as you may see in Bunyan, never did anything else.

A PASSAGE FROM *ROBERT LOUIS STEVENSON* (1928)

Stevenson died swiftly as if struck with an arrow and even over his grave something of a higher frivolity hovers upon wings like a bird; "Glad did I live and gladly die," has a lilt that no repetition can make quite unreal, light as the lifted spires of Spyglass Hill and translucent as the dancing waves; types of a tenuous but tenacious levity and the legend that has made his graveyard a mountain-peak and his epitaph a song.

MARCH 31

Through the tender mercy of our God, with which the Dayspring from on high has visited us . . .
—LUKE 1:78 NKJV

White is a colour. It is not a mere absence of colour; it is a shining and affirmative thing, as fierce as red, as definite as black.

When, so to speak, your pencil grows red-hot, it draws roses; when it grows white-hot, it draws stars. And one of the two or three defiant verities of the best religious morality, of real Christianity, for example, is exactly this same thing; the chief assertion of religious morality is that white is a colour. Virtue is not the absence of vices or the avoidance of moral dangers; virtue is a vivid and separate thing, like pain or a particular smell. Mercy does not mean not being cruel or sparing people revenge or punishment; it means a plain and positive thing like the sun, which one has either seen or not seen.

GKC, AS QUOTED IN *THE OUTLOOK* MAGAZINE (1905)

Legend and epic are in their nature even truer than history; since history is forced to record many things which are exceptional and involuntary, whereas poetry is a full confession of men's hearts.

And in legend and epic we find still the same neglected truth. Achilles is a strong man, but he is also a person of great sensibility. He does not suppress his feelings; he is chiefly occupied in suppressing other people. Of the strong, silent man so popular among moderns, it is often said that he is somewhat hard but not cruel.

In the case of Achilles, as in the case of a child, of a woman, or of other elemental things, exactly the reverse is the case. He is cruel, but he is not hard. He is kind, or can be kind, because others are hurt. He is cruel, or can be cruel, because he can be hurt himself. He butchers and insults his enemies because he is overtaken by evil passions of which in that degree we know little. But he spares his enemies, not because he restrains himself, but because he is overtaken by good passions, things of which we know nothing at all.

APRIL 1

The mystery which has been hidden from ages and from generations . . .

—COLOSSIANS 1:26 NKJV

In 1840 [Browning's poem,] *Sordello*, was published. Its reception by the great majority of readers, including some of the ablest men of the time, was a reception of a kind probably unknown in the rest of literary history, a reception that was neither praise nor blame.

It was perhaps best expressed by Carlyle, who wrote to say that his wife had read *Sordello* with great interest, and wished to know whether *Sordello* was a man, or a city, or a book. Better known, of course, is the story of Tennyson, who said that the first line of the poem "Who will, may hear Sordello's story told," and the last line "Who would has heard Sordello's story told," were the only two lines in the poem that he understood, and they were lies.

Perhaps the best story, however, of all the cycle of *Sordello* legends is that which is related of Douglas Jerrold. He was recovering from an illness; and having obtained permission for the first time to read a little during the day, he picked up a book from a pile beside the bed and began *Sordello*. No sooner had he done so than he turned deadly pale, put down the book, and said, "My God! I'm an idiot. My health is restored, but my mind's gone. I can't understand two consecutive lines of an English poem."

He then summoned his family and silently gave the book into their hands, asking for their opinion on the poem; and as the shadow of perplexity gradually passed over their faces, he heaved a sigh of relief and went to sleep.

These stories, whether accurate or no, do undoubtedly represent the very peculiar reception accorded to *Sordello*, a reception which, as I have said, bears no resemblance whatever to anything in the way of eulogy or condemnation that had ever been accorded to a work of art before. There had been authors whom it was fashionable to boast of admiring and authors whom it was fashionable to boast of despising; but with *Sordello* enters into literary history the Browning of popular badinage, the author whom it is fashionable to boast of not understanding.

DURING THIS MONTH ————————————————————

- In 1915, GKC's first collection of verse, *Poems*, was published.
- In 1932, GKC's study *Chaucer* was published, as was the second edition of his *Collected Poems*.

APRIL 2

And with great power the apostles gave witness to the resurrection of the Lord Jesus. And great grace was upon them all.

—ACTS 4:33 NKJV

[In] The Apostles' Creed ... the word "I" comes before even the word "God." The believer comes first; but he is soon dwarfed by his beliefs, swallowed in the creative whirlwind and the trumpets of the resurrection.

GKC, AS DESCRIBED IN *THE BOOKMAN* (1912)

Among scholars both here and in England will be found his warmest admirers. The late William James, for example, was a loyal Chestertonian.

Manalive *is another of Mr. Chesterton's fairy tales for grown up people, successor to* The Napoleon of Notting Hill, The Man Who Was Thursday, *and* The Ball and the Cross.

Now you cannot surprise a grown up person by making a toad turn into a princess or exhibiting a giant with three heads. So Mr. Chesterton's fairy tales do not turn on what is physically impossible. They turn only on what is socially improbable, which to a grown up person is a far wilder thing. They represent men as acting logically upon some natural impulse which, though innocent and even praiseworthy, it is customary to repress. He delights in the startling effects produced by this simple expedient.

ON THIS DAY ───────────────────────────────

- In 1932, GKC's article "The Symbolism of Syntax" was published in the *Illustrated London News*.

APRIL 3

By Him to reconcile all things to Himself, by Him,
whether things on earth or things in heaven, having made
peace through the blood of His cross.
                                        —COLOSSIANS 1:20 NKJV

Turnbull glanced at the crucifix with a sort of scowling good-humour and then said: "He may look and see His cross defeated."

"The cross cannot be defeated," said MacIan, "for it is Defeat."

GKC'S NOVEL *MANALIVE*, AS DESCRIBED IN *THE BOOKMAN* (1912)

Innocent Smith's endeavours to keep himself alive and enliven others lead naturally to a belief that he is mad. He makes his first appearance leaping a wall and climbing a tree in the garden of a boarding-house. Soon afterward he shoots two holes in the high hat of a very respectable physician, who, aided by an eminent American expert in criminology, investigates his record. They find the clearest evidence that Smith is a criminal lunatic of the most dangerous type. He has been expelled from Cambridge for an attempt to murder the warden of a college. He has committed burglary, bigamy, and probably murder. They are for hurrying him immediately off to court and securing a commitment to an asylum, but finally are induced by the other boarders to try him first before an informal tribunal of their own.

Mr. Chesterton's art of making the fantastic seem plausible has never been employed more effectively than in the account of this absurd trial and the preposterous incidents that lead up to it. Needless to say all the prisoner's hideous crimes turn out to be the innocent experiments of a man bent on the singular mission of reminding himself and others that they are alive. He fired bullets past the Cambridge don because the don was a pessimist and needed to be reminded that life after all had some value to him. He shot off the doctor's hat for the same reason. The burglary consisted in breaking into his own house, that he might learn to covet his own goods, instead of his neighbour's. The young women with whom he successively eloped and whose mysterious disappearance gave rise to the suspicion of murder turned out to be his own wife in successive disguises.

Let us therefore come boldly to the throne of grace, that we
may obtain mercy and find grace to help in time of need.
—HEBREWS 4:16 NKJV

From the Cross from which he had fallen fell the shadow of its
fantastic mercy; and the first three words he spoke in a voice
like a silver trumpet, held men as still as stones. Perhaps if he
had spoken there for an hour in his illumination he might have
founded a religion on Ludgate Hill.

A PASSAGE FROM *MANALIVE* (1912)

A puddle reflects infinity, and is full of light; nevertheless, if anal-
ysed objectively, a puddle is a piece of dirty water spread very thin
on mud. The two great historic universities of England have all this
large and reflective brilliance. They repeat infinity. They are full of
light. Nevertheless, or rather on the other hand, they are puddles . . .
The academic mind reflects infinity, and is full of light by the simple
process of being shallow and standing still.

A PASSAGE FROM *ALL I SURVEY* (1933)

History and sociology can never be "scientific" in the sense of sub-
ject to exact measurement, because there is always the mystery and
doubt inherent in moral evidence affecting one half of the equation,
and generally both.

In the thesis that red-haired men are great men, there are shades of
difference even in red hair, and infinite shades of difference in great-
ness or the pretence of greatness. And not a few modern theorists seem
to me to be strangely lacking in the instinct of what is really great.

APRIL 5

And when they had come to the place called Calvary, there they crucified Him.

—LUKE 23:33 NKJV

The abyss between Christ and all His modern interpreters is that we have no record that He ever wrote a word, except with His finger in the sand. The whole is the history of one continuous and sublime conversation . . . It was not for any pompous proclamation, it was not for any elaborate output of printed volumes; it was for a few splendid and idle words that the cross was set up on Calvary and the earth gaped, and the sun was darkened at noonday.

A PASSAGE FROM *ROBERT LOUIS STEVENSON* (1928)

The real story of Stevenson must end where it began; because it was to that end that he himself perpetually wandered and strove. I said at the beginning that the key to his career was put early into his hands; it was well symbolised by the paint-brush dipped in purple or prussian blue, with which he started to colour the stiff caricatures upon the cardboard of Skelt.

ON THIS DAY ─────────────────────────────

- In 1912, George Bernard Shaw wrote to GKC's wife, Frances: "I have promised to drive somebody to Beaconsfield on Sunday morning; and I shall be in that district more or less for the rest of the day. If you are spending Easter at Overroads, and have no irisfetors who couldn't stand us, we should like to call on you at any time that would be convenient.

The convenience of time depends on a design of my own which I wish to impart to you first. I want to read a play to Gilbert. It began by way of being a music-hall sketch; so it is not 3 hours long as usual: I can get through it in an hour and a half. I want to insult and taunt and stimulate Gilbert with it. It is the sort of thing he could write and ought to write: a religious harlequinade. In fact, he could do it better if a sufficient number of pins were stuck into him."

- And in 1930, GKC's article "Who Moved the Stone?" was published in the *Illustrated London News*.

APRIL 6

This do, as often as you drink it, in remembrance of Me.
—1 CORINTHIANS 11:25 NKJV

And in the high altar of Christianity stands another figure in whose hand also is the cup of the vine. "Drink," he says, "for the whole world is as red as this wine with the crimson of the love and wrath of God. Drink, for the trumpets are blowing for battle, and this is the stirrup cup. Drink, for this is my blood of the New Testament that is shed for you. Drink, for I know whence you come and why. Drink, for I know when you go and where."

A PASSAGE FROM *MANALIVE* (1912)

The idea that Smith is attacking is this. Living in an entangled civilisation, we have come to think certain things wrong which are not wrong at all. We have come to think outbreak and exuberance, banging and barging, rotting and wrecking, wrong. In themselves they are not merely pardonable, they are unimpeachable.

There is nothing wicked about firing off a pistol even at a friend; so long as you do not mean to hit him and know you won't. It is no more wrong than throwing a pebble at the sea—less; for you do occasionally hit the sea. There is nothing wrong in bashing down a chimney-pot and breaking through a roof, so long as you are not injuring the life or property of other men. It is no more wrong to choose to enter a house from the top, than to choose to open a packing case from the bottom. There is nothing wicked about walking around the world and coming back to your own house. It is no more wicked than walking round the garden and coming back to your own house.

And there is nothing wicked about picking up your wife here, there, and everywhere, if, forsaking all others, you keep only to her so long as you both shall live. It is as innocent as playing a game of hide-and-seek in the garden. You associate such acts with blackguardism by a mere snobbish association; as you think there is something vaguely vile about going (or being seen going) into a pawnbroker's or a public house. You think there is something squalid and common-place about such a connection. You are mistaken. This man's spiritual power has been precisely this: that he has distinguished between custom and creed. He has broken the conventions, but he has kept the commandments.

And behold, there was a great earthquake; for an angel
of the Lord descended from heaven, and came and rolled
back the stone.

—MATTHEW 28:2 NKJV

All real scholars who have studied the Greek and Roman culture say one thing about it. They agree that in the ancient world
religion was one thing and philosophy quite another, there was
very little effort to rationalise and at the same time to realise a
real belief in the gods. There was very little pretense of any such
real belief among the philosophers.

But neither had the passion or perhaps the power to per-
secute the others save in particular and peculiar cases; and
neither the philosopher in his school nor the priest in his
temple seems ever to have seriously contemplated his own
concept as covering the world. A priest sacrificing to Artemis
in Calydon did not seem to think that people would some day
sacrifice to her instead of to Isis beyond the sea; a sage following the vegetarian rule of the Neo-Pythagoreans did not
seem to think it would universally prevail and exclude the
methods of Epictetus or Epicurus. We may call this liberality
if we like; I am not dealing with an argument but describing
an atmosphere.

All this, I say, is admitted by all scholars; but what neither the
learned nor the unlearned have fully realised, perhaps, is that
this description is really an exact description of all non-Christian
civilisation today; and especially of the great civilisations of the
East. Eastern paganism really is much more all of a piece, just as
ancient paganism was much more all of a piece, than the modern
critics admit. It is a many-coloured Persian Carpet as the other

was a varied and tessellated Roman pavement; but the one real crack right across that pavement came from the earthquake of the Crucifixion.

APRIL 8

For it was fitting for Him, for whom are all things and by whom are all things, in bringing many sons to glory, to make the captain of their salvation perfect through sufferings.

—HEBREWS 2:10 NKJV

Nothing short of the extreme and strong and startling doctrine of the divinity of Christ will give that particular effect that can truly stir the popular sense like a trumpet; the idea of the king himself serving in the ranks like a common soldier.

By making that figure merely human we make that story much less human. We take away the point of the story which actually pierces humanity; the point of the story which was quite literally the point of a spear. It does not especially humanise the universe to say that good and wise men can die for their opinions; any more than it would be any sort of uproariously popular news in an army that good soldiers may easily get killed. It is no news that King Leonidas is dead any more than that Queen Anne is dead; and men did not wait for Christianity to be men, in the full sense of being heroes.

But if we are describing, for the moment, the atmosphere of what is generous and popular and even picturesque, any knowledge of human nature will tell us that no sufferings of the sons of men, or even of the servants of God, strike the same note as the notion of the master suffering instead of his servants. . . . No mysterious monarch, hidden in his starry pavilion at the base of the cosmic campaign, is in the least like that celestial chivalry of the Captain who carries his five wounds in the front of battle.

APRIL 9

I am He who lives, and was dead, and behold, I am
alive forevermore. Amen. And I have the keys of Hades
and of Death.

—REVELATION 1:18 NKJV

Christendom has had a series of revolutions and in each one of them Christianity has died. Christianity has died many times and risen again; for it had a God who knew the way out of the grave.

GKC, AS QUOTED IN *THE BOOKMAN* (1912)

Mr. G. K. Chesterton [recently] remarked in the Illustrated London News: *"It is perfectly true, as English papers are saying, that some American papers are what we should call both vulgar and vindictive; that they set the pack in full cry upon a particular man; that they are impatient of delay and eager for savage decisions; and that the flags under which they march are often the rags of a reckless and unscrupulous journalism.*

All this is true; but if these be the American faults, it is all the more necessary to emphasise the opposite English faults. Our national evil is exactly the other way: it is to damp everything down; it is to leave every great affair unfinished, to leave every enormous question unanswered."

- In 1906, the American journalist Shane F. Bullock said of GKC in the *Chicago Evening Post*: "it is almost impossible to open a paper that does not contain either an article or review or poem or drawing of his, and his name is better known now to compositors than Bernard Shaw."
- In 1921, GKC gave an address at a luncheon hosted by the Dickens Fellowship in the National Arts Club.

APRIL 10

*For this is My blood of the new covenant, which is shed
for many for the remission of sins.*
—MATTHEW 26:28 NKJV

There are people who say they wish Christianity to remain as a spirit. They mean, very literally, that they wish it to remain as a ghost. But it is not going to remain as a ghost. What follows this process of apparent death is not the lingerings of the shade; it is the resurrection of the body.

These people are quite prepared to shed pious and reverential tears over the Sepulchre of the Son of Man; what they are not prepared for is the Son of God walking once more upon the hills of morning. These people, and indeed most people, were indeed by this time quite accustomed to the idea that the old Christian candle-light would fade into the light of common day. To many of them it did quite honestly appear like that pale yellow flame of a candle when it is left burning in daylight.

It was all the more unexpected, and therefore all the more unmistakable, that the seven branched candle-stick suddenly towered to heaven like a miraculous tree and flamed until the sun turned pale. But other ages have seen the day conquer the candle-light and then the candle-light conquer the day. Again and again, before our time, men have grown content with a diluted doctrine. And again and again there has followed on that dilution, coming as out of the darkness in a crimson cataract, the strength of the red original wine.

APRIL 11

Yes, the Almighty will be your gold and your precious silver.
—Job 22:25 NKJV

"Elder father, though thine eyes
Shine with hoary mysteries,
Canst thou tell what in the heart
Of a cowslip blossom lies?

"Smaller than all lives that be,
Secret as the deepest sea,
Stands a little house of seeds,
Like an elfin's granary.
Speller of the stones and weeds,

"Skilled in Nature's crafts and creeds,
Tell me what is in the heart
Of the smallest of the seeds."

"God Almighty, and with Him
Cherubim and Seraphim,
Filling all eternity—
Adonai Elohim."

ON THIS DAY ——————————————————————————

- In 1931, GKC's article "On American Humanism" was published in the *Illustrated London News*.

APRIL 12

Tell the daughter of Zion, "Behold, your King is coming to you, lowly, and sitting on a donkey, a colt, the foal of a donkey."

—MATTHEW 21:5 NKJV

> *The tattered outlaw of the earth,*
> *Of ancient crooked will;*
> *Starve, scourge, deride me: I am dumb,*
> *I keep my secret still.*
> *"Fools! For I also had my hour;*
> *One far fierce hour and sweet:*
> *There was a shout about my ears,*
> *And palms before my feet."*

GKC, AS DESCRIBED IN *THE BOOKMAN* (1912)

Of course there are times when the most effective way to teach a certain truth is by laughing very hard: consider, as an illustration, Mr. Chesterton's bracing habit of leading us to laugh our way into the very presence of his God.

ON THIS DAY ——————————————————————————

- In 1930, GKC's article "Religion and the New Science" was published in the *Illustrated London News*.

Let thy fountain be blessed: and rejoice with the wife of
thy youth.

—PROVERBS 5:18

PASSAGES FROM THE *DAILY NEWS* (SELECTED BY GKC'S WIFE, FRANCES CHESTERTON)

If there be any value in scaling the mountains, it is only that from
them one can behold the plains.

Variability is one of the virtues of a woman. It obviates the crude
requirements of polygamy. If you have one good wife you are sure to
have a spiritual harem.

I pressed some little way farther through the throng of people,
and caught a glimpse of some things that are never seen in Fleet
Street. I mean real green which is like the grass in the glaring sun,
and real blue that is like the burning sky in another quarter of
the world, and real gold that is like fire that cannot be quenched,
and real red that is like savage roses and the wine that is the
blood of God. Nor was it a contemptible system of ideas that was
supposed to be depicted by these colours of flags and shields and
shining horsemen. It was at least supposed to be England, which
made us all; it was at least supposed to be London, which made
me and better men. I at least am not so made that I can make
sport of such symbols. There in whatever ungainly procession,
there on whatever ugly shields, there was the cross of St. George
and the sword of St. Paul. Even if all men should go utterly away
from everything that is symbolized, the last symbol will impress
them. If no one should be left in the world except a million open

malefactors and one hypocrite, that hypocrite will still remind them of holiness.

ON THIS DAY ─────────────────────────────

- In 1929, GKC's article "Bowing Down to the New Religion" was published in the *Illustrated London News*.

APRIL 14

The darkness is passing away, and the true light is already shining.

—1 JOHN 2:8 NKJV

> *A secret happiness that soaks the heart*
> *As hills are soaked by slow unsealing snow,*
> *Or secret as that wind without a chart*
> *Whereon did the wild leaves of Sibyl go.*
> *O light uplifted from all mortal knowing,*
> *Send back a little of that glimpse of thee,*
> *That of its glory I may kindle glowing*
> *One tiny spark for all men yet to be.*

A PASSAGE FROM THE MAGAZINE *MODERN MEDICINE* (1921)

The brilliant essayist, Mr. G. K. Chesterton, has been lecturing in the United States, and his wit has been emitting sparks. Among them was one which flew in the direction of the modern health movement. We do not doubt that his audience responded reprovingly when he ridiculed the idea that the doctor should be the health officer of the community.

For doctors as doctors, the lecturer said, he had profound respect; but he would knock their heads off if they undertook to make themselves advisers of the community. The doctor was to be called upon extraordinary occasions to deal with abnormal situations. Suppose he [Mr. Chesterton,] were to precipitate himself into the audience and break his leg. A doctor would set the leg. He would be doing his work as a doctor, but the modern idea seemed to be that he was to take charge of unbroken legs, to say when they were to be used to walk, and when they were to be used to dance.

"Take a policeman. He is there to punish crime," Mr. Chesterton continued. "When you and I indulge in murder, he takes charge of us and deals with us according to law. But just imagine what you would say if told that the policeman was there to encourage virtue. What would happen if you and I were always followed by a policeman, and we heard his voice over our shoulder telling us when to do this and not to do that? I think we should soon begin to look upon it as rather a bore."

APRIL 15

He has put down the mighty from their thrones, and exalted the lowly.

—LUKE 1:52 NKJV

> Great God, that bowest sky and star,
> Bow down our towering heights to thee,
> And grant us in a faltering war
> The firm feet of humility.
> Cleanse us from ire of creed or class,
> The anger of the idle kings;
> Sow in our souls, like living grass,
> The laughter of all lowly things.

A PASSAGE FROM *ROBERT LOUIS STEVENSON* (1928)

Fashions change; but this return to the nursery is not a fashion and it does not change. If we turn to the very latest, and we might say loudest, of literary innovators, we still find that in so far as they are saying anything, they are saying that.

Let us suppose that the Stevensonian way of doing it is altogether dated and out of date; let us leave Stevenson behind in the dead past, along with such lumber as Cervantes and Balzac and Charles Dickens. If we shoot forward into the most fashionable fads and fancies, if we rush to the newest salons or listen to the most advanced lectures, we do not escape the challenge of our childhood. There is already a group, we might say a family group, of poets who consider themselves, and are generally considered, the last word in experiment and even extravagance; and who are not without real qualities of deep atmosphere and suggestion. Yet all that is really deep in the best of their work comes out of those depths of garden perspective and large rooms as seen by little children, white with the windows of the morning.

APRIL 16

Consider and hear me, O Lord my God: lighten mine eyes . . .

—Psalm 13:3

To have known the things that from the weak are furled,
Perilous ancient passions, strange and high;
It is something to be wiser than the world,
It is something to be older than the sky.
In a time of sceptic moths and cynic rusts,

And fatted lives that of their sweetness tire,
In a world of flying loves and fading lusts,
It is something to be sure of a desire.
Lo, blessed are our ears for they have heard;
Yea, blessed are our eyes for they have seen:
Let thunder break on man and beast and bird
And the lightning. It is something to have been.

ON THIS DAY

- In 1927, Chesterton wrote memorably in *G. K.'s Weekly* of "the far-flung Titanic figure of the Giant Albion—whom Blake saw in visions, spreading to our encircling seas."
- And in 1932, GKC's article "Climate and Culture" was published in the *Illustrated London News*.

APRIL 17

The Lord is the strength of my life.
—PSALM 27:1 NKJV

Between us, by the peace of God, such truth can now be
*   told;*
Yea, there is strength in striking root, and good in
*   growing old.*

A POEM ABOUT GKC, GIVEN IN *LIFE* MAGAZINE (1921)

If I were G. K. Chesterton,
And G. K.C. were me,
I'd write the fizziest essay
That ever you did see;

> *I'd plant one foot on Betelgeuse,*
> *The other in the sea,*
> *If I were G. K. Chesterton,*
> *And G. K.C. were me.*

GKC, AS QUOTED IN THE YMCA'S *ASSOCIATION MEN* MAGAZINE (1921)

We must hate the world enough to change it, and yet love the world
enough to think it worth changing.

APRIL 18

> *And where the Spirit of the Lord is, there is liberty.*
> —2 Corinthians 3:17 nkjv

And the more I considered Christianity, the more I found that
while it had established a rule and order, the chief aim of that
order was to give room for good things to run wild.

GKC, AS DESCRIBED IN *THE OUTLOOK* MAGAZINE (1921)

Mr. Chesterton has arrived in this country for a visit. He is going to
warn us against the danger of believing things that are not so. He is
going to tell us of the untrustworthiness of the things which, in com-
mon with the rest of humanity, we have been accepting as truths. He
is going to see that the skeptics are hoist with their own petard. He
is going to pierce the hide of conventional heterodoxy. It is probably
without significance that his manager arranged that his first lecture
should be in Boston.

Most of those who will hear Mr. Chesterton will expect him to
serve them paradoxes. Now there are paradoxes and paradoxes,

and it is not difficult to turn off something paradoxical provided one is indifferent to its quality or its substance. Mr. Chesterton's paradoxes, however, are all of one kind, or rather they all serve one end. He is not interested in a paradox as such; he is interested in stating what he believes to be truth in such a way as to indicate his enjoyment of disbelieving untruth.

One reason why the radical, the skeptic, the iconoclast, the heretic, gets a hearing is that he seems interesting. He is different from the crowd, and therefore is conspicuous. He introduces into common life the element of drama. As soon as heresy becomes the accepted belief it ceases to be interesting. Now what Mr. Chesterton has done is to lend interest to orthodoxy . . . To him the exciting thing is not turbulence, but order.

ON THIS DAY

- In 1908, GKC's article "Shakspere and Zola" was published in the *Illustrated London News.*

APRIL 19

For since the creation of the world His invisible attributes are clearly seen, being understood by the things that are made.

—ROMANS 1:20 NKJV

St. Francis was not a lover of nature. Properly understood, a lover of nature was precisely what he was not. The phrase implies accepting the material universe as a vague environment, a sort of sentimental pantheism. In the romantic period of literature, in the age of Byron and Scott, it was easy enough to imagine that a hermit in the ruins of a chapel (preferably by moonlight) might find peace and a mild pleasure in the harmony of solemn forests and silent stars, while he pondered over some scroll or illuminated volume, about the liturgical nature of which the author was a little vague. In short, the hermit might love nature as a background.

Now for St. Francis nothing was ever in the background. We might say that his mind had no background, except perhaps that divine darkness out of which the divine love had called up every coloured creature one by one. He saw everything as dramatic, distinct from its setting, not all of a piece like a picture but in action like a play. A bird went by him like an arrow; something with a story and a purpose.

A PASSAGE FROM *ROBERT LOUIS STEVENSON* (1928)

Nameless universal forces streaming through the subconsciousness, run very truly like that dark and sacred river that wound its way through caverns measureless to man. When this process of shapelessness is complete, it is always possible that men may come upon a shape with something of a sharp surprise; like a geologist finding in featureless rocks the fossil of some wild creature, looking as if petrified in the last wild leap or on the wing. Or it is as if an antiquary, passing through halls and temples of some iconoclastic city, covered with dizzy patterns of merely mathematical beauty, were to come upon the heaving limb or lifted shoulder of some broken statue of the Greeks.

In that condition it may be that the novel will again be novel. And in that condition, in that reaction, certainly no novel will serve its purpose so forcibly, or make its point so plainly, as a novel by Stevenson. The story, the first of childish and the oldest of human pleasures, will nowhere reveal its structure and its end so swiftly and simply as in the tales of Tusitala. The world's great age will in that degree begin anew; the childhood of the earth be rediscovered; for the story-teller will once more have spread his carpet in the dust; and it will really be a magic carpet.

ON THIS DAY ————————————————————————
- In 1930, GKC's article "Novels on the Great War" was published in the *Illustrated London News*.

APRIL 20

Oh, that men would give thanks to the Lord for His goodness, and for His wonderful works to the children of men!

—PSALM 107:31 NKJV

All these profound matters must be suggested in short and imperfect phrases; and the shortest statement of one aspect of this illumination is to say that it is the discovery of an infinite debt. It may seem a paradox to say that a man may be transported with joy to discover that he is in debt. But this is only because in commercial cases the creditor does not generally share the transports of joy; especially when the debt is by hypothesis infinite and therefore unrecoverable. . . .

It is the highest and holiest of the paradoxes that the man who really knows he cannot pay his debt will be for ever paying it. He will be for ever giving back what he cannot give back, and cannot be expected to give back. He will be always throwing things away into a bottomless pit of unfathomable thanks. Men who think they are too modern to understand this are in fact too mean to understand it; we are most of us too mean to practise it. We are not generous enough to be ascetics; one might almost say not genial enough to be ascetics. A man must have magnanimity of surrender, of which he commonly only catches a glimpse in first love, like a glimpse of our lost Eden.

ON THIS DAY ——————————————————————

- In 1929, GKC's article "The Bible and the Sceptics" was published in the *Illustrated London News*.

APRIL 21

Before the mountains were brought forth, or ever You had formed the earth and the world, even from everlasting to everlasting, You are God.

—PSALM 90:2 NKJV

He who has seen the whole world hanging on a hair of the mercy of God has seen the truth; we might almost say the cold truth. He who has seen the vision of his city upside-down has seen it the right way up. . . . the mystical method establishes a very healthy external relation to everything else.

But it must always be remembered that everything else has for ever fallen into a second place, in comparison with this simple fact of dependence on the divine reality. In so far as ordinary social relations have in them something that seems solid and self-supporting, some sense of being at once buttressed and cushioned; in so far as they establish sanity in the sense of security and security in the sense of self-sufficiency, the man who has seen the world hanging on a hair does have some difficulty in taking them so seriously as that.

GKC, AS QUOTED IN *COLLIER'S* MAGAZINE (1910)

"The great deliverers of men," says G. K. Chesterton, "have, for the most part, saved them from calamities which we all recognize as

evil, from calamities which are the ancient enemies of humanity. The great lawgivers saved us from anarchy; the great physicians saved us from pestilence; the great reformers saved us from starvation. But there is a huge and bottomless evil compared with which all these are fleabites, the most desolating curse that can fall upon men or nations, and it has no name—except we call it satisfaction."

APRIL 22

Whom have I in heaven but thee? and there is none upon earth that I desire beside thee.

—PSALM 73:25

Rossetti makes the remark somewhere, bitterly but with great truth, that the worst moment for the atheist is when he is really thankful and has nobody to thank. The converse of this proposition is also true; and it is certain that this gratitude produced, in such men as we are here considering, the most purely joyful moments that have been known to man. The great painter boasted that he mixed all his colours with brains, and [St. Francis,] the great saint may be said to mix all his thoughts with thanks. All goods look better when they look like gifts.

A REVIEW OF GKC'S BOOK, *GEORGE BERNARD SHAW*, FROM *COLLIER'S* MAGAZINE (1909)

Mr. Chesterton reminds us always of a very big, very good-natured, and very shiftless sand-bagger who holds up his passers-by and goes through their mental pockets only to refill them with a very much shinier assortment of ideas than was there originally.

So here, while relieving us of our preconceptions regarding Mr.

Shaw, he hands back a collection of notions about religion, philoso-phy, literature, and life which must be considered a very unselfish exchange. Any wayfaring man not quite a fool might willingly sub-mit to such a robbery.

APRIL 23

> *But I will sing of Your power; yes, I will sing aloud of Your mercy in the morning.*
>
> —PSALM 59:16 NKJV

While it was yet twilight a figure appeared silently and sud-denly on a little hill above the city, dark against the fading darkness. For it was the end of a long and stern night, a night of vigil, not unvisited by stars. [St. Francis] stood with his hands lifted, as in so many statues and pictures, and about him was a burst of birds singing; and behind him was the break of day.

HIGHLIGHTS OF GKC'S FIRST LECTURE AT THE TIMES SQUARE THEATRE, FROM THE *NEW YORK TIMES* (1921)

Gilbert K. Chesterton delivered his first lecture in New York at the Times Square Theatre last night, his subject being "The Ignorance of the Educated." He had appeared earlier in the week in Boston. Nevertheless, Edwin Markham, who presided, tendered him a for-mal "welcome to America."

An overflowing audience heard the brilliant Englishman and heard him clearly, in spite of his apologies for the carrying power of his voice . . . He caused a laugh at the very start, while the audi-ence was still admiring his great size, by saying that his voice was "the original mouse that came out of the mountain." Mr. Markham

*had said that, when Chesterton spoke, his voice was heard on four
continents.*

*"But you will have reason, I fear," said the lecturer, "to gather that
it is not heard in all theatres." [Other memorable statements were:]*

*If Patrick Henry could arise from the dead and revisit the land
of the living, and see the vast system and social organisation and
social science which now controls, he would probably simplify his
observation and say, "Give me death."*

*I do seriously think that the most profound criticism of the culture
of our time can be found in a sentence which, I believe, was written
by Artemus Ward, which runs, I think: "It isn't so much people's
ignorance that does the harm as it is their knowing so many things
that ain't so."*

APRIL 24

*But I have trusted in Your mercy; my heart shall rejoice in
Your salvation.*

—PSALM 13:5 NKJV

We should turn to St. Francis, in the spirit of thanks for what
he has done. He was above all things a great giver; and he cared
chiefly for the best kind of giving which is called thanksgiving.
If another great man wrote a grammar of assent, he may well
be said to have written a grammar of acceptance; a grammar
of gratitude. He understood down to its very depths the theory
of thanks; and its depths are a bottomless abyss. He knew that
the praise of God stands on its strongest ground when it stands
on nothing. He knew that we can best measure the towering

miracle of the mere fact of existence if we realise that but for some strange mercy we should not even exist.

GKC, AS DESCRIBED BY MURRAY HILL, COLUMNIST FOR *THE BOOKMAN* (1921)

I one time wrote an article in which I told with what surprising ease I saw Mr. Chesterton several years ago in England. Without acquaintances in England, some sort of a fit of impudence seized me. I wrote Mr. Chesterton a letter, communicating to him the intelligence that I had arrived in London, that it was my belief that he was one of the noblest and most interesting monuments in England; and I asked him if he supposed that he could be "viewed" by me, at some street corner, say, at a time appointed, as he rumbled past in his triumphal car.

Mrs. Chesterton replied directly in a note that her husband wished to thank me for my letter and to say that he would be pleased if I cared to come down to spend an afternoon with him at Beaconsfield. Mr. Chesterton, I later recollected, had no means readily at hand of ascertaining whether or not I was an American pickpocket; but from the deference of his manner I was led to suspect that he vaguely supposed I was perhaps the owner of the New York Times, *or somebody like that ...*

My recollection of the conversation I had with Mr. Chesterton in 1914 at Beaconsfield is that there was a much more ruddy quality to his voice then than [when I heard him recently], and more, much more, in the turn of his talk—a racy note of the burly world.

To you it was shown, that you might know that the Lord Himself is God; there is none other besides Him.

—DEUTERONOMY 4:35 NKJV

Man can be defined as an animal that makes dogmas. As he piles doctrine on doctrine and conclusion on conclusion in the formation of some tremendous scheme of philosophy and religion, he is, in the only legitimate sense of which the expression is capable, becoming more and more human.

When he drops one doctrine after another in a refined scepticism, when he declines to tie himself to a system, when he says that he has outgrown definitions, when he says that he disbelieves in finality, when, in his own imagination, he sits as God, holding no form of creed but contemplating all, then he is by that very process sinking slowly backwards into the vagueness of the vagrant animals and the unconsciousness of the grass. Trees have no dogmas. Turnips are singularly broadminded. If then, I repeat, there is to be mental advance, it must be mental advance in the construction of a definite philosophy of life. And that philosophy of life must be right and the other philosophies wrong.

GKC, AS DESCRIBED BY MURRAY HILL,
COLUMNIST FOR *THE BOOKMAN* (1921)

A bit later in the course of his answer to the question he had propounded, "Shall We Abolish the Inevitable?", he got an especially good hand when he remarked: "People nowadays do not like statements having authority—but they will accept any statement without authority."

- In 1931, GKC's article "On Modern Half-Truths" was published in the *Illustrated London News*.

APRIL 26

Let us hold fast the confession of our hope without wavering, for He who promised is faithful.

—HEBREWS 10:23 NKJV

Mankind has not passed through the Middle Ages. Rather mankind has retreated from the Middle Ages in reaction and rout. The Christian ideal has not been tried and found wanting. It has been found difficult; and left untried.

GKC, AS DESCRIBED BY MURRAY HILL, COLUMNIST FOR *THE BOOKMAN* (1921)

I am far from being as large as Mr. Chesterton, but the two of us closeted in that compartment [for an interview] was an absurdity. Mr. Chesterton eclipsed a chair, and beamed upon me with an expression of Cheeryble-like brightness.

Upon his arrival in New York he had declared to the press that he would not write a book of his impressions of the United States. I asked him if, after being here a week or so, he had changed his mind as to this determination. "Not definitely," he said, "not definitely. But, of course, one could never tell what one might do."

He might write a book about us, then? Yes, he might. Did he think it at all likely that he would take up residence over here? A very joyous smile. "One's own country is best," he said.

Rumours had several times been afloat that he had entered the Roman Catholic church. Would he say whether there was any likelihood of his doing this? He was an Anglican Catholic, he replied. Not a Roman Catholic—yet. That was not to say that he might not be—if the Church of England should become more Protestant.

APRIL 27

How great are his signs! and how mighty are his wonders!
—DANIEL 4:3

Let us, then, go upon a long journey and enter on a dreadful search. Let us, at least, dig and seek till we have discovered our own opinions. The dogmas we really hold are far more fantastic, and, perhaps, far more beautiful than we think.

GKC, AS PROFILED IN *PUBLISHERS' WEEKLY* (1921)

Gilbert K. Chesterton arrived here from England last Saturday on the Cunarder Kaiserin Augusta Victoria *"to lose his impressions of the United States," at least that is his own way of describing the object of his voyage.*

Altho he announced before he left London that he would not write a book on America, he was immediately beset by interviewers, who wanted to know, his impressions of America and his opinion on all sorts of questions.

"How is the war affecting the literary market in England?" he was asked.

"There have not been many big things resulting from the war yet, because in my opinion it is too early to expect it. There have, however, been a great many little things—quite a lot of excellent poetry."

ON THIS DAY ————————————————————————

- In 1904, GKC and his wife, Frances, hosted Elodie and Hilaire Belloc for dinner. Frances wrote in her diary: "Hilaire, in great form, recited his own poetry with great enthusiasm the whole evening."

APRIL 28

Blessed be the God and Father of our Lord Jesus Christ, who according to His abundant mercy has begotten us again to a living hope through the resurrection of Jesus Christ.

—1 PETER 1:3 NKJV

The fierce poet of the Middle Ages wrote, "Abandon hope all ye who enter here" over the gates of the lower world. The emancipated poets of to-day have written it over the gates of this world.

But if we are to understand the story [of Dickens] which follows, we must erase that apocalyptic writing, if only for an hour. We must recreate the faith of our fathers, if only as an artistic atmosphere. If, then, you are a pessimist, in reading this story, forego for a little the pleasures of pessimism. Dream for one mad moment that the grass is green. Unlearn that sinister learning that you think so clear; deny that deadly knowledge that you think you know. Surrender the very flower of your culture; give up the very jewel of your pride; abandon hopelessness, all ye who enter here.

GKC ON CHARLES DICKENS

Mrs. Micawber is very nearly the best thing in Dickens . . . If we regard David Copperfield *as an unconscious defence of the poetic view of life, we might regard Mrs. Micawber as an unconscious satire on the logical view of life. She sits as a monument of the hopelessness and helplessness of reason in the face of this romantic and unreasonable world.*

APRIL 29

With men it is impossible, but not with God; for with God all things are possible.

—MARK 10:27 NKJV

This world is not to be justified as it is justified by the mechanical optimists; it is not to be justified as the best of all possible worlds. Its merit is not that it is orderly and explicable; its merit is that it is wild and utterly unexplained. Its merit is precisely that none of us could have conceived such a thing, that we should have rejected the bare idea of it as miracle and unreason. It is the best of all impossible worlds.

GKC ON CHARLES DICKENS (1911)

There was a painful moment (somewhere about the eighties) when we watched anxiously to see whether Dickens was fading from the modern world. We have watched a little longer, and with great relief we begin to realise that it is the modern world that is fading. All that universe of ranks and respectabilities in comparison with which Dickens was called a caricaturist, all that Victorian universe in which he seemed vulgar all that is itself breaking up like a cloudland. And only the caricatures of Dickens remain like things carved in stone.

I have read Treasure Island twenty times; nevertheless I know it. But I do not really feel as if I knew all Pickwick; I have not so much read it twenty times as read in it a million times; and it almost seemed as if I always read something new.

We of the true faith look at each other and understand; yes, our master was a magician. I believe the books are alive; I believe that leaves still grow in them, as leaves grow on the trees. I believe that this fairy library flourishes and increases like a fairy forest.

APRIL 30

> *There is a friend who sticks closer than a brother.*
> —PROVERBS 18:24 NKJV

Our ethical societies understand fellowship, but they do not understand good fellowship. Similarly, our wits understand talk, but not what Dr. Johnson called a good talk. In order to have, like Dr. Johnson, a good talk, it is emphatically necessary to be, like Dr. Johnson, a good man—to have friendship and honour and an abysmal tenderness. Above all, it is necessary to be openly and indecently humane, to confess with fulness all the primary pities and fears of Adam. Johnson was a clear-headed humorous man, and therefore he did not mind talking seriously about religion.

GKC ON DICKENS—AND MARRIAGE (1911)

But the wise old fairy tales (which are the wisest things in the world, at any rate the wisest things of worldly origin), the wise old fairy tales never were so silly as to say that the prince and the princess lived peacefully ever afterwards. The fairy tales said that the prince and princess lived happily ever afterwards: and so they did. They lived happily, although it is very likely that from time to time they threw the furniture at each other.

ON THIS DAY ———————————————————————

- In 1932, GKC's article "Tradition and Continuity," celebrating the 90th anniversary of the *Illustrated London News*, was published.

MAY 1

I applied my heart to know, to search and seek out wisdom and the reason of things.

—ECCLESIASTES 7:25 NKJV

It is idle to talk always of the alternative of reason and faith. Reason is itself a matter of faith. It is an act of faith to assert that our thoughts have any relation to reality at all.

If you are merely a sceptic, you must sooner or later ask yourself the question, "Why should *anything* go right; even observation and deduction? Why should not good logic be as misleading as bad logic? They are both movements in the brain of a bewildered ape?"

The young sceptic says, "I have a right to think for myself." But the old sceptic, the complete sceptic, says, "I have no right to think for myself. I have no right to think at all."

GKC ON DICKENS (1911)

If there be anywhere a man who loves good books, that man wishes that there were four Oliver Twists *and at least forty-four* Pickwicks. *If there be any one who loves laughter and creation, he would be glad to read a hundred of* Nicholas Nickleby *and two hundred of* The Old Curiosity Shop.

DURING THIS MONTH

- In 1903, GKC's study *Robert Browning* was published.
- In 1927, GKC's novel *The Return of Don Quixote* was published.

MAY 2

Marvellous are Your works, and that my soul knows very well. My frame was not hidden from You, when I was made in secret.

—Psalm 139:14–15 NKJV

The sense of the miracle of humanity itself should be always more vivid to us than any marvels of power, intellect, art, or civilization. The mere man on two legs, as such, should be felt as something more heart-breaking than any music and more startling than any caricature.

GKC ON DICKENS (1911)

The power of Dickens is shown even in the scraps of Dickens, just as the virtue of a saint is said to be shown in fragments of his property or rags from his robe. It is with such fragments that we are chiefly concerned in the Christmas Stories.

Many of them are fragments in the literal sense; Dickens began them and then allowed some one else to carry them on; they are almost rejected notes. In all the other cases we have been considering the books that he wrote; here we have rather to consider the books that he might have written. And here we find the final evidence and the unconscious stamp of greatness, as we might find it in some broken bust or some rejected moulding in the studio of Michael Angelo.

ON THIS DAY ───────────────────────────────

- In 1908, GKC's article "Ceremonial Regulations and Costumes" was published in the *Illustrated London News*.

MAY 3

But those who seek the Lord shall not lack any good thing.
—PSALM 34:10 NKJV

I am ordinary in the correct sense of the term; which means the acceptance of an order; a Creator and the Creation, the common sense of gratitude for Creation, life and love as gifts permanently good, marriage and chivalry as laws rightly controlling them.

GKC ON DICKENS (1911)

Critics have called Keats and others who died young "the great Might-have-beens of literary history." Dickens certainly was not merely a great Might-have-been. Dickens, to say the least of him, was a great Was.

Yet this fails fully to express the richness of his talent; for the truth is that he was a great Was and also a great Might-have-been. He said what he had to say, and yet not all he had to say. Wild pictures, possible stories, tantalising and attractive trains of thought, perspectives of adventure, crowded so continually upon his mind that at the end there was a vast mass of them left over, ideas that he literally had not the opportunity to develop, tales that he literally had not the time to tell. This is shown clearly in his private notes and letters, which are full of schemes singularly striking and suggestive, schemes which he never carried out.

It is indicated even more clearly by these Christmas Stories, collected out of the chaotic opulence of Household Words and All the Year Round. He wrote short stories actually because he had not time to write long stories. He often put into the short story a deep and branching idea which would have done very well for a long story; many of his long stories, so to speak, broke off short. This is where he differs from most who are called the Might-have-beens of literature. Marlowe and Chatterton failed because of their weakness. Dickens failed because of his force.

ON THIS DAY ───────────────────────────────

- In 1930, GKC's article "The Joy of Dullness" was published in the *Illustrated London News*.

MAY 4

Let no one deceive you with empty words . . .
—EPHESIANS 5:6 NKJV

When scientific evolution was announced, some feared that it would encourage mere animality. It did worse: it encouraged mere spirituality. It taught men to think that so long as they were passing from the ape they were going to the angel. But you can pass from the ape and go to the devil.

GKC ON DICKENS (1911)

For Dickens had hold of one great truth, the neglect of which has, as it were, truncated and made meagre the work of many brilliant modern novelists. Modern novelists try to make long novels out of subtle characters. But a subtle character soon comes to an end, because it works in and in to its own centre and dies there. But a simple character goes on for ever in a fresh interest and energy, because it works out and out into the infinite universe.

A PASSAGE FROM *ROBERT LOUIS STEVENSON* (1928)

It may be that the world will forget Stevenson, a century or so after it has forgotten all the present distinguished detractors of Stevenson. It may be quite the other way, as the poet said; it may be the world will remember Stevenson; will remember him with a start, so to speak, when everybody else has forgotten that there ever was any story in a novel. The dissolution hinted at by Sir Edmund Gosse, whereby fiction which was always a rather vague form shall become utterly formless, may have by that time dropped out of the novel all its original notion of a narrative. Mr. H.G. Wells, if he lives to delight the world so long, will be able to deliver the goods in the form of great masses of admirable analyses of economics and social conditions, without the embarrassment of having to remember at every two hundred pages or so that he has somewhere left a hero in a motor-car or a heroine in a lodging-house.

ON THIS DAY

• In 1929, GKC's article "The Truth About St. George" was published in the *Illustrated London News*.

MAY 5

Where wast thou when I laid the foundations of the earth? declare, if thou hast understanding. Who hath laid the measures thereof, if thou knowest? or who hath stretched the line upon it?

—Job 38:4–5

Most modern histories of mankind begin with the word evolution, and with a rather wordy exposition of evolution.... There is something slow and soothing and gradual about the word and even about the idea.

As a matter of fact, it is not, touching these primary things, a very practical word or a very profitable idea. Nobody can imagine how nothing could turn into something. Nobody can get an inch nearer to it by explaining how something could turn into something else. It is really far more logical to start by saying "In the beginning God created heaven and earth" even if you only mean "In the beginning some unthinkable power began some unthinkable process." For [the name of] God is by its nature a name of mystery, and nobody ever supposed that man could imagine how a world was created any more than he could create one.

GKC ON DICKENS (1911)

When we come to Bleak House, *we come to a change in artistic structure. The thing is no longer a string of incidents; it is a cycle of incidents. It returns upon itself; it has recurrent melody and poetic justice; it has artistic constancy and artistic revenge. It preserves the unities; even to some extent it preserves the unities of time and place.*

The story circles round two or three symbolic places; it does not go straggling irregularly all over England like one of Mr. Pickwick's coaches. People go from one place to another place; but not from one place to another place on the road to everywhere else. Mr. Jarndyce goes from Bleak House to visit Mr. Boythorn; but he comes back to Bleak House. Miss Clare and Miss Summerson go from Bleak House to visit Mr. and Mrs. Bayham Badger; but they come back to Bleak House. The whole story strays from Bleak House and plunges into the foul fogs of Chancery and the autumn mists of Chesney Wold; but the whole story comes back to Bleak House. The domestic title is appropriate; it is a permanent address.

MAY 6

You have set all the borders of the earth; You have made summer and winter.

—PSALM 74:17 NKJV

But to Browning himself hope was traced to something like red toadstools. His mysticism was not of that idle and wordy type which believes that a flower is symbolical of life; it was rather of that deep and eternal type which believes that life, a mere abstraction, is symbolical of a flower. With him the great concrete experiences which God made always come first; his own deductions and speculations about them always second. And in this point we find the real peculiar inspiration of his very original poems.

GKC ON DICKENS (1911)

A picaresque novel is only a very eventful biography; but the opening of Bleak House *is quite another business altogether. It is admirable in quite another way. The description of the fog in the first chapter of* Bleak House *is good in itself; but it is not merely good in itself, like the description of the wind in the opening of* Martin Chuzzlewit; *it is also good in the sense that Maeterlinck is good; it is what the modern people call an atmosphere. Dickens begins in the Chancery fog because he means to end in the Chancery fog. He did not begin in the Chuzzlewit wind because he meant to end in it; he began in it because it was a good beginning. This is perhaps the best short way of stating the peculiarity of the position of* Bleak House. *In this* Bleak House *beginning we have the feeling that it is not only a beginning; we have the feeling that the author sees the conclusion and the whole. The beginning is alpha and omega: the beginning and the end. He means that all the characters and all the events shall be read through the smoky colours of that sinister and unnatural vapour.*

MAY 7

This is the purpose that is purposed upon the whole
earth: and this is the hand that is stretched out upon all
the nations.

—ISAIAH 14:26

One of my first journalistic adventures, or misadventures, concerned a comment on Grant Allen, who had written a book about the Evolution of the Idea of God. I happened to remark that it would be much more interesting if God wrote a book about the evolution of the idea of Grant Allen.

And I remember that the editor objected to my remark on the ground that it was blasphemous; which naturally amused me not a little. For the joke of it was, of course, that it never occurred to him to notice the title of the book itself, which really was blasphemous; for it was, when translated into English, "I will show you how this nonsensical notion that there is God grew up among men." My remark was strictly pious and proper confessing the divine purpose even in its most seemingly dark or meaningless manifestations.

A PASSAGE FROM *ROBERT LOUIS STEVENSON* (1928)

I have admitted that some part of Stevenson's deliberate choice of
childishness was a reaction from ill-chosen surroundings and courses
of conduct in the periods of passion and of youth. But the younger writ-
ers, who boast of choosing for themselves, seem just as unsuccessful in
making passion identical with pleasure; and just as unsuccessful in
preserving the youthful spirit of youth. I have admitted that when he
made his dash for liberty and happiness, it may have appeared that
there was no other alternative but that of Puritanism or pessimism.

But the new writers who are not threatened with Puritanism seem to be just as much moved to pessimism. There seems no explanation of the two tempers; except that the apostle of childhood was at least seeking pleasure where it could be found, while the apostles of youth are seeking it where it cannot be found.

What awaits us after all these episodes I will not pretend to prophesy; I will only profess to hope that it may be the rebuilding of the great and neglected Christian philosophy, to which all contributions will be thankfully received, especially those of atheists and anarchists.

MAY 8

For my thoughts are not your thoughts, neither are your ways my ways, saith the Lord.

—ISAIAH 55:8

Poetry is sane because it floats easily in an infinite sea; reason seeks to cross the infinite sea, and so make it finite. The result is mental exhaustion, like the physical exhaustion of Mr. Holbein. To accept everything is an exercise, to understand everything a strain. The poet only desires exaltation and expansion, a world to stretch himself in. The poet only asks to get his head into the heavens. It is the logician who seeks to get the heavens into his head. And it is his head that splits.

GKC ON DICKENS (1911)

The fog of the first chapter [in Bleak House*] never lifts. In this twilight he traced wonderful shapes. Those people who fancy that Dickens was a mere clown; that he could not describe anything delicate or deadly in the human character, those who fancy this* *are mostly people whose position is explicable in many easy ways. The vast majority of the fastidious critics have, in the quite strict and solid sense of the words, never read Dickens at all; hence their opposition is due to and inspired by a hearty innocence which will certainly make them enthusiastic Dickensians if they ever, by some accident, happen to read him.*

A PASSAGE FROM *ROBERT LOUIS STEVENSON* (1928)

The naturalistic philosophies did not only contradict Christianity. The naturalistic philosophies also contradicted the naturalistic novels. Their own exercise of their own right of expression was quite enough to show that the mere combination of the maturity of reason with the pleasures of passion does not in fact produce a Utopia. We need not debate here whether the Zolaists were justified in so laboriously describing horrors. If mere liberty had really led to happiness, they would have been describing happiness. It would not have been necessary for a grown man with a library of modern literature to hide himself in a twopenny toy theatre in order to be happy.

This very simple truth is probably too simple to be seen; because, like many such things, it is too large to be seen. But certainly it is still there to be seen, if any of the moderns could enlarge their minds enough to see it.

MAY 9

When His lamp shone upon my head, and when by His
light I walked through darkness ...

—JOB 29:3 NKJV

"Do you see this lantern?" cried Syme in a terrible voice. "Do you see the cross carved on it, and the flame inside? You did not make it. You did not light it. Better men than you, men who could believe and obey, twisted the entrails of iron and preserved the legend of fire. There is not a street you walk on, there is not a thread you wear, that was not made as this lantern was, by denying your philosophy of dirt and rats. You can make nothing. You can only destroy. You will destroy mankind; you will destroy the world. Let that suffice you. Yet this one old Christian lantern you shall not destroy."

GKC ON DICKENS (1911)

Dickens had a singularly just mind. He was wild in his caricatures, but very sane in his impressions. Many of his books were devoted, and this book is partly devoted, to a denunciation of aristocracy of the idle class that lives easily upon the toil of nations. But he was fairer than many modern revolutionists, and he insisted on satirising also those who prey on society not in the name of rank or law, but in the name of intellect and beauty.

ON THIS DAY ———————————————————

- In 1904, GKC and his wife, Frances, attended a Literary Fund Dinner presided over by J.M. Barrie, the author of *Peter Pan*.

- And in 1908, GKC's article "On the World Getting Smaller" was published in the *Illustrated London News*.

MAY 10

My people have been lost sheep. Their shepherds have led them astray . . . They have forgotten their resting place.
—JEREMIAH 50:6 NKJV

Man has always lost his way. He has been a tramp ever since Eden; but he always knew, or thought he knew, what he was looking for. Every man has a house somewhere in the elaborate cosmos; his house waits for him waist deep in slow Norfolk rivers or sunning itself upon Sussex downs. Man has always been looking for that home which is the subject matter of this book.

But in the bleak and blinding hail of skepticism to which he has been now so long subjected, he has begun for the first time to be chilled, not merely in his hopes, but in his desires. For the first time in history he begins really to doubt the object of his wanderings on the earth. He has always lost his way; but now he has lost his address.

A PASSAGE FROM *ROBERT LOUIS STEVENSON* (1928)

For the truth is that there really is no sense or meaning, in this continuous tribute of the poets to the poetry of early childhood, unless it be, as Traherne says, that the world of sin comes between us and something more beautiful or, as Wordsworth says, that we came first from God who is our home.

- In 1930, GKC's article "The Poet Laureate in Our Time" was published in the *Illustrated London News*.

MAY 11

> ... *that your faith should not be in the wisdom of men*
> *but in the power of God.*
>
> —1 CORINTHIANS 2:5 NKJV

Charity is a fashionable virtue in our time; it is lit up by the gigantic firelight of Dickens. Hope is a fashionable virtue today; our attention has been arrested for it by the sudden and silver trumpet of Stevenson.

But faith is unfashionable, and it is customary on every side to cast against it the fact that it is a paradox. Everybody mockingly repeats the famous childish definition that faith is "the power of believing that which we know to be untrue." Yet it is not one atom more paradoxical than hope or charity. Charity is the power of defending that which we know to be indefensible. Hope is the power of being cheerful in circumstances which we know to be desperate.

GKC ON DICKENS (1911)

A collection of the works of Dickens would be incomplete in an essential as well as a literal sense without his Child's History of England. *It may not be important as a contribution to history, but it is important as a contribution to biography; as a contribution to the character and the career of the man who wrote it, a typical man of his time. That he had made no personal historical researches, that he had no special historical learning, that he had not had, in truth, even anything that could be called a good education, all this only accentuates not the merit but at least the importance of the book. For here we may read in plain popular language, written by a man whose genius for popular exposition has never been surpassed among men, a brief account of the origin and meaning of England as it seemed to the average Englishman of that age. When subtler views of our history, some more false and some more true than his, have become popular, or at least well known, when in the near future Carlylean or Catholic or Marxian views of history have spread themselves among the reading public, this book will always remain as a bright and brisk summary.*

MAY 12

Happy are the people whose God is the Lord!
—PSALM 144:15 NKJV

The supreme and most practical value of poetry is this, that in poetry, as in music, a note is struck which expresses beyond the power of rational statement a condition of mind, and all actions arise from a condition of mind.

Prose can only use a large and clumsy notation; it can only say that a man is miserable, or that a man is happy; it is forced to ignore that there are a million diverse kinds of misery and a million diverse kinds of happiness. Poetry alone, with the first throb of its metre, can tell us whether the depression is the kind of depression that drives a man to suicide, or the kind of depression that drives him to the Tivoli. Poetry can tell us whether the happiness is the happiness that sends a man to a restaurant, or the much richer and fuller happiness that sends him to church.

ON THIS DAY

- In 1904, GKC and his wife, Frances, "went to see Max Beerbohm's caricature of Gilbert at the Carfax Gallery." It bore the title: "G.K.C.—Humanist—Kissing the World." Frances told her diary: "It's more like Thackeray, very funny though."

MAY 13

And I heard a loud voice from heaven saying, "Behold, the tabernacle of God is with men, and He will dwell with them, and they shall be His people. God Himself will be with them and be their God."

—Revelation 21:3 NKJV

All my modern Utopian friends look at each other rather doubtfully, for their ultimate hope is the dissolution of all special ties. But again I seem to hear, like a kind of echo, an answer from beyond the world. "You will have real obligations, and therefore real adventures when you get to my Utopia. But the hardest obligation and the steepest adventure is to get there."

GKC ON DICKENS (1911)

The fault of Dickens is not (as is often said) that he "applies the same moral standard to all ages." Every sane man must do that: a moral standard must remain the same or it is not a moral standard.

Dickens, through being a living and fighting man of his own time, kept the health of his own heart, and so saw many truths with a single eye: truths that were spoilt for subtler eyes. He was much more really right than Carlyle; immeasurably more right than Froude. He was more right precisely because he applied plain human morals to all facts as he saw them.

MAY 14

He sets on high those who are lowly.
—JOB 5:11 NKJV

The most marvellous of those mystical cavaliers who wrote intricate and exquisite verse in England in the seventeenth century, I mean Henry Vaughan, put the matter in one line, intrinsically immortal and practically forgotten—

Oh holy hope and high humility.

That adjective "high" is not only one of the sudden and stunning inspirations of literature; it is also one of the greatest and gravest definitions of moral science. However far aloft a man may go, he is still looking up, not only at God (which is obvious), but in a manner at men also: seeing more and more all that is towering and mysterious in the dignity and destiny of the lonely house of Adam.

GKC ON DICKENS (1911)

The time will soon come when the mere common-sense of Dickens, like the mere common-sense of Macaulay (though his was poisoned by learning and Whig politics), will appear to give a plainer and therefore truer picture of the mass of history than the mystical perversity of a man of genius writing only out of his own temperament, like Carlyle or Taine. If a man has a new theory of ethics there is one thing he must not be allowed to do. Let him give laws on Sinai, let him dictate a Bible, let him fill the world with cathedrals if he can. But he must not be allowed to write a history of England; or a history of any country. All history was conducted on ordinary morality: with his extraordinary morality he is certain to read it all askew.

ON THIS DAY

• In 1932, GKC's article "The Language of Convention" was published in the *Illustrated London News.*

MAY 15

Therefore He is also able to save to the uttermost those who come to God through Him.

—HEBREWS 7:25 NKJV

In the fairy tale an incomprehensible happiness rests upon an incomprehensible condition. A box is opened, and all evils fly out. A word is forgotten, and cities perish. A lamp is lit, and love flies away. A flower is plucked, and human lives are forfeited. An apple is eaten, and the hope of God is gone.

GKC ON DICKENS (1911)

I have heard that in some debating clubs there is a rule that the members may discuss anything except religion and politics. I cannot imagine what they do discuss; but it is quite evident that they have ruled out the only two subjects which are either important or amusing.

The thing is a part of a certain modern tendency to avoid things because they lead to warmth; whereas, obviously, we ought, even in a social sense, to seek those things specially. The warmth of the discussion is as much a part of hospitality as the warmth of the fire.

MAY 16

Now may the God of hope fill you with all joy and peace in believing, that you may abound in hope by the power of the Holy Spirit.

—ROMANS 15:13 NKJV

But we are always praying that our eyes may behold greatness, instead of praying that our hearts may be filled with it.

GKC ON DICKENS (1911)

Dickens was capable of loving all men; but he refused to love all opinions. The modern humanitarian can love all opinions, but he cannot love all men; he seems, sometimes, in the ecstasy of his humanitarianism, even to hate them all. He can love all opinions, including the opinion that men are unlovable.

In feeling Dickens as a lover we must never forget him as a fighter, and a fighter for a creed; but indeed there is no other kind of fighter. The geniality which he spread over all his creations was geniality spread from one centre, from one flaming peak.

ON THIS DAY ————————————————————

- In 1931, GKC's article "Einstein on War" was published in the *Illustrated London News*.

MAY 17

*When I consider thy heavens, the work of thy fingers, the
moon and the stars, which thou hast ordained . . .*

—PSALM 8:3

The Christian is quite free to believe that there is a considerable amount of settled order and an inevitable development in the universe. But the materialist is not allowed to admit into his spotless machine the slightest speck of spiritualism or miracle.

GKC ON DICKENS (1911)

Everywhere in Dickens's work these angles of his absolute opinion stood up out of the confusion of his general kindness, just as sharp and splintered peaks stand up out of the soft confusion of the forests. Dickens is always generous, he is generally kind-hearted, he is often sentimental, he is sometimes intolerably maudlin; but you never know when you will not come upon one of the convictions of Dickens; and when you do come upon it you do know it. It is as hard and as high as any precipice or peak of the mountains. The highest and hardest of these peaks is Hard Times.

ON THIS DAY ————————————————————

- In 1930, GKC's article "The Creeds and the Modernist" was published in the *Illustrated London News*.

MAY 18

So God created man in His own image; in the image of
God He created him; male and female He created them.
— GENESIS 1:27 NKJV

And almost without exception all the great men have come out of this atmosphere of equality. Great men may make despotisms; but democracies make great men. The other main factory of heroes besides a revolution is a religion. And a religion again, is a thing which, by its nature, does not think of men as more or less valuable, but of men as all intensely and painfully valuable, a democracy of eternal danger. For religion all men are equal, as all pennies are equal, because the only value in any of them is that they bear the image of the King.

GKC ON DICKENS (1911)

Great Expectations *is melancholy in a sense; but it is doubtful of everything, even of its own melancholy.* The Tale of Two Cities *is a great tragedy, but it is still a sentimental tragedy. It is a great drama, but it is still a melodrama. But this tale of* Hard Times *is in some way harsher than all these. For it is the expression of a righteous indignation which cannot condescend to humour and which cannot even condescend to pathos. Twenty times we have taken Dickens's hand and it has been sometimes hot with revelry and sometimes weak with weariness; but this time we start a little, for it is inhumanly cold; and then we realise that we have touched his gauntlet of steel.*

ON THIS DAY

- In 1929, GKC's article "The Sophistication—and Simplicity—of the Young" was published in the *Illustrated London News.*

MAY 19

He shall be like a tree planted by the rivers of water, that brings forth its fruit in its season.

—PSALM 1:3 NKJV

Real development is not leaving things behind, as on a road, but drawing life from them, as from a root.

GKC ON DICKENS (1911)

Now the really odd thing about England in the nineteenth century is this that there was one Englishman who happened to keep his head. The men who lost their heads lost highly scientific and philosophical heads; they were great cosmic systematisers like Spencer, great social philosophers like Bentham, great practical politicians like Bright, great political economists like Mill. The man who kept his head kept a head full of fantastic nonsense; he was a writer of rowdy farces, a demagogue of fiction, a man without education in any serious sense whatever, a man whose whole business was to turn ordinary cockneys into extraordinary caricatures.

Yet when all these other children of the revolution went wrong he, by a mystical something in his bones, went right. He knew nothing of the Revolution; yet he struck the note of it. He returned to the original sentimental commonplace upon which it is forever founded, as the Church is founded on a rock. In an England gone mad about a minor theory, he reasserted the original idea the idea that no one in the State must be too weak to influence the State. This man was Dickens.

But there is a spirit in man, and the breath of the
Almighty gives him understanding.

—JOB 32:8 NKJV

Mysticism keeps men sane. As long as you have mystery, you have health; when you destroy mystery you create morbidity. The ordinary man has always been sane because the ordinary man has always been a mystic. He has permitted the twilight. He has always had one foot in the earth and the other in fairyland. He has always left himself free to doubt his gods but (unlike the agnostic of today) free also to believe in them. He has always cared more for truth than for consistency . . .

It is exactly this balance of apparent contradictions that has been the whole buoyancy of the healthy man. The whole secret of mysticism is this: that man can understand everything by the help of what he does not understand.

ON THIS DAY

- In 1905, GKC and his wife, Frances, attended a reunion dinner of J. D. C., a club founded by Chesterton and several friends during their school-days before going up to university. Of this event, Frances said, "Words fail me when I try to recall the sensation aroused by a J. D. C. dinner. It seems so odd to think of these men as boys, to realize what their school life was and what a powerful element the J. D. C. was in the lives of all. And there were husbands and wives, and the tie so strong, and the long, long thoughts of schoolboys and schoolgirls fell on us."

MAY 21

Then shall thy light break forth as the morning.
—Isaiah 58:8

Only in our romantic country do you have the romantic thing called weather—beautiful and changeable as a woman. The great English landscape painters (neglected now, like everything that is English) have this salient distinction, that the weather is not the atmosphere of their pictures: it is the subject of their pictures. They paint portraits of the weather. The weather sat to Constable; the weather posed for Turner—and the deuce of a pose it was. In the English painters the climate is the hero; in the case of Turner a swaggering and fighting hero, melodramatic but magnificent. The tan and terrible protagonist robed in rain, thunder, and sunlight, fills the whole canvas and the whole foreground.

Rich colours actually look more luminous on a grey day, because they are seen against a dark background, and seem to be burning with a lustre of their own.... There is this value about the colour that men call colourless: that it suggests in some way the mixed and troubled average of existence, especially in its quality of strife and expectation and promise. Grey is a colour that always seems on the eve of changing to some other colour; of brightening into blue, or blanching into white or breaking into green or gold. So we may be perpetually reminded of the indefinite hope that is in doubt itself; and when there is grey weather on our hills or grey hair on our heads perhaps they may still remind us of the morning.

ON THIS DAY

- In 1932, GKC's article "The Brevity of Modern Poems" was published in the *Illustrated London News*.

MAY 22

Consider the lilies how they grow: they toil not, they spin not; and yet I say unto you, that Solomon in all his glory was not arrayed like one of these.

—LUKE 12:27

> *Beneath the gnarled old Knowledge-tree*
> *Sat, like an owl, the evil sage:*
> *"The world's a bubble," solemnly*
> *He read, and turned a second page.*
> *"A bubble, then, old crow," I cried,*
> *"God keep you in your weary wit!*
> *A bubble—have you ever spied*
> *The colours I have seen on it?"*

GKC ON DICKENS (1911)

Dickens is the one living link between the old kindness and the new, between the good will of the past and the good works of the future. He links May Day with Bank Holiday, and he does it almost alone. All the men around him, great and good as they were, were in comparison puritanical, and never so puritanical as when they were also atheistic. He is a sort of solitary pipe down which pours to the twentieth century the original river of Merry England.

And although this Hard Times *is, as its name implies, the hardest of his works, although there is less in it perhaps than in any of the others of the abandon and the buffoonery of Dickens, this only emphasises the more clearly the fact that he stood almost alone for a more humane and hilarious view of democracy. None of his great and much more highly-educated contemporaries could help him in this. Carlyle was as gloomy on the one side as Herbert Spencer on the other. He protested against the commercial oppression simply and solely because it was not only an oppression but a depression. And this protest of his was made specially in the case of the book before us. It may be bitter, but it was a protest against bitterness. It may be dark, but it is the darkness of the subject and not of the author. He is by his own account dealing with hard times, but not with a hard eternity, not with a hard philosophy of the universe.*

MAY 23

Then Jesus called his disciples unto him.
—Matthew 15:32

Our civilization has decided, and very justly decided, that determining the guilt or innocence of men is a thing too important to be trusted to trained men. If it wishes for light upon that awful matter, it asks men who know no more law than I know, but who can feel the things that I felt in the jury-box. When it wants a library catalogued, or the solar system discovered, or any trifle of that kind, it uses up its specialists.

But when it wishes anything done which is really serious, it collects twelve of the ordinary men standing round. The same thing was done, if I remember right, by the Founder of Christianity.

ON THIS DAY ─────────────────────────────────

- In 1919, GKC wrote a candid letter to his friend the poet and novelist Maurice Baring, saying: "I remember . . . the only time I ever talked to Swinburne. I had regarded (and resisted) him in my boyhood as a sort of Antichrist in purple, like Nero holding his lyre, and I found him more like a very well-read Victorian old maid, almost entirely a *laudator temporis acti* disposed to say that none of the young men would ever come up to Tennyson—which may be quite true for all I know."
- And in 1931, GKC's article "A Tax on Talking" was published in the *Illustrated London News*.

MAY 24

But I will sing of thy power; yea, I will sing aloud of thy mercy in the morning.

—PSALM 59:16

Great men like Ariosto, Rabelais, and Shakespeare fall in foul places, flounder in violent but venial sin, sprawl for pages, exposing their gigantic weakness, are dirty, are indefensible; and then they struggle up again and can still speak with a convincing kindness and an unbroken honour of the best things in the world: Rabelais, of the instruction of ardent and austere youth; Ariosto, of holy chivalry; Shakespeare, of the splendid stillness of mercy.

GKC ON DICKENS (1911)

Hard Times *is harsh; but then* Hard Times *is a social pamphlet; perhaps it is only harsh as a social pamphlet must be harsh.* Bleak House *is a little sombre; but then* Bleak House *is almost a detective story; perhaps it is only sombre in the sense that a detective story must be sombre.* A Tale of Two Cities *is a tragedy; but then* A Tale of Two Cities *is a tale of the French Revolution; perhaps it is only a tragedy because the French Revolution was a tragedy.* The Mystery of Edwin Drood *is dark; but then the mystery of anybody must be dark.*

ON THIS DAY

- In 1905, GKC and his wife, Frances, went to see the poet George Meredith.
- And in 1930, GKC's article "The Place of Mysticism" was published in the *Illustrated London News*.

MAY 25

Strength and beauty are in His sanctuary.
—PSALM 96:6 NKJV

Painting the town red is a delightful thing until it is done. It would be splendid to see the cross of St. Paul's as red as the cross of St. George, and the gallons of red paint running down the dome or dripping from the Nelson Column. But when it is done, when you have painted the town red, an extraordinary thing happens. You cannot see any red at .all. I can see, as in a sort of vision, the successful artist standing in the midst of that frightful city, hung on all sides with the scarlet of his shame.

And then, when everything is red, he will long for a red rose in a green hedge and long in vain; he will dream of a red leaf and be unable even to imagine it. He has desecrated the divine colour, and he can no longer see it, though it is all around. I see him, a single black figure against the red-hot hell that he has kindled, where spires and turrets stand up like immobile flames: he is stiffened in a sort of agony of prayer. Then the mercy of Heaven is loosened, and I see one or two flakes of snow very slowly begin to fall.

ON THIS DAY

- In 1929, GKC's article "The Exhaustion of the Vote" was published in the *Illustrated London News*.

MAY 26

Most gladly therefore will I rather glory in my infirmities, that the power of Christ may rest upon me.
—2 CORINTHIANS 12:9

All the jokes about men sitting down on their hats are really theological jokes; they are concerned with the Dual Nature of Man. They refer to the primary paradox that man is superior to all the things around him and yet is at their mercy.

GKC ON DICKENS (1911)

It is quite true that [Dickens's] jokes are often on the same subjects as the jokes in a halfpenny comic paper. Only they happen to be good jokes. He does make jokes about drunkenness, jokes about mothers-in-law, jokes about henpecked husbands, jokes (which is much more

really unpardonable) about spinsters, jokes about physical coward-
ice, jokes about fatness, jokes about sitting down on one's hat.

He does make fun of all these things; and the reason is not
very far to seek. He makes fun of all these things because all these
things, or nearly all of them, are really very funny.

But a large number of those who might otherwise read and enjoy
Dickens are undoubtedly "put off" (as the phrase goes) by the fact
that he seems to be echoing a poor kind of claptrap in his choice of
incidents and images. Partly, of course, he suffers from the very fact
of his success; his play with these topics was so good that every one
else has played with them increasingly since; he may indeed have
copied the old jokes, but he certainly renewed them.

MAY 27

But blessed are your eyes for they see, and your ears for
they hear.

—MATTHEW 13:16 NKJV

We shall be left defending not only the incredible virtues and
sanities of human life, but something more incredible still, this
huge impossible universe which stares us in the face. We shall
fight for visible prodigies as if they were invisible. We shall look
on the impossible grass and skies with a strange courage. We
shall be of those who have seen and believed.

GKC ON DICKENS (1911)

The second element to be found in all such festivity and all such
romance is the element which is represented as well as it could be
represented by the mere fact that Christmas occurs in the winter. It

is the element not merely of contrast, but actually of antagonism. It preserves everything that was best in the merely primitive or pagan view of such ceremonies or such banquets. If we are carousing, at least we are warriors carousing. We hang above us, as it were, the shields and battle-axes with which we must do battle with the giants of the snow and hail.

All comfort must be based on discomfort. Man chooses when he wishes to be most joyful the very moment when the whole material universe is most sad. It is this contradiction and mystical defiance which gives a quality of manliness and reality to the old winter feasts which is not characteristic of the sunny felicities of the Earthly Paradise. And this curious element has been carried out even in all the trivial jokes and tasks that have always surrounded such occasions as these . . .

About all Christmas things there is something a little nobler, if only nobler in form and theory, than mere comfort; even holly is prickly. It is not hard to see the connection of this kind of historic instinct with a romantic writer like Dickens. The healthy novelist must always play snapdragon with his principal characters; he must always be snatching the hero and heroine like raisins out of the fire.

MAY 28

> How much more will your Father who is in heaven give
> good things to those who ask Him!
>
> —MATTHEW 7:11 NKJV

I have often been haunted with a fancy that the creeds of men might be paralleled and represented in their beverages. Wine might stand for genuine Catholicism, and ale for genuine Protestantism; for these at least are real religions with comfort and strength in them.

Clean cold Agnosticism would be clean cold water—an excellent thing if you can get it. Most modern ethical and idealistic movements might be well represented by soda-water—which is a fuss about nothing. Mr. Bernard Shaw's philosophy is exactly like black coffee—it awakens, but it does not really inspire.

Modern hygienic materialism is very like cocoa; it would be impossible to express one's contempt for it in stronger terms than that. Sometimes one may come across something that may honestly be compared to milk, an ancient and heathen mildness, an earthly yet sustaining mercy—the milk of human kindness. You can find it in a few pagan poets and a few old fables; but it is everywhere dying out.

ON THIS DAY

- In 1932, GKC's article "On Private Property and Modern Education" was published in the *Illustrated London News*.

MAY 29

Yet for us there is one God, the Father, of whom are all things, and we for Him; and one Lord Jesus Christ, through whom are all things, and through whom we live.
—1 CORINTHIANS 8:6 NKJV

When once one believes in a creed, one is proud of its complexity, as scientists are proud of the complexity of science. It shows how rich it is in discoveries. If it is right at all, it is a compliment to say that it's elaborately right. A stick might fit a hole or a stone a hollow by accident. But a key and a lock are both complex. And if a key fits a lock, you know it is the right key.

A PASSAGE FROM *ALL I SURVEY* (1933)

Each one of us has probably found his own favourite piece of folly, in an advertisement or an epitaph or a corner of a newspaper; and the thing has remained almost as private as a family joke. To keep a record of all these individual discoveries would need not an anthology but a library of lunacy; a Bodleian of Bad Verse.

ON THIS DAY ─────────────────────────────────

- In 1874, G. K. Chesterton was born at 23 Sheffield Terrace, Campden Hill, London.

MAY 30

And a time to laugh ...
—ECCLESIASTES 3:4 NKJV

Laughter and love are everywhere. The cathedrals, built in the ages that loved God, are full of blasphemous grotesques. The mother laughs continually at the child, the lover laughs continually at the lover, the wife at the husband, the friend at the friend.

A PASSAGE FROM *ALL I SURVEY* (1933)

In ultimate philosophy, as in ultimate theology, men are not capable of creation, but only of combination. But there is a workable meaning of the word, which I take to be this: some image evoked by the individual imagination which might never have been evoked by any other imagination, and adds something to the imagery of the world. I call it Creative to write "the multitudinous seas Incarnadine." I call it Creative by three real and even practical tests: first, that nobody need ever have thought of such a thing if Mr. William Shakespeare had not happened to think of it; second, that while it is an apocalyptic, or titanic, it is not really an anarchic idea; it is gigantic, but it does not merely sprawl; it fits into the frame of thought exactly as the sea fits into all the fretted bays and creeks of the world. Also, in passing, with all its tragic occasion, it is a jolly image: it gives the mere imagination a positive and passionate joy of colour, like the joy of drinking a purple sea of wine.

ON THIS DAY

- In 1931, GKC's article "Sound and Sense in Poetry" was published in the *Illustrated London News*.

MAY 31

Great and marvellous are thy works, Lord God Almighty.
—REVELATION 15:3

For religion the mountains are lifted up suddenly like waves. Those who quote that fine passage which says that in God's sight a thousand years are as yesterday that is passed as a watch in the night, do not realise the full force of the meaning. To God a thousand years are not only a watch but an exciting watch. For God time goes at a gallop, as it does to a man reading a good tale.

A PASSAGE FROM *ALL I SURVEY* (1933)

We are the only men in all history who fell back upon bragging about the mere fact that to-day is not yesterday. I fear that some in the future will explain it by saying that we had precious little else to brag about. For, whatever the medieval faults, they went with one merit. Medieval people never worried about being medieval; and modern people do worry horribly about being modern.

To begin with, note the queer, automatic assumption that it must always mean throwing mud at a thing to call it a relic of medievalism. The modern world contains a good many relics of medievalism, and most of us would be surprised if the argument were logically enforced even against the things that are commonly called medieval. We should express some regret if somebody blew up Westminster Abbey, because it is a relic of medievalism. Doubts would trouble us if the Government burned all existing copies of Dante's Divine Comedy and Chaucer's Canterbury Tales, because they are quite certainly relics of medievalism.

ON THIS DAY ——————————————————————————

- In 1917, during World War I, GKC censured the behaviour of some pacifist groups in *The New Witness*: "How many pacifists or semi-pacifists . . . resisted the detailed destruction of all liberty for the populace *before the war*? It is a bitter choice between freedom and patriotism, but how many fought for freedom before it gave them the chance of fighting against patriotism?"

JUNE 1

Glad and merry in heart for the goodness that the Lord had shewed.

—2 CHRONICLES 7:10

For [Pickwick] is a good man, and therefore even his dulness is beautiful, just as is the dulness of the animal. We can leave

Pickwick a little while by the fire to think; for the thoughts of Pickwick, even if they were to go slowly, would be full of all the things that all men care for—old friends and old inns and memory and the goodness of God.

A PASSAGE FROM *ALL I SURVEY* (1933)

After all, Stevenson died at about the time of life when Dickens had only just written David Copperfield, *and had not yet attempted so new a departure as* Hard Times *or* Great Expectations; *at an age when any number of great men had still their fullest and most mature work to do.*

And when he died he was already writing what is quite obviously a much fuller and more mature work, and in many ways quite a new departure. The fragments of Weir of Hermiston *are like the fragments of a colossal god lying broken in the desert, compared with many of the slender ivory statuettes that he had carved before.*

DURING THIS MONTH

- In 1905, GKC's apologia, *Heretics*, was published.
- In the summer of 1908, GKC and his wife, Frances, rented a home in Rye, No. 4 Mermaid Street, which was next to Lamb House, the residence of the American expatriate novelist, Henry James.
- In 1910, GKC's collection of essays *What's Wrong with the World* was published. In 1926, GKC's collection of mystery stories *The Incredulity of Father Brown* was published.
- And in 1933, Chesterton stated this in *G. K.'s Weekly*: "The English were not wrong in loving liberty. They were only wrong in losing it."

JUNE 2

These wait all upon thee; that thou mayest give them their
meat in due season.

—PSALM 104:27

Dickens displayed again a quality that was very admirable in him—I mean a disposition to see things sanely. . . . He loved that great Christian carelessness that seeks its meat from God.

GKC IN THE PAGES OF THE *ATLANTIC MONTHLY* (1921)

[In The New Jerusalem,*] we catch fleeting glimpses of battle-mented walls, of a striped landscape, of a snow-storm, of a pageant of colours, creeds, and races; but before the picture is formed, it fades . . .*

Needless to say, there are brilliant passages, such, for example, as the description of Godfrey de Bouillon's scaling of the walls of Jerusalem in the First Crusade. There are nights of wit and fancy, such as only Mr. Chesterton has the talent and the courage to perpetrate. He takes his essential self and his lamp-post with him where he goes; and the reader delights in meeting and recognizing him at every turn.

JUNE 3

Or do you despise the riches of His goodness, forbearance,
and longsuffering, not knowing that the goodness of God
leads you to repentance?

—ROMANS 2:4 NKJV

Dickens does not alter [this character of his story] in any vital
point. The thing he does alter is us. He makes us lively where
we were bored, kind where we were cruel, and above all, free
for an universal human laughter where we were cramped in a
small competition about that sad and solemn thing, the intellect. His enthusiasm fills us, as does the love of God, with a
glorious shame.

A PASSAGE FROM *CHARLES DICKENS: A CRITICAL STUDY* (1906)

[Dickens's] power, then, lay in the fact that he expressed with an
energy and brilliancy quite uncommon the things close to the com-
mon mind.

But with this mere phrase, the common mind, we collide with
a current error. Commonness and the common mind are now gen-
erally spoken of as meaning in some manner inferiority and the
inferior mind; the mind of the mere mob. But the common mind
means the mind of all the artists and heroes; or else it would not
be common. Plato had the common mind; Dante had the common
mind; or that mind was not common. Commonness means the
quality common to the saint and the sinner, to the philosopher and
the fool; and it was this that Dickens grasped and developed. In
everybody there is a certain thing that loves babies, that fears death,
that likes sunlight: that thing enjoys Dickens.

JUNE 4

In my Father's house are many mansions: if it were not
so, I would have told you. I go to prepare a place for you.
—JOHN 14:2

But we have a long way to travel before we get back to what Dickens meant: and the passage is along a rambling English road, a twisting road such as Mr. Pickwick travelled.

But this at least is part of what he meant; that comradeship and serious joy are not interludes in our travel; but that rather our travels are interludes in comradeship and joy, which through God shall endure for ever. The inn does not point to the road; the road points to the inn.

A PASSAGE FROM *CHARLES DICKENS: A CRITICAL STUDY* (1906)

There are popular phrases so picturesque that even when they are intentionally funny they are unintentionally poetical. I remember, to take one instance out of many, hearing a heated Secularist in Hyde Park apply to some parson or other the exquisite expression, "a sky-pilot." Subsequent inquiry has taught me that the term is intended to be comic and even contemptuous; but in that first freshness of it I went home repeating it to myself like a new poem. Few of the pious legends have conceived so strange and yet celestial a picture as this of the pilot in the sky, leaning on his helm above the empty heavens, and carrying his cargo of souls higher than the loneliest cloud.

JUNE 5

> *The sacrifices of God are a broken spirit, a broken and a*
> *contrite heart—these, O God, You will not despise.*
> —PSALM 51:17 NKJV

We have now reached the great break in the life of Francis of Assisi; the point at which something happened to him that must remain greatly dark to most of us, who are ordinary and selfish men whom God has not broken to make anew.

A PASSAGE FROM *CHARLES DICKENS: A CRITICAL STUDY* (1906)

Now, among a million of such scraps of inspired slang there is one which describes a certain side of Dickens better than pages of explanation. The phrase, appropriately enough, occurs at least once in his works, and that on a fitting occasion. When Job Trotter is sent by Sam on a wild chase after Mr. Perker, the solicitor, Mr. Perker's clerk condoles with Job upon the lateness of the hour, and the fact that all habitable places are shut up.

"My friend," says Mr. Perker's clerk, "you've got the key of the street." Mr. Perker's clerk, who was a flippant and scornful young man, may perhaps be pardoned if he used this expression in a flippant and scornful sense; but let us hope that Dickens did not. Let us hope that Dickens saw the strange, yet satisfying, imaginative justice of the words; for Dickens himself had, in the most sacred and serious sense of the term, the key of the street . . .

His earth was the stones of the street; his stars were the lamps of the street; his hero was the man in the street. He could open the inmost door of his house—the door that leads into that secret passage which is lined with houses and roofed with stars.

JUNE 6

For the pillars of the earth are the Lord's, and he hath set
the world upon them.

—1 Samuel 2:8

If a man saw the world upside down, with all the trees and towers hanging head downwards as in a pool, one effect would be to emphasise the idea of dependence. There is a Latin and literal connection; for the very word dependence only means hanging. It would make vivid the Scriptural text which says that God has hanged the world upon nothing.

A PASSAGE FROM *CHARLES DICKENS: A CRITICAL STUDY* (1906)

[Dickens] was a dreamy child, thinking mostly of his own dreary prospects. Yet he saw and remembered much of the streets and squares he passed. Indeed, as a matter of fact, he went the right way to work unconsciously to do so. He did not go in for "observation," a priggish habit; he did not look at Charing Cross to improve his mind or count the lamp-posts in Holborn to practise his arithmetic.

But unconsciously he made all these places the scenes of the monstrous drama in his miserable little soul. He walked in darkness under the lamps of Holborn, and was crucified at Charing Cross. So for him ever afterwards these places had the beauty that only belongs to battlefields.

ON THIS DAY

- In 1931, GKC's article "Cliques in the Literary World" was published in the *Illustrated London News*.

JUNE 7

> For in him we live, and move, and have our being; as
> certain also of your own poets have said.
>
> —ACTS 17:28

The transition from the good man to the saint is a sort of revolution; by which one for whom all things illustrate and illuminate God becomes one for whom God illustrates and illuminates all things.

A PASSAGE FROM *CHARLES DICKENS: A CRITICAL STUDY* (1906)

So Dickens did not stamp these places on his mind; he stamped his mind on these places. For him ever afterwards these streets were mortally romantic; they were dipped in the purple dyes of youth and its tragedy, and rich with irrevocable sunsets . . .

Dickens himself has given a perfect instance of how these nightmare minutes grew upon him in his trance of abstraction. He mentions among the coffee-shops into which he crept in those wretched days "one in St. Martin's Lane, of which I only recollect that it stood near the church, and that in the door there was an oval glass plate with 'COFFEE ROOM' painted on it, addressed towards the street. If I ever find myself in a very different kind of coffee-room now, but where there is such an inscription on glass, and read it backwards on the wrong side, MOOR EEFFOC (as I often used to do then in a dismal reverie), a shock goes through my blood."

That wild word, "Moor Eeffoc," is the motto of all effective realism! it is the masterpiece of the good realistic principle—the principle that the most fantastic thing of all is often the precise fact. And that elvish kind of realism Dickens adopted everywhere.

His world was alive with inanimate objects. The date on the door danced over Mr. Grewgius, the knocker grinned at Mr. Scrooge, the Roman on the ceiling pointed down at Mr. Tulkinghorn, the elderly armchair leered at Tom Smart—these are all moor eeffocish *things. A man sees them because he does not look at them.*

And so the little Dickens Dickensized London. He prepared the way for all his personages. Into whatever cranny of our city his characters might crawl, Dickens had been there before them.

JUNE 8

There is none like unto the God of Jeshurun, who rideth upon the heaven . . . and in his excellency on the sky.
—DEUTERONOMY 33:26

Unless the sky is beautiful, nothing is beautiful. Unless the background of all things is good, it is no substitute to make the foreground better: it may be right to do so for other reasons, but not for the reason that is the root of religion.

Materialism says the universe is mindless; and faith says it is ruled by the highest mind. Neither will be satisfied with the new progressive creed, which declares hopefully that the universe is half-witted.

A PASSAGE FROM *ALL THINGS CONSIDERED* (1908)

It is not only possible to say a great deal in praise of play; it is really possible to say the highest things in praise of it. It might reasonably be maintained that the true object of all human life is play. Earth is a task garden; heaven is a playground. To be at last in such secure innocence that one can juggle with the universe and the stars, to be so good that one can treat everything as a joke—that may be, per-haps, the real end and final holiday of human souls. When we are really holy we may regard the Universe as a lark.

JUNE 9

> *By humility and the fear of the Lord are riches, and honour, and life.*
>
> —PROVERBS 22:4

But the heraldry of humility was richer than the heraldry of pride; for it saw all these things that God had given as something more precious and unique than the blazonry that princes and peers had only given to themselves. Indeed out of the depths of that surrender it rose higher than the highest titles of the feudal age; than the laurel of Caesar or the Iron Crown of Lombardy.

A PASSAGE FROM *ALL THINGS CONSIDERED* (1908)

With Francis Thompson we lose the greatest poetic energy since Browning. His energy was of somewhat the same kind. Browning was intellectually intricate because he was morally simple. He was too simple to explain himself; he was too humble to suppose that other people needed any explanation.

But his real energy, and the real energy of Francis Thompson, was best expressed in the fact that both poets were at once fond of immensity and also fond of detail. Any common Imperialist can have large ideas so long as he is not called upon to have small ideas also. Any common scientific philosopher can have small ideas so long as he is not called upon to have large ideas as well.

But great poets use the telescope and also the microscope. Great poets are obscure for two opposite reasons; now, because they are talking about something too large for any one to understand, and now again because they are talking about something too small for any one to see. Francis Thompson possessed both these infinities.

ON THIS DAY

- In 1904, GKC and his wife, Frances, attended a "political dinner" at Mrs. Sidney Webb's, where they saw two future prime ministers, Winston Churchill and David Lloyd George.

JUNE 10

Through faith we understand that the worlds were framed by the word of God, so that things which are seen were not made of things which do appear.
—HEBREWS 11:3

[St. Francis] knew that the praise of God stands on its strongest ground when it stands on nothing. He knew that we can best measure the towering miracle of the mere fact of existence if we realise that but for some strange mercy we should not even exist.

G. N. SHUSTER ON GKC'S POEM "THE BALLAD OF THE WHITE HORSE"

"The Ballad of the White Horse" is an ambitious poem that contains a great number of the best things [Chesterton] has to say. Founded upon the popular traditions of King Alfred, the tale

becomes symbolic of the contest which Chesterton is most inter-ested in: the constant battle between Christendom that came from Rome and the heathens who have remained outside. The inspira-tion and the vigour of expression are alike remarkable. A simple ballad stanza is deftly interwoven with supple rhythms and iri-descent diction, while the sweep of the narrative is sustained by a series of lyric stanzas that are strong or tender, that snatch at the heart or carry it aloft. More important even is the characterization. Alfred the Great, anxious to reconquer his kingdom from the invad-ing Danes, goes for aid to three men—Eldred, a Saxon, Mark, a Roman, and Colan, a Gael. The three represent their races as the Danish chieftains are made to typify theirs, and the interpretative sympathy of the author marks the poem as the one great English epic of the twentieth century. The symbolism inherent in the story will not escape the attentive reader. It reveals the character of the eternal contest between heathen and Christian with the subtle insight of perfect music, giving to each side its due but deciding the victory with magnificent fervour. "The Ballad of the White Horse" is a poem to love and even to sing, which are more important mat-ters than putting it on a shelf and calling it great.

JUNE 11

> For unto you is born this day in the city of David a Saviour,
> which is Christ the Lord.
>
> —LUKE 2:11

Human nature simply cannot subsist without a hope and aim of some kind; as the sanity of the Old Testament truly said, where there is no vision the people perisheth. But it is precisely because an ideal is necessary to man that the man without ideals is in permanent danger of fanaticism. There is nothing which is so likely to leave a man open to the sudden and irresistible inroad of an unbalanced vision as the cultivation of business habits. All of us know angular business men who think that the earth is flat . . . or that men are graminivorous, or that Bacon wrote Shakespeare. Religious and philosophical beliefs are, indeed, as dangerous as fire, and nothing can take from them that beauty of danger. But there is only one way of really guarding ourselves against the excessive danger of them, and that is to be steeped in philosophy and soaked in religion.

FROM *THE SPECTATOR'S* REVIEW OF *ALL THINGS CONSIDERED* (1908)

In reading these sincere, enthusiastic, endlessly witty little essays [Mr. Chesterton] seems to be at the mercy of every fancy, of every casual hint, of every caprice of mind. He is a kind of literary Hotspur with endless energy, pugnacity, and courage . . .

He scorns the last insult of the modern reviewer,—the charge of being "brilliant." None the less he is "brilliant." His wordy rockets soar desperately into the dark, pause, break into a cascade of stars, and, clear to our astonished gaze, lies momentarily revealed the peaceful landscape of simple truth.

JUNE 12

*The Lord is my shepherd; I shall not want. He maketh
me to lie down in green pastures: He leadeth me beside
the still waters. He restoreth my soul: He leadeth me in
the paths of righteousness for His name's sake.*

—Psalm 23:1–3

But there is another aspect of the popular element as represented by the shepherds [of the Christmas story] which has not perhaps been so fully developed; and which is more directly relevant here.

Men of the people, like the shepherds, men of the popular tradition, had everywhere been the makers of the mythologies. . . . They had best understood that the soul of a landscape is a story and the soul of a story is a personality. . . .

Upon all such peasantries everywhere there was descending a dusk and twilight of disappointment, in the hour when these few men discovered what they sought. Everywhere else Arcadia was fading from the forest. Pan was dead and the shepherds were scattered like sheep. And though no man knew it, the hour was near which was to end and to fulfil all things; and though no man heard it, there was one far-off cry in an unknown tongue upon the heaving wilderness of the mountains. The shepherds had found their Shepherd.

ON THIS DAY

- In 1915, GKC wrote to George Bernard Shaw in the midst of his recovery from a nearly-fatal illness: "My dear Bernard Shaw, I ought to have written to you a long time ago, to thank you for your kind letter which I received when I had recovered and still more for many other kindnesses that seem to have come from you during the time before the recovery. I am not a vegetarian; and I am only in a very comparative sense a skeleton. Indeed I am afraid you must reconcile yourself to the dismal prospect of my being more or less like what I was before." (Shaw's reply appears under the date June 22.)

JUNE 13

To shew forth thy lovingkindness in the morning . . .
—PSALM 92:2

Lady, the stars are falling pale and small,
Lady, we will not live if life be all,
Forgetting those good stars in heaven hung,
When all the world was young;
For more than gold was in a ring,
and love was not a little thing,
Between the trees in Ivywood,
when all the world was young.

JUNE 14

And the peace of God, which passeth all understanding,
shall keep your hearts and minds through Christ Jesus.
—PHILIPPIANS 4:7

Gazing at some detail like a bird or a cloud, we can all ignore its awful blue background; we can neglect the sky; and precisely because it bears down upon us with an annihilating force it is felt as nothing.

A thing of this kind can only be an impressing and a rather subtle impression; but to me it is a very strong impression made by pagan literature and religion. I repeat that in our special sacramental sense there is, of course, the absence of the presence of God. But there is in a very real sense the presence of the absence of God. We feel it in the unfathomable sadness of pagan poetry; for I doubt if there was ever in all the marvellous manhood of antiquity a man who was happy as St. Francis was happy.

ON THIS DAY ───────────────────────────

- In 1936, G. K. Chesterton died at his home in Beaconsfield, England.

JUNE 15

Now the first day of the week Mary Magdalene went to the tomb early, while it was still dark, and saw that the stone had been taken away from the tomb.

—JOHN 20:1 NKJV

On the third day the friends of Christ coming at daybreak to the place found the grave empty and the stone rolled away. In varying ways they realised the new wonder; but even they hardly realised that the world had died in the night.

What they were looking at was the first day of a new creation, with a new heaven and a new earth; and in a semblance of the gardener God walked again in the garden, in the cool not of the evening but the dawn.

- In 1929, GKC's article "Mr. Epstein and Religious Art" was published in the *Illustrated London News*.

JUNE 16

But made himself of no reputation, and took upon him the form of a servant, and was made in the likeness of men . . .

—PHILIPPIANS 2:7

If the moderns really want a simple religion of love, they must look for it in the Athanasian Creed. The truth is that the trumpet of true Christianity, the challenge of the charities and simplicities of Bethlehem or Christmas Day never rang out more arrestingly and unmistakably than in the defiance of Athanasius to the cold compromise of the Arians. It was emphatically he who really was fighting for a God of Love against a God of colourless and remote cosmic control; the God of the stoics and the agnostics. It was emphatically he who was fighting for the Holy Child against the grey deity of the Pharisees and the Sadducees.

A PASSAGE FROM *HERETICS* (1905)

When Christianity was heavily bombarded in the last century upon no point was it more persistently and brilliantly attacked than upon that of its alleged enmity to human joy. Shelley and Swinburne and all their armies have passed again and again over the ground, but they have not altered it. They have not set up a single new trophy or ensign for the world's merriment to rally to.

A PASSAGE FROM *THE BALL AND THE CROSS* (1909)

All the tools of Professor Lucifer were the ancient human tools gone mad, grown into unrecognisable shapes, forgetful of their origin, forgetful of their names.

JUNE 17

> *And if there is any other commandment, all are summed up in this saying, namely, "You shall love your neighbour as yourself."*
>
> —ROMANS 13:9 NKJV

The Bible tells us to love our neighbours, and also to love our enemies; probably because they are generally the same people.

And there is a real human reason for this. You think of a remote man merely as a man; that is, you think of him in the right way. Suppose I say to you suddenly—"Oblige me by brooding on the soul of the man who lives at 351 High Street, Islington." Perhaps (now I come to think of it) you *are* the man who lives at 351 High Street, Islington. In that case substitute some other unknown address and pursue the intellectual sport.

Now you will probably be broadly right about the man in Islington whom you have never seen or heard of, because you will begin at the right end—the human end. The man in Islington is at least a man. The soul of the man in Islington is certainly a soul. He also has been bewildered and broadened by youth; he also has been tortured and intoxicated by love; he also is sublimely doubtful about death. You can think about the soul of that nameless man who is a mere number in Islington High Street.

But you do not think about the soul of your next-door

neighbour. He is not a man; he is an environment. He is the barking of a dog; he is the noise of a pianola; he is a dispute about a party wall; he is drains that are worse than yours, or roses that are better than yours.

A PASSAGE FROM *THE BALL AND THE CROSS* (1909)

Through the dense London atmosphere they could see below them the flaming London lights; lights which lay beneath them in squares and oblongs of fire. The fog and fire were mixed in a passionate vapour; you might say that the fog was drowning the flames; or you might say that the flames had set the fog on fire. Beside the ship and beneath it (for it swung just under the ball), the immeasurable dome itself shot out and down into the dark like a combination of voiceless cataracts. Or it was like some cyclopean sea-beast sitting above London and letting down its tentacles bewilderingly on every side, a monstrosity in that starless heaven. For the clouds that belonged to London had closed over the heads of the voyagers sealing up the entrance of the upper air. They had broken through a roof and come into a temple of twilight.

JUNE 18

And the Lord God formed man of the dust of the ground, and breathed into his nostrils the breath of life; and man became a living soul.

—GENESIS 2:7

When I was young, it was very generally assumed that any man was a fool who was in possession of a faith. It was the fashion to assume that reason is the same as rationalism, and that rationalism is the same as scepticism; though it has since become obvious that the first real act of scepticism is to be doubtful about reason.

Bullet-headed atheists went about in clubs and public-houses, who hit the table and said, "Prove it!" if anybody suggested that anybody had a soul. Now there has certainly been a very strong and healthy reaction against this very dull and dowdy negation.

A PASSAGE FROM *HERETICS* (1905)

Religious and philosophical beliefs are, indeed, as dangerous as fire, and nothing can take from them that beauty of danger.

A PASSAGE FROM *THE BALL AND THE CROSS* (1909)

"What you say is perfectly true," said Michael, with serenity. "But we like contradictions in terms. Man is a contradiction in terms; he is a beast whose superiority to other beasts consists in having fallen. That cross is, as you say, an eternal collision; so am I."

JUNE 19

*For I neither received it of man, neither was I taught it,
but by the revelation of Jesus Christ.*

—GALATIANS 1:12

The moral of all this is an old one: that religion is revelation. In other words it is a vision, and a vision received by faith; but it is a vision of reality. The faith consists in a conviction of its reality.

A PASSAGE FROM *HERETICS* (1905)

The strong old literature is all in praise of the weak ... The forlorn hope is not only a real hope, it is the only real hope of mankind.

A PASSAGE FROM *THE BALL AND THE CROSS* (1909)

He was a young man, born in the Bay of Arisaig, opposite Rum and the Isle of Skye. His high, hawklike features and snaky black hair bore the mark of that unknown historic thing which is crudely called Celtic, but which is probably far older than the Celts, whoever they were. He was in name and stock a Highlander of the Macdonalds; but his family took, as was common in such cases, the name of a subordinate kept as a surname, and for all the purposes which could be answered in London, he called himself Evan MacIan. He had been brought up in some loneliness and seclusion as a strict Roman Catholic, in the midst of that little wedge of Roman Catholics which is driven into the Western Highlands. And he had found his way as far as Fleet Street.

JUNE 20

Whereupon are the foundations [of the earth] fastened? or who laid the corner stone thereof; when the morning stars sang together, and all the sons of God shouted for joy?

—JOB 38:6–7

When we say that a poet praises the whole creation, we commonly mean only that he praises the whole cosmos. But this sort of poet does really praise creation, in the sense of the act of creation. He praises the passage or transition from nonentity to entity; there falls here also the shadow of that archetypal image of the bridge, which has given to the priest his archaic and mysterious name.

The mystic who passes through the moment when there is nothing but God does in some sense behold the beginningless beginnings in which there was really nothing else. He not only appreciates everything but the nothing of which everything was made. In a fashion he endures and answers even the earthquake irony of the Book of Job; in some sense he is there when the foundations of the world are laid, with the morning stars singing together and the sons of God shouting for joy.

A PASSAGE FROM *HERETICS* (1905)

The usual verdict of educated people on the Salvation Army is expressed in some such words as these: "I have no doubt they do a great deal of good, but they do it in a vulgar and profane style; their aims are excellent, but their methods are wrong." To me, unfortunately, the precise reverse of this appears to be the truth. I do not know whether the aims of the Salvation Army are excellent, but I am quite sure their methods are admirable. Their methods are the methods of all intense and hearty religions; they are popular like all religion, military like all religion, public and sensational like all religion.

JUNE 21

I wait for the Lord, my soul doth wait, and in his word do
I hope.

—PSALM 130:5

It is only when everything is hopeless that hope begins to be a strength at all. Like all the Christian virtues, it is as unreasonable as it is indispensable.

A PASSAGE FROM *HERETICS* (1905)

And the Salvation Army, though their voice has broken out in a mean environment . . . are really the old voice of glad and angry faith, hot as the riots of Dionysius, wild as the gargoyles of Catholicism, not to be mistaken for a philosophy. Professor Huxley, in one of his clever phrases, called the Salvation Army "corybantic Christianity." Huxley was the last and noblest of those Stoics who have never understood the Cross. If he had understood Christianity he would have known that there never has been, and never can be, any Christianity that is not corybantic.

A PASSAGE FROM *THE BALL AND THE CROSS* (1909)

Like so many men and nations who grow up with nature and the common things, he understood the supernatural before he understood the natural. He had looked at dim angels standing knee-deep in the grass before he had looked at the grass. He knew that Our Lady's robes were blue before he knew the wild roses round her feet were red.

The deeper his memory plunged into the dark house of child-hood the nearer and nearer he came to the things that cannot be named. *All through his life he thought of the daylight world as a sort of divine debris, the broken remainder of his first vision. The skies and mountains were the splendid offscourings of another place.*

JUNE 22

Then you will understand the fear of the Lord, and find the knowledge of God.

—PROVERBS 2:5 NKJV

"There are degrees of seriousness," replied Syme. "I have never doubted that you were perfectly sincere in this sense, that you thought what you said well worth saying, that you thought a paradox might wake men up to a neglected truth."

A PASSAGE FROM *THE BALL AND THE CROSS* (1909)

"But to talk in a public place about one's most sacred and private sentiments—well, I call it bad taste," Vane said. "I call it irreverent. I call it irreverent, and I'm not specially orthodox either."

"I see you are not," said Evan, "but I am."

ON THIS DAY

- In 1915, having received a letter from GKC (as he recovered from a life-threatening illness), George Bernard Shaw wrote: "My dear Chesterton, I am delighted to learn under your own hand that you have recovered all your health and powers with an unimpaired figure. You have also the gratification of knowing that you have carried out a theory of mine that every man of genius has a critical illness at 40,

Nature's object being to make him go to bed for several months.

Sometimes Nature overdoes it: Schiller and Mozart died. Goethe survived, though he very nearly followed Schiller into the shades. I did the thing myself quite handsomely by spending eighteen months on crutches, having two surgical operations, and breaking my arm. I distinctly noticed, that instead of my recuperation beginning when my breakdown ended, it began before that. The ascending curve cut through the tail of the descending one; and I was consummating my collapse and rising for my next flight simultaneously."

- And in 1929, GKC's article "On Criticising the Modern Poets" was published in the *Illustrated London News*.

JUNE 23

That they should seek the Lord . . . and find him, though He be not far from every one of us.

—ACTS 17:27

Have you ever known what it is to walk along a road in such a frame of mind that you thought you might meet God at any turn of the path?

A PASSAGE FROM *HERETICS* (1905)

History unanimously attests the fact that it is only mysticism which stands the smallest chance of being understood of the people. Common sense has to be kept as an esoteric secret in the dark temple of culture.

A PASSAGE FROM *THE BALL AND THE CROSS* (1909)

To me this whole strange world is homely, because in the heart of it there is a home; to me this cruel world is kindly, because higher than the heavens there is something more human than humanity. If a man must not fight for this, may he fight for anything?

ON THIS DAY ───────────────────────────────

- In 1915, or nearly so, we don't have the date of the letter, H.G. Wells wrote to GKC with warm congratulations at the news of his ongoing recovery: "Good old G.K.C., I'm so delighted to get a letter from you again. As soon as I can I will come to Beaconsfield and see you."

JUNE 24

For the Lord himself shall descend from heaven with a shout, with the voice of the archangel, and with the trump of God: and the dead in Christ shall rise.
                              —1 THESSALONIANS 4:16

People, if you have any prayers
Say prayers for me.
And bury me underneath a stone
In the stones of Battersea.
Bury me underneath a stone,
With the sword that was my own;
To wait till the holy horn is blown
And all poor men are free.

A PASSAGE FROM *HERETICS* (1905)

A man who has faith must be prepared not only to be a martyr, but to be a fool.

A PASSAGE FROM *THE BALL AND THE CROSS* (1909)

The duellists had from their own point of view escaped or conquered the chief powers of the modern world. They had satisfied the magistrate, they had tied the tradesman neck and heels, and they had left the police behind. As far as their own feelings went they had melted into a monstrous sea; they were but the fare and driver of one of the million hansoms that fill London streets. But they had forgotten something; they had forgotten journalism. They had forgotten that there exists in the modern world, perhaps for the first time in history, a class of people whose interest is not that things should happen well or happen badly, should happen successfully or happen unsuccessfully, should happen to the advantage of this party or the advantage of that party, but whose interest simply is that things should happen.

JUNE 25

The voice of the Lord is full of majesty.
—PSALM 29:4 NKJV

With Browning's knaves we have always this eternal interest, that they are real somewhere, and may at any moment begin to speak poetry. We are talking to a peevish and garrulous sneak; we are watching the play of his paltry features, his evasive eyes, and babbling lips.

And suddenly the face begins to change and harden, the eyes glare like the eyes of a mask, the whole face of clay becomes a common mouthpiece, and the voice that comes forth is the voice of God, uttering His everlasting soliloquy.

A PASSAGE FROM *HERETICS* (1905)

Christmas remains to remind us of those ages, whether Pagan or Christian, when the many acted poetry instead of the few writing it. In all the winter in our woods there is no tree in glow but the holly.

JUNE 26

And give thanks at the remembrance...
—PSALM 30:4 NKJV

Mere existence reduced to its most primary limits, was extraordinary enough to be exciting. Anything was magnificent as compared with nothing. Even if the very daylight were a dream, it was a day-dream; it was not a nightmare. The mere fact that one could wave one's arms and legs about... showed that it had not the mere paralysis of a nightmare. Or if it was a nightmare, it was an enjoyable nightmare.

In fact, I had wandered to a position not very far from the phrase of my Puritan grandfather, when he said that he would thank God for his creation if he were a lost soul. I hung on to the remains of religion by one thin thread of thanks. I [had discovered a] way of looking at things, with a sort of mystical minimum of gratitude.

A PASSAGE FROM *HERETICS* (1905)

Rationally there appears no reason why we should not sing and give each other presents in honour of anything—the birth of Michael Angelo or the opening of Euston Station. But it does not work. As a fact, men only become greedily and gloriously material about something spiritualistic. Take away the Nicene Creed and similar things, and you do some strange wrong to the sellers of sausages. Take away the strange beauty of the saints, and what has remained to us is the far stranger ugliness of Wandsworth. Take away the supernatural, and what remains is the unnatural.

JUNE 27

The horse is prepared against the day of battle: but safety is of the Lord.

—PROVERBS 21:31

That high note of the forlorn hope, of a host at bay and a battle against odds without end, is the note on which [*The Song of Roland*] ends. I know nothing more moving in poetry than that strange and unexpected ending; that splendidly inconclusive conclusion. Charlemagne the Christian emperor has at last established his empire in quiet; has done justice almost in the manner of a day of judgement, and sleeps as it were upon his throne with a peace almost like that of Paradise.

And there appears to him the angel of God crying aloud that his arms are needed in a new and distant land, and that he must take up again the endless march of his days. And the great king tears his long white beard and cries out against his restless life. The poem ends, as it were with a vision and vista of wars against the barbarians; and the vision is true. For that war is never ended, which defends the sanity of the world against all the stark anarchies and rending negations which rage against it.

ON THIS DAY ────────────────────────────────

- In 1936, Monsignor Knox spoke of GKC's novel *The Man Who Was Thursday* during a tribute sermon at Westminster Cathedral. It was, he said, "an extraordinary book, written as if the publisher had commissioned him to write something rather like *The Pilgrim's Progress* in the style of *The Pickwick Papers*."

    Speaking of GKC's lasting legacy, Knox stated: "He will almost certainly be remembered as a prophet, in an age of false prophets."

JUNE 28

To an inheritance incorruptible, and undefiled, and that fadeth not away, reserved in heaven . . .

—1 PETER 1:4

In the specially Christian case we have to react against the heavy bias of fatigue. It is almost impossible to make the facts vivid, because the facts are familiar; and for fallen men it is often true that familiarity is fatigue.

I am convinced that if we could tell the supernatural story of Christ word for word as of a Chinese hero, call him the Son of Heaven instead of the Son of God, and trace his rayed nimbus in the gold thread of Chinese embroideries or the gold lacquer of Chinese pottery, instead of in the gold leaf of our own old

Catholic paintings, there would be a unanimous testimony to the spiritual purity of the story. We should hear nothing then of the injustice of substitution or the illogicality of atonement, of the superstitious exaggeration of the burden of sin or the impossible insolence of an invasion of the laws of nature. We should admire the chivalry of the Chinese conception of a god who fell from the sky to fight the dragons and save the wicked from being devoured by their own fault and folly. We should admire the subtlety of the Chinese view of life, which perceives that all human imperfection is in very truth a crying imperfection. We should admire the Chinese esoteric and superior wisdom, which said there are higher cosmic laws than the laws we know.

ON THIS DAY

- In 1901, G. K. Chesterton and Frances Blogg were wed.

> *But I saw her cheek and forehead*
> *Change, as at a spoken word,*
> *And I saw her head uplifted*
> *Like a lily to the Lord.*
> *Nought is lost, but all transmuted,*
> *Ears are sealed, yet eyes have seen;*
> *Saw her smiles (O soul be worthy!),*
> *Saw her tears (O heart be clean!).*

JUNE 29

For I am not come to call the righteous, but sinners to
repentance.

—MATTHEW 9:13

When the world goes wrong, it proves rather that the Church is
right. The Church is justified, not because her children do not
sin, but because they do.

A PASSAGE FROM *HERETICS* (1905)

And now I have to touch upon a very sad matter. There are in
the modern world an admirable class of persons who really make
protest on behalf of that antiqua pulchritudo *of which Augustine*
spoke, who do long for the old feasts and formalities of the childhood
of the world. William Morris and his followers showed how much
brighter were the dark ages than the age of Manchester. Mr. W.B.
Yeats frames his steps in prehistoric dances, but no man knows and
joins his voice to forgotten choruses that no one but he can hear . . .

There are innumerable persons with eye-glasses and green gar-
ments who pray for the return of the maypole or the Olympian
games. But there is about these people a haunting and alarming
something which suggests that it is just possible that they do not
keep Christmas. It is painful to regard human nature in such a
light, but it seems somehow possible that Mr. George Moore does
not wave his spoon and shout when the pudding is set alight. It is
even possible that Mr. W.B. Yeats never pulls crackers. If so, where
is the sense of all their dreams of festive traditions? Here is a solid
and ancient festive tradition still plying a roaring trade in the
streets, and they think it vulgar. If this is so, let them be very cer-
tain of this, that they are the kind of people who in the time of the
maypole would have thought the maypole vulgar; who in the time

of the Canterbury pilgrimage would have thought the Canterbury pilgrimage vulgar . . .

Nor can there be any reasonable doubt that they were vulgar . . . Wherever you have belief you will have hilarity, wherever you have hilarity you will have some dangers.

ON THIS DAY ─────────────────────────

- In 1905, GKC was told that Prime Minister A.J. Balfour "was very impressed with *Heretics.*"

JUNE 30

For since by man came death, by man came also the resurrection of the dead. For as in Adam all die, even so in Christ shall all be made alive.

—1 CORINTHIANS 15:21–22

The dignity of the artist lies in his duty of keeping awake the sense of wonder in the world. In this long vigil he often has to vary his methods of stimulation; but in this long vigil he is also himself striving against a continual tendency to sleep.

There are some to whom this may even seem a sombre version of human existence, but not to me; for I have long believed that the only really happy and hopeful faith is a faith in the Fall of Man.

PASSAGES FROM *HERETICS* (1905)

Happiness is a mystery like religion, and should never be rationalised.

"Wine," says the Scripture, "maketh glad the heart of man," but only of the man who has a heart. The thing called high spirits is possible

only to the spiritual. Ultimately a man cannot rejoice in anything except the nature of things. Unfortunately a man can enjoy nothing except religion.

JULY 1

> *Doth not their excellency which is in them go away? they die, even without wisdom.*
>
> —JOB 4:21

Some years ago I was asked to write a little book on Victorian literature, for a series edited by good academic authorities. They were very complimentary and courteous, but they thought it their duty to preface the book with a note explaining that they were not responsible for my opinions, with the implication that the opinions were rather wild. As a matter of fact, in so far as the opinions implied were more or less mystical, they belonged to what is by far the commonest, the most cosmopolitan, and the most popular sort of mysticism.

Anyhow, they thought it necessary to protect their own impartiality. Many of them were men I greatly admire; nor was their action one which I in any way resent. But I confess I was amused some time after in opening a book in the same series called "A History of Free Thought," or some such name, by an ordinary academic agnostic. This book was devoted entirely, down to the last detail, to demonstrating the proposition that religion has been a nonsensical nightmare from first to last, that Christianity is dead, and that the world is well rid of it.

There was no preliminary note of apology to that. There was no warning against that bias; there was no disavowal of that partisanship. Nor can it be explained by supposing that it referred to the facts and not the theories of the agnostic and myself. I could easily imagine that my information was sometimes incorrect; but it is quite sufficient to save me from supposing that his was always correct. There were no dates in my book, so they could not be put right; but it was afterwards shown that the dates in his book were wildly wrong.

No; the simple explanation is that the editors did not think his bias was a bias. They thought that sort of secularism was simply sanity; what has been called the religion of all sensible men. As a matter of fact, there are many more sensible men, many more intelligent and instructed men, in modern Europe agreeing with me than agreeing with them. But they lived in a rather limited world, and within it they acted honestly according to their lights.

DURING THIS MONTH ———————————————————

- In 1911, GKC's collection of mystery stories *The Innocence of Father Brown* was published.

JULY 2

Having a form of godliness, but denying the power thereof . . .

—2 Timothy 3:5

Now that little comedy is constantly being acted in the intellectual world. Men reform a thing by removing the reality from it, and then do not know what to do with the unreality that is left. Thus they would reform religious institutions by removing the religion . . .

To keep the temple without the god is to be hag-ridden with superstitious vigilance about a hollow temple—about a mere shell made of brick and stone. To support the palace and not support the king is simply to pay for an empty palace.

A PASSAGE FROM *HERETICS* (1905)

I will have nothing to do with simplicity which lacks the fear, the astonishment, and the joy alike. I will have nothing to do with the devilish vision of a child who is too simple to like toys.

The child is, indeed, in these, and many other matters, the best guide. And in nothing is the child so righteously childlike, in nothing does he exhibit more accurately the sounder order of simplicity, than in the fact that he sees everything with a simple pleasure, even the complex things. The false type of naturalness harps always on the distinction between the natural and the artificial. The higher kind of naturalness ignores that distinction. To the child the tree and the lamp-post are as natural and as artificial as each other; or rather, neither of them are natural but both supernatural. For both are splendid and unexplained.

The flower with which God crowns the one, and the flame with which Sam the lamplighter crowns the other, are equally of the gold of fairy-tales. In the middle of the wildest fields the most rustic child is, ten to one, playing at steam-engines. And the only spiritual or philosophical objection to steam-engines is not that men pay for them or work at them, or make them very ugly, or even that men are killed by them; but merely that men do not play at them. The evil is that the childish poetry of clockwork does not remain. The wrong is not that engines are too much admired, but that they are not admired enough. The sin is not that engines are mechanical, but that men are mechanical.

JULY 3

My God, my God, why hast thou forsaken me?
—PSALM 22:1

We say that Pebblewick-on-Sea is a God-forsaken place, without committing ourselves to the highly heretical dogma that it is really forsaken of God. For it is a heresy to suggest that even a successful watering-place can really be an exception, either to the divine omnipresence or to the divine charity and forgiveness.

But that single phrase "God-forsaken," in itself so tragic, is also itself a tragedy. I mean it is a marked example of this tragedy of the gradual weakening of words. For it is in itself a very powerful and even appalling phrase. It is not a piece of sound theology, but is a piece of vigorous and vivid literature. It reminds us of some great phrase in "Paradise Lost," giving a glimpse of a sort of lurid negation and ruinous quiet; not light, but rather darkness visible.

A PASSAGE FROM *THE BALL AND THE CROSS* (1909)

It is the one great weakness of journalism as a picture of our modern existence, that it must be a picture made up entirely of exceptions. We announce on flaring posters that a man has fallen off a scaffolding. We do not announce on flaring posters that a man has not fallen off a scaffolding. Yet this latter fact is fundamentally more exciting, as indicating that that moving tower of terror and mystery, a man, is still abroad upon the earth. That the man has not fallen off a scaffolding is really more sensational; and it is also some thousand times more common. But journalism cannot reasonably be expected thus to insist upon the permanent miracles. Busy editors cannot be expected to put on their posters, "Mr. Wilkinson Still

Safe," or "Mr. Jones, of Worthing, Not Dead Yet." They cannot announce the happiness of mankind at all.

ON THIS DAY

- In 1909, GKC wrote to Father John O'Connor (the real-life inspiration for the lead character in *The Father Brown Mysteries*): "you combine so unusually in your own single personality the characters of (1) priest, (2) human being, (3) man of the world, (4) man of the other world, (5) man of science, (6) old friend, (7) new friend, not to mention Irishman and picture dealer."

JULY 4

Thou hast prepared the light and the sun.
—PSALM 74:16

Against a dark sky all flowers look like fireworks. There is something strange about them, at once vivid and secret, like flowers traced in fire in the phantasmal garden of a witch. A bright blue sky is necessarily the high light of the picture; and its brightness kills all the bright blue flowers.

But on a grey day the larkspur looks like fallen heaven; the red daisies are really the red lost eyes of day; and the sunflower is the vice-regent of the sun.

ON THIS DAY

- In 1931, GKC's article "Our Recent Satirists" was published in the *Illustrated London News*.

JULY 5

*. . . and strangers from the covenants of promise, having
no hope, and without God in the world.*

—EPHESIANS 2:12

Here is a phrase, for instance, which I heard the other day from
a very agreeable and intelligent person, and which we have
all heard hundreds of times from hundreds of such persons.
A young mother remarked to me, "I don't want to teach my
child any religion. I don't want to influence him; I want him to
choose for himself when he grows up."

That is a very ordinary example of current argument,
which is frequently repeated and yet never really applied. Of
course the mother is always influencing the child. Of course
the mother might just as well of said, "I hope he will choose
his own friends when he grows up; so I won't introduce him
to any Aunts or Uncles." The grown-up person cannot in any
case escape from the responsibility of influencing the child, not
even if she accepts the enormous responsibility of not influencing the child.

The mother can bring up a child without choosing a religion for him, but not without choosing an environment for
him. If she chooses to leave out the religion, she is choosing
the environment—and an infernally dismal, unnatural environment too. The mother can bring up the child alone on
a solitary island in the middle of a large lake, lest the child
should be influenced by superstitions and social conditions.
But the mother is choosing the island and the lake and the
loneliness.

- In 1904, GKC visited the poet Algernon Swinburne.
- In 1905, GKC "dined at the Asquiths," and met the former prime minister, Lord Rosebery.
- And in 1930, GKC's article "The American Behaviourists" was published in the *Illustrated London News*.

JULY 6

> For the good that I would I do not: but the evil which I
> would not, that I do.
>
> —ROMANS 7:19

The command of Christ is impossible, but it is not insane; it is rather sanity preached to a planet of lunatics. If the whole world was suddenly stricken with a sense of humour it would find itself mechanically fulfilling the Sermon on the Mount. It is not the plain facts of the world which stand in the way of that consummation, but its passions of vanity.

RAVI ZACHARIAS ON GKC

G. K. Chesterton once quipped that before you remove any fence, always ask first why it was put there in the first place. You see, every boundary set by God points to something worth protecting, and if you are to protect the wonder of existence, God's instruction book is the place to turn.

A PASSAGE FROM *HERETICS* (1905)

The truth is that there are no things for which men will make such herculean efforts as the things of which they know they are unworthy. There never was a man in love who did not declare that, if he strained every nerve to breaking, he was going to have his desire. And there never was a man in love who did not declare also that he ought not to have it. The whole secret of the practical success of Christendom lies in the Christian humility, however imperfectly fulfilled. For with the removal of all question of merit or payment, the soul is suddenly released for incredible voyages. If we ask a sane man how much he merits, his mind shrinks instinctively and instantaneously. It is doubtful whether he merits six feet of earth. But if you ask him what he can conquer—he can conquer the stars. Thus comes the thing called Romance, a purely Christian product. A man cannot deserve adventures; he cannot earn dragons and hippogriffs. The mediaeval Europe which asserted humility gained Romance.

JULY 7

Then God said, "Let Us make man in Our image, according to Our likeness."

—Genesis 1:26 NKJV

But take the case of a common phrase; a common sneer with the art critics. I mean the phrase "a picture that tells a story." There could not be a sharper instance of the difference between the old hero who was man and more than man and the new hero who is not man at all.

A picture by Leonardo da Vinci tells a story. A picture by Paul Veronese tells a story. A picture by Titian or Tintoretto tells a story. The first and most important Question is, what story?

Most medieval and Renaissance pictures tell the story; the story on which all our European civilisation is founded, and is founded as finally if the thing is a fairy tale or if the thing is a truth. The objection to pictures which "tell a story" only began in our time, for the very simple reason that the story was a dull story. I will not discuss here whether the great story of God made Man has been destroyed. I will confine myself to saying that it has certainly not been replaced.

JULY 8

Do not be deceived, God is not mocked; for whatever a man sows, that he will also reap.

—GALATIANS 6:7 NKJV

I do not believe in a fate that falls on men however they act; but I do believe in a fate that falls upon them unless they act . . .

I do not believe that a nation dies save by suicide. To the very last every problem is a problem of will; and if we will we can be whole. But it involves facing our failures as well as counting our successes.

A PASSAGE FROM *HERETICS* (1905)

In this matter, then, as in all the other matters treated in this book, our main conclusion is that it is a fundamental point of view, a philosophy or religion which is needed, and not any change in habit or social routine.

The things we need most for immediate practical purposes are all abstractions. We need a right view of the human lot, a right view of the human society.

A merry heart doeth good.
—PROVERBS 17:22

I need not say I do not mind being called fat; for deprived of that jest, I should be almost a serious writer. I do not even mind being supposed to mind being called fat. But being supposed to be contented, and contented with the present institutions of modern society, is a mortal slander I will not take from any man.

A PASSAGE FROM *HERETICS* (1905)

"But seek first the kingdom of God and His righteousness, and all these things shall be added unto you." Those amazing words are not only extraordinarily good, practical politics; they are also super-latively good hygiene. The one supreme way of making all those processes go right, the processes of health, and strength, and grace, and beauty, the one and only way of making certain of their accu-racy, is to think about something else.

JULY 10

And the Lord turned the captivity of Job . . .
—JOB 42:10

The Book of Job is chiefly remarkable . . . for the fact that it does not end in a way that is conventionally satisfactory. Job is not told that his misfortunes were due to his sins or a part of any plan for his improvement. But in the prologue we see Job tormented not because he was the worst of men, but because he was the best.

It is the lesson of the whole work that man is most comforted by paradoxes. Here is the very darkest and strangest of the paradoxes; and it is by all human testimony the most reassuring. I need not suggest what a high and strange history awaited this paradox of the best man in the worst fortune. I need not say that in the freest and most philosophical sense there is one Old Testament figure who is truly a type; or say what is pre-figured in the wounds of Job.

A PASSAGE FROM *THE BALL AND THE CROSS* (1909)

"They are gone!" screamed Beatrice, hiding her head. "O God! They are lost!"

Evan put his arm about her, and remembered his own vision.

"No, they are not lost," he said. "They are saved. He has taken away no souls with him, after all."

He looked vaguely about at the fire that was already fading, and there among the ashes lay two shining things that had survived the fire, his sword and Turnbull's, fallen haphazard in the pattern of a cross.

JULY 11

I am the resurrection, and the life: he that believeth in me,
though he were dead, yet shall he live.

—JOHN 11:25

> After one moment when I bowed my head
> And the whole world turned over and came upright,
> And I came out where the old road shone white.
> I walked the ways and heard what all men said,
> Forests of tongues, like autumn leaves unshed,
> Being not unlovable but strange and light;
> Old riddles and new creeds, not in despite
> But softly, as men smile about the dead.
> The sages have a hundred maps to give
> That trace their crawling cosmos like a tree,
> They rattle reason out through many a sieve
> That stores the sand and lets the gold go free:
> And all these things are less than dust to me
> Because my name is Lazarus and I live.

ON THIS DAY

- In 1931, GKC's article "Thoughts on the Sun" was published in the *Illustrated London News*.

JULY 12

But He answered and said to them, "I tell you that if these
should keep silent, the stones would immediately cry out."
—LUKE 19:40 NKJV

But if there was one thing the early medievals liked it was rep-
resenting people doing something—hunting or hawking, or
rowing boats, or treading grapes, or making shoes, or cooking
something in a pot . . .

The Middle Ages is full of that spirit in all its monuments
and manuscripts. Chaucer retains it in his jolly insistence
on everybody's type of trade and toil. It was the earliest and
youngest resurrection of Europe, the time when social order
was strengthening, but had not yet become oppressive; the
time when religious faiths were strong, but had not yet been
exasperated.

For this reason the whole effect of Greek and Gothic carving is different. The figures in the Elgin marbles, though often
rearing their steeds for an instant in the air, seem frozen for ever
at that perfect instant. But a mass of medieval carving seems
actually a sort of bustle or hubbub in stone. Sometimes one cannot help feeling that the groups actually move and mix, and the
whole front of a great cathedral has the hum of a huge hive.

ON THIS DAY

- In 1930, GKC's article "Quackery About the Family" was
  published in the *Illustrated London News*.

JULY 13

In Him was life, and the life was the light of men.
—JOHN 1:4 NKJV

There was a man who dwelt in the east centuries ago,
And now I cannot look at a sheep or a sparrow,
A lily or a cornfield, a raven or a sunset,
A vineyard or a mountain, without thinking of him.

JULY 14

You shall make the trumpet to sound throughout all
your land.
—LEVITICUS 25:9 NKJV

But the great men of those days did not hesitate between the King and the Republic as we hesitate between a hundred new religions and stale philosophies. There is nothing feeble-minded about playing the flute, considered as playing the flute. But if the trumpet give an uncertain sound, who shall prepare himself for the battle?

A PASSAGE FROM *HERETICS* (1905)

Whatever may be the meaning of the contradiction, it is [a] fact that the only kind of hope that is any use in battle is a hope that denies arithmetic.

JULY 15

Remember the days of old, consider the years of many generations.

—Deuteronomy 32:7 nkjv

The things of which England has most reason to be proud are the things which England has preserved out of the ancient culture of the Christian world, when all the rest of the world has neglected them.

A PASSAGE FROM *HERETICS* (1905)

Mr. Bernard Shaw . . . has based all his brilliancy and solidity upon the hackneyed, but yet forgotten, fact that truth is stranger than fiction. Truth, of course, must of necessity be stranger than fiction, for we have made fiction to suit ourselves.

JULY 16

Do not be wise in your own eyes; fear the Lord.

—Proverbs 3:7 nkjv

There are two kinds of people in the world, the conscious dogmatists and the unconscious dogmatists. I have always found myself that the unconscious dogmatists were by far the most dogmatic.

Thus they are wandering about the world, at any given moment, a very large number of unconscious missionaries. They do as a fact preach wherever they go; sometimes they are so fanatical as to practise what they preach; but they never know that they are preaching. They are under the extraordinary delusion that the thing they practise is universally regarded as practical politics.

ON THIS DAY ────────────────────────────

- In 1905, GKC "went to see Mrs. Grenfell at Taplow." There, he met the prime minister, Arthur Balfour, as well as Austen Chamberlain (the brother of future prime minister Neville Chamberlain), and George Wyndham—the distinguished editor of *The Poems of Shakespeare*, and cabinet minister.

──

JULY 17

For Your mercy is great above the heavens, and Your truth reaches to the clouds.

—PSALM 108:4 NKJV

Now, poetical people like Francis Thompson will, as things stand, tend away from secular society and towards religion for the reason above described: that there are crowds of symbols in both, but that those of religion are simpler and mean more . . .

A poet like Thompson could deduce perpetually rich and branching meanings out of two plain facts like bread and wine; with bread and wine he can expand everything to everywhere.

A PASSAGE FROM *HERETICS* (1905)

The ritual which is comparatively rude and straightforward is the ritual which people call "ritualistic." It consists of plain things like bread and wine and fire, and men falling on their faces.

But the ritual which is really complex, and many coloured, and elaborate, and needlessly formal, is the ritual which people enact without knowing it. It consists not of plain things like wine and fire, but of really peculiar, and local, and exceptional, and ingenious things—things like door-mats, and door-knockers, and electric bells, and silk hats, and white ties, and shiny cards, and confetti. The truth is that the modern man scarcely ever gets back to very old and simple things.

JULY 18

But He was wounded for our transgressions, He was bruised for our iniquities; the chastisement for our peace was upon Him, and by His stripes we are healed.
                                               —ISAIAH 53:5 NKJV

This doctrine that the best man suffers most is, of course, the supreme doctrine of Christianity: millions have found not merely an elevating but a soothing story in the undeserved sufferings of Christ; had the sufferings been deserved we should all have been pessimists.

[Robert Louis] Stevenson's great ethical and philosophical value lies in the fact he realised this great paradox that life becomes more fascinating the darker it grows, that life is worth living only so far as it is difficult to live.

PASSAGES FROM *HERETICS* (1905)

Stevenson had found that the secret of life lies in laughter and humility. Self is the gorgon.

Every instant of conscious life is an unimaginable prodigy.

JULY 19

> *Blessed are they that keep His testimonies, and that seek*
> *Him with the whole heart.*
> —PSALM 119:2

This at least had come to be my position about all that was called optimism, pessimism, and improvement. Before any cosmic act of reform we must have a cosmic oath of allegiance. A man must be interested in life, then he could be disinterested in his views of it. "My son give me thy heart"; the heart must be fixed on the right thing.

A LINE FROM *HERETICS* (1905)

Life is not a thing from outside, but a thing from inside.

A PASSAGE FROM *THE BALL AND THE CROSS* (1909)

The other two came up along the slow course of the path talking and talking. No one but God knows what they said (for they certainly have forgotten), and if I remembered it I would not repeat it. When they parted at the head of the walk she put out her hand again . . .

"If it is really always to be like this," he said, thickly, "it would not matter if we were here for ever."

"You tried to kill yourself four times for me," she said, unsteadily, "and I have been chained up as a madwoman for you. I really think that after that."

"Yes, I know," said Evan in a low voice, looking down. "After that we belong to each other. We are sort of sold to each other—until the stars fall." Then he looked up suddenly, and said: "By the way, what is your name?"

"My name is Beatrice Drake."

JULY 20

In this was manifested the love of God toward us, because that God sent his only begotten Son into the world, that we might live through him.

—1 JOHN 4:9

My acceptance of the universe is not optimism, it is more like patriotism. It is a matter of primary loyalty. The world is not a lodging-house at Brighton, which we are to leave because it is miserable. It is the fortress of our family, with the flag flying on the turret, and the more miserable it is the less we should leave it.

The point is not that this world is too sad to love or too glad not to love; the point is that when you do love a thing, its gladness is a reason for loving it, and its sadness a reason for loving it more.

A PASSAGE FROM *ROBERT LOUIS STEVENSON* (1928)

The new criticism of Stevenson is still a criticism of Stevenson rather than of Stevenson's work; it is always a personal criticism, and often, I think, rather a spiteful criticism. It is simply nonsense, for instance, for a distinguished living novelist to suggest that Stevenson's correspondence is a thin stream of selfish soliloquy devoid of feeling for anybody but himself. It teems with lively expressions of longing for particular people and places; it breaks out everywhere with delight into that broad Scots idiom which, as Stevenson truly said elsewhere, gives a special freedom to all the terms of affection.

Stevenson might be lying, of course, though I know not why a busy author should lie at such length for nothing. But I cannot see how any man could say any more to suggest his dependence on the society of friends. These are positive facts of personality that can never be proved or disproved. I never knew Stevenson; but I knew very many of his favourite friends and correspondents. I knew Henry James and William Archer; I have still the honour of knowing Sir James Barrie and Sir Edmund Gosse. And anybody who knows them, even most slightly and superficially, must know they are not the men to be in confidential correspondence for years with a silly, greedy and exacting egoist without seeing through him.

ON THIS DAY ───────────────────────────────

- In 1929, GKC's article "Finding Influences in Poetry" was published in the *Illustrated London News*.

JULY 21

> *My help cometh from the Lord, which made heaven
> and earth.*
>
> —PSALM 121:2

I wrote some part of these rambling remarks on a high ridge of rock and turf overlooking a stretch of the central counties; the rise was slight enough in reality, but the immediate ascent had been so steep and sudden that one could not avoid the fancy that on reaching the summit one would look down at the stars.

But one did not look down at the stars, but rather up at the cities; seeing as high in heaven the palace town of Alfred like a lit sunset cloud, and away in the void spaces, like a planet in eclipse, Salisbury.

So, it may be hoped, until we die you and I will always look up rather than down at the labours and the habitations of our race; we will lift up our eyes to the valleys from whence cometh our help.

A PASSAGE FROM *HERETICS* (1905)

This colour as of a fantastic narrative ought to cling to the family and to our relations with it throughout life. Romance is the deepest thing in life; romance is deeper even than reality.

A PASSAGE FROM *ROBERT LOUIS STEVENSON* (1928)

The original quality in any man of imagination is imagery. It is a thing like the landscapes of his dreams; the sort of world he would wish to make or in which he would wish to wander; the strange flora and fauna of his own secret planet.

JULY 22

And he doeth great wonders . . .
—REVELATION 13:13

Life is always a novel. Our existence may cease to be a song; it may cease even to be a beautiful lament. Our existence may not be an intelligible justice, or even a recognizable wrong. But our existence is still a story. In the fiery alphabet of every sunset is written, "to be continued in our next."

A PASSAGE FROM *HERETICS* (1905)

The thing which keeps life romantic and full of fiery possibilities is the existence of these great plain limitations which force all of us to meet the things we do not like or do not expect.

JULY 23

For my strength is made perfect in weakness.
—2 CORINTHIANS 12:9 NKJV

Many modern Englishmen talk of themselves as the sturdy descendants of their sturdy Puritan fathers. As a fact, they would run away from a cow. If you asked one of their Puritan fathers, if you asked Bunyan, for instance, whether he was sturdy, he would have answered, with tears, that he was as weak as water. And because of this he would have borne tortures.

A PASSAGE FROM *HERETICS* (1905)

To be in a romance is to be in uncongenial surroundings. To be born into this earth is to be born into uncongenial surroundings, hence to be born into a romance. Of all these great limitations and frameworks which fashion and create the poetry and variety of life, the family is the most definite and important.

JULY 24

Yea, he did fly upon the wings of the wind.
—Psalm 18:10

> *But in this grey morn of man's life*
> *Cometh sometime to the mind*
> *A little light that leaps and flies,*
> *Like a star blown on the wind.*

A PASSAGE FROM *HERETICS* (1905)

Moderns . . . imagine that romance would exist most perfectly in a complete state of what they call liberty. They think that if a man makes a gesture it would be a startling and romantic matter that the sun should fall from the sky.

But the startling and romantic thing about the sun is that it does not fall from the sky. They are seeking under every shape and form a world where there are no limitations—that is, a world where there are no outlines; that is, a world where there are no shapes. There is nothing baser than that infinity. They say they wish to be as strong as the universe, but they really wish the whole universe as weak as themselves.

JULY 25

Until the day dawn, and the day star arise in your
hearts . . .

—2 PETER 1:19

If seeds in the black earth can turn into such beautiful roses,
what might not the heart of man become in its long journey
towards the stars?

But I began to make for myself a sort of rudimentary philosophy . . . which was founded on the first principle that it is,
after all, a precious and wonderful privilege to exist at all. It was
simply what I should express now by saying that we must praise
God for creating us out of nothing.

But I expressed it then in a little book of poems, now happily extinct, which described (for example) the babe unborn as
promising to be good if he were only allowed to be anything,
or which asked what terrible transmigrations of martyrdom
I had gone through before birth, to be made worthy to see a
dandelion. In short, I thought, as I think still, that merely to
exist for a moment, and see a white patch of daylight on a gray
wall, ought to be an answer to all the pessimism of that period.

ON THIS DAY

- In 1919, GKC wrote in *The New Witness* of the close of
  World War I: "On Peace Day I set up outside my house two
  torches, and twined them with laurel; because I thought at
  least there was nothing pacifist about laurel.

  But that night, after the bonfire and the fire works
  had faded, a wind grew and blew with gathering violence,
  blowing away the rain. And in the morning I found one

of the laurelled posts torn off and lying at random on the
rainy ground; while the other still stood erect, green and
glittering in the sun. I thought that the pagans would
certainly have called it an omen; and it was one that
strangely fitted my own sense of some great work half fulfilled and half frustrated. And I thought vaguely of that
man in Virgil, who prayed that he might slay his foe and
return to his country; and the gods heard half the prayer,
and the other half was scattered to the winds. For I knew
we were right to rejoice; since the tyrant was indeed slain
and his tyranny fallen for ever; but I know not when we
shall find our way back to our own land."

JULY 26

Of whom the world was not worthy . . .
—HEBREWS 11:38 NKJV

The Secularists laboriously explain that martyrdoms do not
prove a faith to be true, as if anybody was ever such a fool as to
suppose that they did. What they did prove, or, rather, strongly
suggest, was that something had entered human psychology
which was stronger than strong pain.

A PASSAGE FROM *ROBERT LOUIS STEVENSON* (1928)

*Now everybody knows what was in this sense the atmosphere and
architecture of Poe. Dark wine, dying lamps, drugging odours, a
sense of being stifled in curtains of black velvet, a substance which is
at once utterly black and unfathomably soft, all carried with them*

a sense of indefinite and infinite decay . . . The stars are not clean in his sight; but are rather more worlds made for worms.

ON THIS DAY

- In 1930, GKC's article "The Guilt of the Churches" was published in the *Illustrated London News.*

JULY 27

Ye men of Athens . . . as I passed by, and beheld your devotions, I found an altar with this inscription, TO THE UNKNOWN GOD . . . Him declare I unto you.
—ACTS 17:22–23

Let [Mr. Blatchford] doubt more, and he will believe more; for belief was always born out of doubt. Once before, the world went through an equinox of doubt, of cultured, serious, philosophical, cosmopolitan doubt; the result was Christianity.

PASSAGES FROM *HERETICS* (1905)

Every man in the street must hold a metaphysical system, and hold it firmly. The utmost possibility is that he may have held it so firmly and so long as to have forgotten all about its existence.

The modern world is filled with men who hold dogmas so strongly that they do not even know that they are dogmas.

JULY 28

But ye are a chosen generation . . . a peculiar people; that
ye should shew forth the praises of him who hath called
you out of darkness into his marvellous light.

—1 PETER 2:9

Christ did not tell his apostles that they were only the excellent people, or the only excellent people, but that they were the exceptional people; the permanently incongruous and incompatible people; and the text about the salt of the earth is really as sharp and shrewd and tart as the taste of salt. It is because they were the exceptional people, that they must not lose their exceptional quality.

A PASSAGE FROM *HERETICS* (1905)

When Christ at a symbolic moment was establishing His great society, He chose for its corner-stone neither the brilliant Paul nor the mystic John, but a shuffler, a snob, a coward—in a word, a man.

JULY 29

Yet of myself I will not boast, except in my infirmities.

—2 CORINTHIANS 12:5 NKJV

Until we realize that things might not be, we cannot realize that things are. Until we see the background of darkness we cannot admire the light as a single and created thing. As soon as we have seen that darkness, all light is lightening, sudden, blinding, and divine. Until we picture nonentity we underrate the victory of God, and can realize none of the trophies of His ancient war. It is one of the million wild jests of truth that we know nothing until we know nothing.

A PASSAGE FROM *ROBERT LOUIS STEVENSON* (1928)

The first fact about the imagery of Stevenson is that all his images stand out in very sharp outline; and are, as it were, all edges. It is something in him that afterwards attracted him to the abrupt and angular black and white of woodcuts. It is to be seen from the first, in the way in which his eighteenth-century figures stand up against the skyline, with their cutlasses and cocked hats. The very words carry the sound and the significance. It is as if they were cut out with cutlasses; as was that unforgettable chip or wedge that was hacked by the blade of Billy Bones out of the wooden sign of the "Admiral Benbow."

That sharp indentation of the wooden square remains as a sort of symbolic shape expressing Stevenson's type of literary attack; and if all the colours should fade from me and the scene of all that romance grow dark, I think that black wooden sign with a piece bitten out of it would be the last shape that I should see.

JULY 30

Therefore, brethren, stand fast and hold the traditions which you were taught.

—2 Thessalonians 2:15 NKJV

The act of defending any of the cardinal virtues has to-day all the exhilaration of a vice. Moral truisms have been so much disputed that they have begun to sparkle like so many brilliant paradoxes. And especially (in this age of egoistic idealism) there is about one who defends humility something inexpressibly rakish.

A PASSAGE FROM *ORTHODOXY* (1908)

Towers that vanish upwards above the loneliest star are the creations of humility. For towers are not tall unless we look up at them; and giants are not giants unless they are larger than we. All this gigantesque imagination, which is, perhaps, the mightiest of the pleasures of man, is at bottom entirely humble. It is impossible without humility to enjoy anything—even pride.

A PASSAGE FROM *ROBERT LOUIS STEVENSON* (1928)

Just as all the form can best be described as clean-cut, so all the colour is conspicuously clear and bright. That is why such figures are so often seen standing against the sea. Everybody who has been at the seaside has noted how sharp and highly coloured, like painted caricatures, appear even the most ordinary figures as they pass in profile to and fro against the blue dado of the sea. There is something also of that hard light that falls full and pale upon ships and open shores; and even more, it need not be said, of a certain salt and acrid clearness in the air. But it is notably the case in the outlines of these maritime figures. They are all edges and they stand by the sea, that is the edge of the world.

JULY 31

*And he said unto them, I beheld Satan as lightning fall
from heaven.*

—LUKE 10:18

"Then, what," asked Turnbull, very slowly, as he softly picked a
flower, "what is the difference between Christ and Satan?"

"It is quite simple," replied the Highlander. "Christ descended
into hell; Satan fell into it."

"Does it make much odds?" asked the free thinker.

"It makes all the odds," said the other. "One of them wanted
to go up and went down; the other wanted to go down and
went up."

AUGUST 1

*I have fought the good fight, I have finished the race, I
have kept the faith.*

—2 TIMOTHY 4:7 NKJV

> *O well for him that loves the sun,*
> *That sees the heaven-race ridden or run,*
> *The splashing seas of sunset won,*
> *And shouts for victory.*

A PASSAGE FROM *HERETICS* (1905)

*The truth is, that all genuine appreciation rests on a certain
mystery of humility and almost of darkness. The man who said,*

"Blessed is he that expecteth nothing, for he shall not be disappointed," put the eulogy quite inadequately and even falsely. The truth is, "Blessed is he that expecteth nothing, for he shall be gloriously surprised."

DURING THIS MONTH ———————————————

- In 1906, GKC's book *Charles Dickens: A Critical Study* was published.
- In 1909, GKC's book *George Bernard Shaw* was published.
- And in 1911, GKC's epic poem *The Ballad of the White Horse* was published.

AUGUST 2

Oh, how great is Your goodness, which You have laid up for those who fear You, which You have prepared for those who trust in You.

—PSALM 31:19 NKJV

But the main point here is simpler. It is merely that Blake did not mean that meekness was true and the lamb only a pretty fable. If anything he meant that meekness was a mere shadow of the everlasting lamb.

The distinction is essential to anyone at all concerned for this rooted spirituality which is the only enduring sanity of mankind. The personal is not a mere figure for the impersonal; rather the impersonal is a clumsy term for something more personal than common personality. God is not a symbol of goodness. Goodness is a symbol of God.

ON THIS DAY ────────────────────────

- In 1930, GKC's article "On Remembering Everything in a Poem" was published in the *Illustrated London News*.

AUGUST 3

For You created all things, and by Your will they exist and were created.

—REVELATION 4:11 NKJV

No true mystic ever loved darkness rather than light. No pure mystic ever loved mere mystery. The mystic does not bring doubts or riddles: the doubts and riddles exist already. We all feel the riddle of the earth without anyone to point it out.

The mystery of life is the plainest part of it. The clouds and curtains of darkness, the confounding vapours, these are the daily weather of this world. Whatever else we have grown accustomed to, we have grown accustomed to the unaccountable. Every stone or flower is a hieroglyphic of which we have lost the key.

ON THIS DAY ────────────────────────

- In 1929, GKC's article "The Paradoxes of Internationalism" was published in the *Illustrated London News*.

AUGUST 4

He who is faithful in what is least is faithful also in much.
—LUKE 16:10 NKJV

To love anything is to see it at once under lowering skies of danger. Loyalty implies loyalty in misfortune.

A PASSAGE FROM *ORTHODOXY* (1908)

Had Christianity felt what I felt, but could not (and cannot) express—this need for a first loyalty to things, and for a ruinous reform of things? Then I remembered that it was actually the charge against Christianity that it combined these two things which I was wildly trying to combine. Christianity was accused, at one and the same time, of being too optimistic about the universe and of being too pessimistic about the world. The coincidence made me suddenly stand still.

AUGUST 5

You are the light of the world. A city that is set on a hill cannot be hidden.
—MATTHEW 5:14 NKJV

For this idea, this modern idea that sanctity is identical with secrecy, there is one thing at least to be said. It is for all practical purposes an entirely new idea; it was unknown to all the ages in which the idea of sanctity really flourished.

The record of the great spiritual movements of mankind is dead against the idea that spirituality is a private matter. The most awful secret of every man's soul, its most lonely and individual need, its most primal and psychological relationship, the thing called worship, the communication between the soul and the last reality—this most private matter is the most public spectacle in the world.

Anyone who chooses to walk into a large church on Sunday morning may see a hundred men each alone with his Maker. He stands, in truth, in the presence of one of the strangest spectacles in the world—a mob of hermits. And in thus definitely espousing publicity by making public the most internal mystery, Christianity acts in accordance with its earliest origins and its terrible beginning. It was surely by no accident that the spectacle which darkened the sun at noonday was set upon a hill.

AUGUST 6

> *For better is a neighbour that is near.*
> —PROVERBS 27:10

I was alone in the flat fields out of sight of the city. On one side of the road was one of those small, thin woods which are common in all countries, but of which, by a coincidence, the mystical painters of Flanders were very fond. The night was closing in with cloudy purple and grey; there was one ribbon of silver, the last rag of the sunset. Through the wood went one little path, and somehow it suggested that it might lead to some sign of life— there was no other sign of life on the horizon. I went along it, and soon sank into a sort of dancing twilight of all those tiny trees.

There is something subtle and bewildering about that sort of frail and fantastic wood. A forest of big trees seems like a bodily barrier; but somehow that mist of thin lines seems like a spiritual barrier. It is as if one were caught in a fairy cloud or could not pass a phantom.

When I had well lost the last gleam of the high road a curious and definite feeling came upon me. Now I suddenly felt something much more practical and extraordinary—the absence of humanity: inhuman loneliness. Of course, there was nothing really lost in my state; but the mood may hit one anywhere. I wanted men—any men; and I felt our awful alliance over all the globe. And at last, when I had walked for what seemed a long time, I saw a light too near the earth to mean anything except the image of God.

ON THIS DAY ───────────────────────────

- In 1915, George Bernard Shaw wrote a famously farcical letter to GKC, describing the Fabian activism of Mrs. Sidney Webb.

AUGUST 7

Along the road I saw a light from heaven.
　　　　　—ACTS 26:13 NKJV

> *Far from your sunny uplands set*
> *I saw the dream; the streets I trod*
> *The lit straight streets shot out and met*
> *The starry streets that point to God.*

A PASSAGE FROM *ORTHODOXY* (1908)

My first and last philosophy, that which I believe in with unbroken certainty, I learnt in the nursery. I generally learnt it from a nurse;

that is, from the solemn and star-appointed priestess at once of democracy and tradition. The things I believed most then, the things I believe most now, are the things called fairy tales. They seem to me to be the entirely reasonable things. They are not fantasies: compared with them other things are fantastic. Compared with them religion and rationalism are both abnormal, though religion is abnormally right and rationalism abnormally wrong. Fairyland is nothing but the sunny country of common sense. It is not earth that judges heaven, but heaven that judges earth; so for me at least it was not earth that criticised elfland, but elfland that criticised the earth.

AUGUST 8

> For it is known that he is man; and he cannot contend
> with Him who is mightier than he.
> —ECCLESIASTES 6:10 NKJV

If humility has been discredited as a virtue at the present day, it is not wholly irrelevant to remark that this discredit has arisen at the same time as a great collapse of joy in current literature and philosophy.

Men have revived the splendour of Greek self-assertion at the same time that they have revived the bitterness of Greek pessimism. A literature has arisen which commands us to arrogate to ourselves the liberty of self-sufficing deities.

A PASSAGE FROM *TWELVE TYPES* (1903)

We [moderns] insist, however, upon treating this matter tail foremost. We insist that the ascetics were pessimists because they gave

up threescore years and ten for an eternity of happiness. We forget
that the bare proposition of an eternity of happiness is by its very
nature ten thousand times more optimistic than ten thousand
pagan saturnalias.

ON THIS DAY ─────────────────────────────────

- In 1931, GKC's article "The Rotting of Certain Lies" was
  published in the *Illustrated London News*.

AUGUST 9

> But Jesus called them to Him and said, "Let the little
> children come to Me . . . for of such is the kingdom of God."
> —LUKE 18:16 NKJV

The humorous look of children is perhaps the most endearing
of all the bonds that hold the cosmos together. Their top-heavy
dignity is more touching than any humility; their solemnity
gives us more hope for all things than a thousand carnivals of
optimism; their large and lustrous eyes seem to hold all the
stars in their astonishment; their fascinating absence of nose
seems to give to us the most perfect hint of the humour that
awaits us in the kingdom of heaven.

A PASSAGE FROM *TWELVE TYPES* (1903)

But great comedy, the comedy of Shakespeare or Sterne, not only can
be, but must be, taken seriously. There is nothing to which a man
must give himself up with more faith and self-abandonment than to
genuine laughter. In such comedies one laughs with the heroes and
not at them. The humour which steeps the stories of Falstaff and

Uncle Toby is a cosmic and philosophic humour, a geniality which goes down to the depths.

ON THIS DAY ────────────────────

• In 1930, GKC's article "The Error of the Spiritualists" was published in the *Illustrated London News*.

AUGUST 10

And in Your book they all were written, the days fashioned for me, when as yet there were none of them.
—PSALM 139:16 NKJV

Here I am only trying to describe the enormous emotions which cannot be described. And the strongest emotion was that life was as precious as it was puzzling. It was an ecstasy because it was an adventure; it was an adventure because it was an opportunity. The goodness of the fairy tale was not affected by the fact that there might be more dragons than princesses; it was good to be in a fairy tale. The test of all happiness is gratitude; and I felt grateful, though I hardly knew to whom. Children are grateful when Santa Claus puts in their stockings gifts of toys or sweets. Could I not be grateful to Santa Claus when he put in my stockings the gift of two miraculous legs? We thank people for birthday presents of cigars and slippers. Can I thank no one for the birthday present of birth?

A PASSAGE FROM *ROBERT LOUIS STEVENSON* (1928)

The main point to be seized here is that [Stevenson's writing possessed] coloured pictures of a particular kind. The colours faded, but in a certain sense the forms remained fixed; that is, that though they were slowly discoloured by the light of common day, yet when the lantern was again lit from within, the same magic-lantern slides glowed upon the blank screen. They were still pictures of pirates and red gold and bright blue sea, as they were in his childhood. And this fact is very important in the story of his mind; as we shall see when his mind reverted to them. For the time was to come when he was truly, like Jim Hawkins, to be rescued by a leering criminal with crutch and cutlass from destiny worse than death and men worse than Long John Silver—from the last phase of the enlightened nineteenth century and the leading thinkers of the age.

ON THIS DAY ───────────────────────────────

- In 1929, GKC's article "The Health of the Mind" was published in the *Illustrated London News*.

AUGUST 11

A fountain of gardens, a well of living waters, and streams from Lebanon.

—Song of Solomon 4:15

The grass seemed signalling to me with all its fingers at once; the crowded stars seemed bent upon being understood. The sun would make me see him if he rose a thousand times. The recurrences of the universe rose to the maddening rhythm of an incantation, and I began to see an idea.

All the towering materialism which dominates the modern mind rests ultimately upon one assumption; a false assumption. It is supposed that if a thing goes on repeating itself it is probably dead; a piece of clockwork. People feel that if the universe was personal it would vary; if the sun were alive it would dance. This is a fallacy even in relation to known fact. For the variation in human affairs is generally brought into them, not by life, but by death; by the dying down or breaking off of their strength or desire.

A man varies his movements because of some slight element of failure or fatigue. He gets into an omnibus because he is tired of walking; or he walks because he is tired of sitting still. But if his life and joy were so gigantic that he never tired of going to Islington, he might go to Islington as regularly as the Thames goes to Sheerness. The very speed and ecstasy of his life would have the stillness of death. The sun rises every morning. I do not rise every morning; but the variation is due not to my activity, but to my inaction. Now, to put the matter in a popular phrase, it might be true that the sun rises regularly because he never gets tired of rising. His routine might be due, not to a lifelessness, but to a rush of life.

AUGUST 12

To every thing there is a season, and a time to every purpose under the heaven.

—ECCLESIASTES 3:1

The repetition in Nature may not be a mere recurrence; it may be a theatrical encore. Heaven may encore the bird who laid an egg. If the human being conceives and brings forth a human child instead of bringing forth a fish, or a bat, or a griffin, the reason may not be that we are fixed in an animal fate without life or purpose. It may be that our little tragedy has touched the gods, that they admire it from their starry galleries, and that at the end of every human drama man is called again and again before the curtain. Repetition may go on for millions of years, by mere choice, and at any instant it may stop. Man may stand on the earth generation after generation, and yet each birth be his positively last appearance.

This was my first conviction; made by the shock of my childish emotions meeting the modern creed in mid-career. I had always vaguely felt facts to be miracles in the sense that they are wonderful: now I began to think them miracles in the stricter sense that they were wilful. I mean that they were, or might be, repeated exercises of some will. In short, I had always believed that the world involved magic: now I thought that perhaps it involved a magician. And this pointed a profound emotion always present and sub-conscious; that this world of ours has some purpose; and if there is a purpose, there is a person. I had always felt life first as a story: and if there is a story there is a story-teller.

AUGUST 13

Yet You have said, "I know you by name."
—EXODUS 33:12 NKJV

We have all read in scientific books, and, indeed, in all romances, the story of the man who has forgotten his name. This man walks about the streets and can see and appreciate everything; only he cannot remember who he is.

Well, every man is that man in the story. Every man has forgotten who he is. One may understand the cosmos, but never the ego; the self is more distant than any star. Thou shalt love the Lord thy God; but thou shalt not know thyself. We are all under the same mental calamity; we have all forgotten our names. We have all forgotten what we really are.

A PASSAGE FROM *TWELVE TYPES* (1903)

Scott is separated, then, from much of the later conception of fiction by this quality of eloquence. The whole of the best and finest work of the modern novelist (such as the work of Mr Henry James) is primarily concerned with that delicate and fascinating speech which burrows deeper and deeper like a mole; but we have wholly forgotten that speech which mounts higher and higher like a wave and falls in a crashing peroration.

AUGUST 14

"For I know the thoughts that I think toward you," says the Lord, "thoughts of peace and not of evil, to give you a future and a hope."

—JEREMIAH 29:11 NKJV

We look at the rise of Christianity, and conceive it as a rise of self-abnegation and almost of pessimism. It does not occur to us that the mere assertion that this raging and confounding universe is governed by justice and mercy is a piece of staggering optimism fit to set all men capering.

The detail over which these monks went mad with joy was the universe itself; the only thing really worthy of enjoyment. The white daylight shone over all the world, the endless forests stood up in their order. The lightning awoke and the tree fell and the sea gathered into mountains and the ship went down, and all these disconnected and meaningless and terrible objects were all part of one dark and fearful conspiracy of goodness, one merciless scheme of mercy.

A PASSAGE FROM *TWELVE TYPES* (1903)

Why was he a monk, and not a troubadour? These questions are far too large to be answered fully here, but in any life of Francis they ought at least to have been asked; we have a suspicion that if they were answered we should suddenly find that much of the enigma of this sullen time of ours was answered also. So it was with the monks. The two great parties in human affairs are only the party which sees life black against white, and the party which sees it white against black, the party which macerates and blackens itself with sacrifice because the background is full of the blaze of an universal mercy, and the party which crowns itself with flowers and lights itself with bridal torches because it stands against a black curtain of incalculable night. The revellers are old, and the monks are young. It was the monks who were the spendthrifts of happiness, and we who are its misers.

AUGUST 15

But Mary kept all these things, and pondered them in her heart.

—LUKE 2:19

A PASSAGE FROM *WILLIAM BLAKE* (1910)

England was called in Catholic days the garden of Mary.

SELECTION FROM CHESTERTON'S POEMS

The standing whirlpool of the stars,
The wheel of all the world,
Is a ring on Our Lady's finger

With the suns and moons empearled
With stars for stones to please her
Who sits playing with her rings
With the great heart that a woman has
And the love of little things.

AUGUST 16

I am persuaded that neither death nor life, nor angels nor
principalities nor powers, nor things present nor things to
come, nor height nor depth, nor any other created thing,
shall be able to separate us from the love of God which is
in Christ Jesus our Lord.

—ROMANS 8:38–39 NKJV

At least five times, therefore, with the Arian and the Albigensian, with the Humanist sceptic, after Voltaire and after Darwin, the Faith has to all appearance gone to the dogs. In each of these five cases it was the dog that died . . .

Both in fact and figure there is something deeply disturbing about this, and that for an essential reason. A dead thing can go with the stream, but only a living thing can go against it.

A PASSAGE FROM *TWELVE TYPES* (1903)

Savonarola and his republic fell. The drug of despotism was admin-
istered to the people, and they forgot what they had been. There are
some at the present day who have so strange a respect for art and
letters, and for mere men of genius, that they conceive the reign of
the Medici to be an improvement on that of the great Florentine
republican.

It is such men as these and their civilisation that we have at the present day to fear. We are surrounded on many sides by the same symptoms as those which awoke the unquenchable wrath of Savonarola—a hedonism that is more sick of happiness than an invalid is sick of pain, an art sense that seeks the assistance of crime since it has exhausted nature. In many modern works we find veiled and horrible hints of a truly Renaissance sense of the beauty of blood, the poetry of murder. The bankrupt and depraved imagination does not see that a living man is far more dramatic than a dead one.

ON THIS DAY

- In 1930, GKC's article "The Menace of Spiritualism" was published in the *Illustrated London News*.

AUGUST 17

> *. . . the house of God, which is the church of the living God, the pillar and ground of the truth.*
>
> —1 TIMOTHY 3:15 NKJV

MacIan burst out like a man driven back and explaining everything.

"The Church is not a thing like the Athenaeum Club," he cried. "If the Athenaeum Club lost all its members, the Athenaeum Club would dissolve and cease to exist. But when we belong to the Church we belong to something which is outside all of us; which is outside everything you talk about, outside the Cardinals and the Pope. They belong to it, but it does not belong to them. If we all fell dead suddenly, the Church would still somehow exist in God."

A PASSAGE FROM *ROBERT LOUIS STEVENSON* (1928)

[Stevenson] found no foothold on those steep streets of his beautiful and precipitous city; and as he looked forth over the litter of little islands in the large and shining estuary, he may have had some foreshadowing of that almost vagabond destiny which ended in the ends of the earth.

ON THIS DAY ────────────────────────────

- In 1929, GKC's article "Trent's Last Case" was published in the *Illustrated London News*.

AUGUST 18

But now they desire a better, that is, a heavenly country...
—HEBREWS 11:16 NKJV

Comradeship is at most only one half of human life; the other half is love, a thing so different that one might fancy it had been made for another universe.

A PASSAGE FROM *TWELVE TYPES* (1903)

For the universe is like everything in it; we have to look at it repeatedly and habitually before we see it. It is only when we have seen it for the hundredth time that we see it for the first time. The more consistently things are contemplated, the more they tend to unify themselves and therefore to simplify themselves. The simplification of anything is always sensational. Thus monotheism is the most sensational of things: it is as if we gazed long at a design full of disconnected objects, and, suddenly, with a stunning thrill, they came together into a huge and staring face.

A PASSAGE FROM *ROBERT LOUIS STEVENSON* (1928)

Treasure Island, if hardly a historical novel, was essentially a historical event. The rise or revolt of R.L.S. must be taken in relation to history, to the history of the whole European mind and mood. It was, first and last, a reaction against pessimism.

There was thrown across all that earth and sky the gigantic shadow of Schopenhauer. At least it seemed gigantic then, though some of us may already have suspected that the shadow was larger than the man. Anyhow, in that period we might almost say that pessimism was another name for culture. Cheerfulness was associated with the Philistine, like the broad grin with the bumpkin. Pessimism could be read between the lines of the lightest triolet or most elegant essay . . .

Stevenson . . . stood up suddenly amid all these things and shook himself with a sort of impatient sanity; a shrug of scepticism about scepticism. His real distinction is that he had the sense to see that there is nothing to be done with Nothing. He saw that in that staggering universe it was absolutely necessary to stand somehow on something; and instead of falling about anyhow with all the other lunatics, he did seek for a ledge on which he could really stand.

AUGUST 19

Looking unto Jesus the author and finisher of our faith ...
—HEBREWS 12:2

God has given us not so much the colours of a picture as the colours of a palette. But He has also given us a subject, a model, a fixed vision. We must be clear about what we want to paint.

A PASSAGE FROM *TWELVE TYPES* (1903)

But if ever this gradual and genuine movement of our time towards beauty—not backwards, but forwards—does truly come about, Morris will be the first prophet of it. Poet of the childhood of nations, craftsman in the new honesties of art, prophet of a merrier and wiser life, his full-blooded enthusiasm will be remembered when human life has once more assumed flamboyant colours and proved that this painful greenish grey of the aesthetic twilight in which we now live is, in spite of all the pessimists, not of the greyness of death, but the greyness of dawn.

A PASSAGE FROM *ROBERT LOUIS STEVENSON* (1928)

Stevenson seemed to say to the semi-suicides drooping round him at the café tables; drinking absinthe and discussing atheism: "Hang it all, the hero of a penny-dreadful play was a better man than you are! A Penny Plain and Twopence Coloured was an art more worthy of living men than the art that you are all professing. Painting pasteboard figures of pirates and admirals was better worth doing than all this, it was fun; it was fighting; it was a life and a lark; and if I can't do anything else, dang me but I will try to do that again!"

So was presented to the world this entertaining spectacle; of the art student surrounded by easels on which other artists were debating the fine shades of Corot and Renoir, while he himself was gravely painting mariners a bright prussian blue of a shilling paint-box and shedding their blood in streams of unmistakable crimson lake.

AUGUST 20

Every good gift and every perfect gift is from above, and comes down from the Father of lights.

—JAMES 1:17 NKJV

... go to inns to dine;
Where the bacon's on the rafter
And the wine is in the wood,
And God that made good laughter
Has seen that they are good.

A PASSAGE FROM *TWELVE TYPES* (1903)

One of the most genuinely poetical of our younger poets says, as the one thing certain, that

From quiet home and first beginning
Out to the undiscovered ends
There's nothing worth the wear of winning
But laughter and the love of friends.
—Hilaire Belloc

Here we have a perfect example of the main important fact, that all true joy expresses itself in terms of asceticism.

AUGUST 21

Give us this day our daily bread.
—MATTHEW 6:11 NKJV

[Dickens's] thirst was for things as humble, as human, as laughable as that daily bread for which we cry to God.

A PASSAGE FROM *THE USES OF DIVERSITY* (1920)

I am sorry that the comic costume festival which was organized for Christmas by one of the chief Dickensian societies has unavoidably fallen through. It is not for me to reproach those traitors who found it impossible to turn up: for I was one of those traitors myself. Whatever character it was that I was expected to appear in—Jingle, I suppose, or possibly Uriah Heep—was, under a final press of business, refused by me.

These Dickensian enthusiasts were going to have a Christmas party at Rochester, where they would brew punch and drink punch, and drive coaches and fall off coaches, and do all the proper Pickwickian things. How many of them were ready to make a hole in the ice, to be wheeled about in a wheelbarrow, or to wait all night outside a ladies' school, the official documents have not informed me. But I would gladly take a moderate part.

AUGUST 22

> *Thus saith the Lord, the heaven is my throne, and the*
> *earth is my footstool.*
>
> —ISAIAH 66:1

Earth is not even earth without heaven, as a landscape is not a landscape without the sky. And in a universe without God there is not room enough for a man.

A PASSAGE FROM *THE USES OF DIVERSITY* (1920)

There is a new plan for a new universe, which may be expected to last for many a long month to come. It is the view that seems to have satisfied Mr. Wells, or, at any rate, Mr. Britling. It is the view which has been more than once suggested by Mr. Shaw, and is repeated in the skeleton of certain lectures he is delivering.

It is much more supernatural and even superstitious than my imaginary thesis; for instead of giving to man more of the powers of God, it arbitrarily imagines a God and then limits him with the impotence of man. He is not limited, as in the theologies, by his own reason or justice or desire for the freedom of man. He is limited by unreason and injustice and the impossibility of freedom even for himself. But I do not make this note upon the new development with any intention of discussing it thoroughly in its theological aspect; though there is one aspect of that aspect which may respectfully be called amusing.

When I was a boy, Christianity was blamed by the freethinkers for its anthropomorphic demigod, substituted by savages for the Unknown God who made all things. Now Christianity is blamed for the flat contrary; because its God is unknown and not anthropomorphic enough. Thirty years ago we only needed the First Person of the Trinity; and thirty years later we have discovered that we only need the Second. This sort of fashion-plate philosophy will no doubt go on as usual.

ON THIS DAY

- In 1931, GKC's article "On Assuming Too Much in Debate" was published in the *Illustrated London News*.

AUGUST 23

The lion hath roared, who will not fear? the Lord God hath spoken.

—AMOS 3:8

[The] town of Belfort is famous for one of the most typical and powerful of the public monuments of France. From the café table at which I sit I can see the hill beyond the town on which hangs the high and flat-faced citadel, pierced with many windows, and warmed in the evening light. On the steep hill below it is a huge stone lion, itself as large as a hill. It is hacked out of the rock with a sort of gigantic impression.

No trivial attempt has been made to make it like a common statue; no attempt to carve the mane into curls, or to distinguish the monster minutely from the earth out of which he rises, shaking the world. The face of the lion has something of the bold conventionality of Assyrian art. The mane of the lion is left like a shapeless cloud of tempest, as if it might literally be said of him that God had clothed his neck with thunder.

A PASSAGE FROM *ROBERT LOUIS STEVENSON* (1928)

The great scenes in Kidnapped, *the defence of the Round House or the confrontation of Uncle Ebenezer and Alan Breck, are full of those snapping phrases that seem to pick things off like pistol shots. A whole essay on the style of Stevenson, such as I shall attempt forlornly and ineffectually on another page, might be written by a real critic on the phrase, "His sword flashed like quicksilver into the huddle of our fleeing enemies."*

ON THIS DAY ────────────────────────────────

- In 1930, GKC's article "False Ideas About the Primitive" was published in the *Illustrated London News*.

AUGUST 24

For who hath known the mind of the Lord? or who hath been his counsellor?

—ROMANS 11:34

[Thomas Hardy] personifies the universe in order to give it a piece of his mind. But the fight is unequal for the old philosophical reason: that the universe had already given [him] a piece of its mind to fight with.

A PASSAGE FROM *THE USES OF DIVERSITY* (1920)

When I was a boy, people used to talk about something which they called the quarrel between religion and science. It would be very tedious to recount the quarrel now; the rough upshot of it was something like this: that some traditions too old to be traced came in vague conflict with some theories much too new to be tested. Many things three thousand years old had forgotten their reason for existing; many things a few years old had not yet discovered theirs. To this day this remains roughly true of all the relations between science and religion.

ON THIS DAY ──────────────────────────

- In 1929, GKC's article "What Does Mr. Hoover Mean?" was published in the *Illustrated London News*.

AUGUST 25

He hath scattered the proud in the imagination of their hearts.

—LUKE 1:51

Mr. Bernard Shaw has put the view in a perfect epigram: "The golden rule is that there is no golden rule." We are more and more to discuss details in art, politics, literature. A man's opinion on tramcars matters; his opinion on Botticelli matters; his opinion on all things does not matter. He may turn over and explore a million objects, but he must not find that strange object, the universe; for if he does he will have a religion, and be lost.

A PASSAGE FROM *THE USES OF DIVERSITY* (1920)

Our real error in such a case is that we do not know or care about the creed itself, from which a people's customs, good or bad, will necessarily flow. We talk much about "respecting" this or that person's religion; but the way to respect a religion is to treat it as a religion: to ask what are its tenets and what are their consequences.

But modern tolerance is deafer than intolerance. The old religious authorities, at least, defined a heresy before they condemned it.

AUGUST 26

> *Behold, I stand at the door, and knock: if any man hear*
> *my voice, and open the door, I will come in to him, and*
> *will sup with him, and he with me.*
>
> —REVELATION 3:20

> *Good news: but if you ask me what it is, I know not;*
> *It is a track of feet in the snow,*
> *It is a lantern showing a path,*
> *It is a door set open.*

A PASSAGE FROM *THE USES OF DIVERSITY* (1920)

For the meaning of [A Midsummer Night's Dream] is that the little things of life as well as the great things stray on the borderland of the unknown. That as a man may fall among devils for a morbid crime, or fall among angels for a small piece of piety or pity, so also he may fall among fairies through an amiable flirtation or a fanciful jealousy.

The fact that a back door opens into elfland is all the more reason for keeping the foreground familiar, and even prosaic. For even the fairies are very neighbourly and firelight fairies; therefore the human beings ought to be very human in order to effect the fantastic contrast. And in Shakespeare they are very human.

AUGUST 27

*Therefore, my beloved brethren, be steadfast, immovable,
always abounding in the work of the Lord.*
—1 CORINTHIANS 15:58 NKJV

A man with a definite belief always appears bizarre, because
he does not change with the world; he has climbed into a fixed
star, and the earth whizzes below him like a zoetrope.

A PASSAGE FROM *THE USES OF DIVERSITY* (1920)

*[A love of] the elementary things . . . is an essential of any poetry and
any religion. It must appeal to the origins and deal with the first things,
however much or little it may say about them. It must be at home in
the homeless void, before the first star was made. The one thing every
man knows about the unknowable is that it is the Indispensable.*

AUGUST 28

Be peaceable, gentle, showing all humility to all men.
—TITUS 3:2 NKJV

*Pride juggles with her toppling towers,
They strike the sun and cease,
But the firm feet of humility
They grip the ground like trees.*

A PASSAGE FROM *THE USES OF DIVERSITY* (1920)

The weakness of the proposition that marriage is good for the common herd, but can be advantageously violated by special "experimenters" and pioneers, is that it takes no account of the problem of the disease of pride.

AUGUST 29

> *For the same cause also do ye joy . . .*
> —PHILIPPIANS 2:18

And similarly, if [Mr. McCabe] had ever had, as Mr. Shaw and I have had, the impulse to what he calls paradox, he would have discovered that paradox again is not a frivolous thing, but a very serious thing. He would have found that paradox simply means a certain defiant joy which belongs to belief.

ON THIS DAY ———————————————————

- In 1931, GKC's article "Thinking in Scraps and Patches" was published in the *Illustrated London News*.

His compassions fail not. They are new every morning:
great is thy faithfulness.

—LAMENTATIONS 3:22–23

The world will never starve for want of wonders; but only for want of wonder.

A PASSAGE FROM *THE USES OF DIVERSITY* (1920)

But certainly it is not the mere sound of [a] word that makes it unworkable in the literature of wonder or beauty. "Omnibus" may seem at first sight a more difficult thing to swallow—if I may be allowed a somewhat gigantesque figure of speech. This, it may be said, is a Cockney and ungainly modern word, as it is certainly a Cockney and ungainly modern thing.

But even this is not true. The word "omnibus" is a very noble word with a very noble meaning and even tradition. It is derived from an ancient and adamantine tongue which has rolled it with very authoritative thunders: quod ubique, quod semper, quod ab omnibus. It is a word really more human and universal than republic or democracy. A man might very consistently build a temple for all the tribes of men, a temple of the largest pattern and the loveliest design, and then call it an omnibus.

ON THIS DAY ————————————————

- In 1930, GKC's article "The Way the World is Going" was published in the *Illustrated London News*.

AUGUST 31

> *Let the earth hear, and all that is therein; the world, and all things that come forth of it.*
>
> —ISAIAH 34:1

The optimism which talks about this as "the best of all possible worlds" misses the point altogether. The precise fact which makes the world so wonderful and valuable is the fact that you cannot compare it with anything. It is everything. . . . It is not the best of all possible worlds: but it is the best of all possible things that a world should exist.

A PASSAGE FROM *THE CATHOLIC WORLD* (1922)

Confidence in the value of existence, and in the intrinsic victory of virtue, is not optimism, but religion.

ON THIS DAY

- In 1929, GKC's article "The Art of Thinking" was published in the *Illustrated London News*.

SEPTEMBER 1

> *I am the way, the truth, and the life: no man cometh unto the Father, but by me.*
>
> —JOHN 14:6

On the other side our idealist pessimists were represented by the old remnant of the Stoics. Marcus Aurelius and his friends had really given up the idea of any god in the universe and looked only to the god within. They had no hope of any virtue in nature, and hardly any hope of any virtue in society. They had not enough interest in the outer world really to wreck or revolutionise it. They did not love the city enough to set fire to it.

Thus the ancient world was exactly in our own desolate dilemma. The only people who really enjoyed this world were busy breaking it up; and the virtuous people did not care enough about them to knock them down. In this dilemma (the same as ours) Christianity suddenly stepped in and offered a singular answer, which the world eventually accepted as the answer. It was the answer then, and I think it is the answer now.

DURING THIS MONTH ————————————————

- In 1908, GKC's apologia *Orthodoxy* was published.
- In 1909, GKC's collection of essays *Tremendous Trifles* was published.
- In 1925, GKC's apologia *The Everlasting Man* was published.
- In 1927, GKC's collection of mystery stories *The Secret of Father Brown* was published.
- And in 1933, GKC's study *St. Thomas Aquinas* was published.

SEPTEMBER 2

And ye shall know the truth, and the truth shall make you free.

—JOHN 8:32

According to most philosophers, God in making the world enslaved it. According to Christianity, in making it, He set it free. God had written, not so much a poem, but rather a play; a play he had planned as perfect, but which had necessarily been left to human actors and stage-managers, who had since made a great mess of it.

ORSON WELLES ON GKC (1938)

G. K. C., Gilbert Keith Chesterton, great, greatly articulate Roman convert and liberal, has been dead now for two years. For a unique brand of common sense enthusiasm, for a singular gift of paradox, for a deep reverence and a high wit, and most of all for a free and shamelessly beautiful English prose, he will never be forgotten.

SEPTEMBER 3

> *Praise Him, sun and moon; praise Him, all you stars of light! Praise Him, you heavens of heavens, and you waters above the heavens! Let them praise the name of the Lord, for He commanded and they were created.*
> —PSALM 148:3–5 NKJV

One of the deepest and strangest of all human moods is the mood which will suddenly strike us perhaps in a garden at night, or deep in sloping meadows, the feeling that every flower and leaf has just uttered something stupendously direct and important, and that we have by a prodigy of imbecility not heard or understood it. There is a certain poetic value, and that a genuine one, in this sense of having missed the full meaning of things. There is beauty, not only in wisdom, but in this dazed and dramatic ignorance.

LINES FROM GKC'S POEM IN HONOUR OF EDMUND CLERIHEW BENTLEY

But we were young; we lived to see God break their
    bitter charms,
God and the good Republic come riding back in arms:
We have seen the city of Mansoul, even as it rocked,
    relieved—
Blessed are they who did not see, but being blind,
    believed.

SEPTEMBER 4

Behold their sitting down, and their rising up; I am their
music.

—LAMENTATIONS 3:63

Music is mere beauty; it is beauty in the abstract, beauty in solution. It is a shapeless and liquid element of beauty.

LINES FROM THE POEM, "THE STRANGE MUSIC"

In your strings is hid a music that no hand hath ere let fall,
In your soul is sealed a pleasure that you have not known
    at all;
Pleasure subtle as your spirit, strange and slender as your
    frame,
Fiercer than the pain that folds you, softer than your
    sorrow's name.

SEPTEMBER 5

Ye shall find the babe wrapped in swaddling clothes, lying in a manger.

—Luke 2:12

I found my way back to the city, and some time afterwards I actually saw in the street my two men talking, no doubt still saying, one that Science had changed all in Humanity, and the other that Humanity was now pushing the wings of the purely intellectual. But for me Humanity was hooked on to an accidental picture. I thought of a low and lonely house in the flats, behind a veil or film of slight trees, a man breaking the ground as men have broken from the first morning, and a huge grey horse champing his food within a foot of a child's head, as in the stable where Christ was born.

ON THIS DAY

- In 1931, GKC's article "The Way to Get International Peace" was published in the *Illustrated London News*.

SEPTEMBER 6

Yea, the fir trees rejoice at thee.
—Isaiah 14:8

A sunset of copper and gold had just broken down and gone to pieces in the west, and grey colours were crawling over everything in earth and heaven; also a wind was growing, a wind that laid a cold finger upon flesh and spirit. The bushes at the back of my garden began to whisper like conspirators; and then to wave like wild hands in signal.

A PASSAGE FROM *THE MAN WHO WAS THURSDAY* (1908)

This particular evening, if it is remembered for nothing else, will be remembered in that place for its strange sunset. It looked like the end of the world. All the heaven seemed covered with a quite vivid and palpable plumage; you could only say that the sky was full of feathers, and of feathers that almost brushed the face. Across the great part of the dome they were grey, with the strangest tints of violet and mauve and an unnatural pink or pale green; but towards the west the whole grew past description, transparent and passionate, and the last red-hot plumes of it covered up the sun like something too good to be seen.

ON THIS DAY

- In 1906, George Bernard Shaw wrote to GKC in praise of his book *Charles Dickens: A Critical Study*.
- And in 1930, GKC's article "Another Defence of the Primitive" was published in the *Illustrated London News*.

SEPTEMBER 7

And if I go and prepare a place for you, I will come again, and receive you unto myself; that where I am, there ye may be also.

—JOHN 14:3

[Tennyson] was a Victorian in the bad as well as the good sense; he could not keep priggishness out of long poems. Or again, take the case of *In Memoriam*. I will quote one verse . . . which has always seemed to me splendid, and which does express what the whole poem should express but hardly does.

> *That we may lift from out the dust,*
> *A voice as unto him that hears*
> *A cry above the conquered years*
> *Of one that ever works, and trust.*

The poem should have been a cry above the conquered years. It might well have been that if the poet could have said sharply at the end of it, as a pure piece of dogma, "I've forgotten every feature of the man's face: I know God holds him alive."

ON THIS DAY ───────────────────────────────────

- In 1929, GKC's article "The Language of Commerce" was published in the *Illustrated London News*.

SEPTEMBER 8

> *Now when Jesus was born in Bethlehem of Judaea in*
> *the days of Herod the king, behold, there came wise men*
> *from the east to Jerusalem.*
>
> —MATTHEW 2:1

> *Step softly, under snow or rain,*
> *To find the place where men can pray;*
> *The way is all so very plain*
> *That we may lose the way.*
> *Oh we have learnt to peer and pore,*
> *On tortured puzzles from our youth.*

We know all labyrinthine lore,
We are the three Wise Men of yore,
And we know all things but the truth.
Go humbly . . . it has hailed and snowed . . .
With voices low and lanterns lit,
So very simple is the road,
That we may stray from it . . .
The house from which the heavens are fed,
The old strange house that is our own . . .

SEPTEMBER 9

O taste and see that the Lord is good: blessed is the man
that trusteth in him.

—PSALM 34:8

The test of true religion is that . . . it is always trying to make men feel truths as facts; always trying to make abstract things as plain and solid as concrete things; always trying to make men, not merely admit the truth, but see, smell, handle, hear, and devour the truth.

A LINE FROM *THE MAN WHO WAS THURSDAY* (1908)

Truth is . . . terrible, even in fetters.

SEPTEMBER 10

Behold, this is the joy of his way . . .
　　　　　　　　　　—JOB 8:19

But if the question turn on the primary pivot of the cosmos, then there was more cosmic contentment in the narrow and bloody streets of Florence than in the theatre of Athens or the open garden of Epicurus. Giotto lived in a gloomier town than Euripides, but he lived in a [happier] universe.

The mass of men have been forced to be [happy] about the little things, but sad about the big ones. Nevertheless (I offer my last dogma defiantly) it is not native to man to be so. Man is more himself, man is more manlike, when joy is the fundamental thing in him, and grief the superficial. Melancholy should be an innocent interlude, a tender and fugitive frame of mind; praise should be the permanent pulsation of the soul.

A LINE FROM *THE MAN WHO WAS THURSDAY* (1908)

Syme, you are a poet. Stare at those morning clouds, and tell me or anyone the truth about morning clouds. But I tell you this, that you will have found out the truth of the last tree and the topmost cloud before the truth about me. You will understand the sea, and I shall be still a riddle; you shall know what the stars are, and not know what I am.

SEPTEMBER 11

*God created man in His own image; in the image of God
He created him; male and female He created them.*

—GENESIS 1:27 NKJV

An Englishman . . . may at least understand what Jefferson and Lincoln meant, and he may possibly find some assistance in this task by reading what they said. He may realise that equality is not some crude fairy tale about all men being equally tall or equally tricky . . . It is an absolute of morals by which all men have a value invariable and indestructible.

A PASSAGE FROM *VARIED TYPES* (1903)

I cannot feel myself that art has any dignity higher then the indwelling and divine dignity of human nature.

A PASSAGE FROM *TREMENDOUS TRIFLES* (1909)

*Tragedy is the highest expression of the
infinite value of human life.*

ON THIS DAY

- In 1909, GKC stated in the *Illustrated London News*: "Idolatry is committed, not merely by setting up false gods, but also by setting up false devils; by making men afraid of war or alcohol, or economic law, when they should be afraid of spiritual corruption and cowardice."

SEPTEMBER 12

He maketh them also to skip like a calf; Lebanon and
Sirion like a young unicorn.

—PSALM 29:6

Nature was a solemn mother to Wordsworth or to Emerson. But Nature is not solemn to Francis of Assisi or to George Herbert. To St. Francis, Nature is a sister, and even a younger sister: a little, dancing sister, to be laughed at as well as loved.

A LINE FROM *THE MAN WHO WAS THURSDAY* (1908)

There were a thousand other such objects, however. There was a dancing lamp-post, a dancing apple tree, a dancing ship. One would have thought that the untameable tune of some mad musician had set all the common objects of field and street dancing an eternal jig. And long afterwards, when Syme was middle-aged and at rest, he could never see one of those particular objects—a lamp-post, or an apple tree, or a windmill—without thinking that it was a strayed reveller from that revel of masquerade.

ON THIS DAY

- In 1931, GKC's article "Victorian Literary Fashions—and Our Own" was published in the *Illustrated London News*.

SEPTEMBER 13

That it might be fulfilled which was spoken by the prophet,
saying, I will open my mouth in parables.
—MATTHEW 13:35

Christ had even a literary style of his own, not to be found, I
think, elsewhere; it consists of an almost furious use of the *a*
fortiori. His "how much more" is piled one upon another like
castle upon castle in the clouds.

The diction used about Christ has been, and perhaps
wisely, sweet and submissive. But the diction used by Christ
is quite curiously gigantesque; it is full of camels leaping
through needles and mountains hurled into the sea. Morally
it is equally terrific; he called himself a sword of slaughter,
and told men to buy swords if they sold their coats for them.

ON THIS DAY

- In 1930, GKC's article "The Trouble with Our Pagans" was
  published in the *Illustrated London News*.

SEPTEMBER 14

That I may open my mouth boldly, to make known the
mystery of the gospel . . .
—EPHESIANS 6:19

It is of course the very element of confidence which has in our
day become least common and least possible. We know we are
brilliant and distinguished, but we do not know we are right.

We swagger in fantastic artistic costumes; we praise ourselves; we fling epigrams right and left; we have the courage to play the egoist and the courage to play the fool, but we have not the courage to preach.

A PASSAGE FROM *ORTHODOXY* (1908)

Courage is almost a contradiction in terms. It means a strong desire to live taking the form of a readiness to die. "He that will lose his life, the same shall save it," is not a piece of mysticism for saints and heroes. It is a piece of everyday advice for sailors or mountaineers.

SEPTEMBER 15

The moon and the stars, which thou hast ordained . . .
—PSALM 8:3

The grass seemed signalling to me with all its fingers at once; the crowded stars seemed bent upon being understood.

G. N. SHUSTER ON GKC'S BOOK *HERETICS*

The point about [Chesterton's] famous book of protests, Heretics, is that the world is full of enemies worth fighting. That is probably the most satisfactory reason for being a philosopher, or, at least, for worrying about philosophy. One of the most characteristic modern ideas is that it really doesn't matter what a man believes; and were he to believe in nothing whatever it would generally be supposed that his happiness was complete. In his book Chesterton "pointed out" (a favorite phrase) that it does make a great deal of difference what opinions a man holds, particularly if he wishes to be happy.

SEPTEMBER 16

Prove all things; hold fast that which is good.
—1 Thessalonians 5:21

This world can be made beautiful again by beholding it as a battlefield. When we have defined and isolated the evil thing, the colours come back into everything else. When evil things have become evil, good things, in a blazing apocalypse, become good.

A PASSAGE FROM *ORTHODOXY* (1908)

Christianity spoke again and said: "I have always maintained that men were naturally backsliders; that human virtue tended of its own nature to rust or to rot; I have always said that human beings as such go wrong, especially happy human beings, especially proud and prosperous human beings. This eternal revolution, this suspicion sustained through centuries, you (being a vague modern) call the doctrine of progress. If you were a philosopher you would call it, as I do, the doctrine of original sin. You may call it the cosmic advance as much as you like; I call it what it is—the Fall."

I have spoken of orthodoxy coming in like a sword; here I confess it came in like a battleaxe. For really (when I came to think of it) Christianity is the only thing left that has any real right to question the power of the well-nurtured or the well-bred.

SEPTEMBER 17

> *Therefore, as the elect of God, holy and beloved, put*
> *on tender mercies, kindness, humility, meekness,*
> *longsuffering . . .*
> —COLOSSIANS 3:12 NKJV

There is the lesson of "Cinderella," which is the same as that of the Magnificat—*exaltavit humiles*. There is the great lesson of "Beauty and the Beast"; that a thing must be loved before it is loveable.

A PASSAGE FROM *TREMENDOUS TRIFLES* (1910)

I met a man the other day who did not believe in fairy tales. I do not mean that he did not believe in the incidents narrated in them— that he did not believe that a pumpkin could turn into a coach. He did, indeed, entertain this curious disbelief. And, like all the other people I have ever met who entertained it, he was wholly unable to give me an intelligent reason for it.

He tried the laws of nature, but he soon dropped that. Then he said that pumpkins were unalterable in ordinary experience, and that we all reckoned on their infinitely protracted pumpkinity. But I pointed out to him that this was not an attitude we adopt specially towards impossible marvels, but simply the attitude we adopt towards all unusual occurrences. If we were certain of miracles we should not count on them. Things that happen very seldom we all leave out of our calculations, whether they are miraculous or not . . .

If I had seen a pumpkin turned into a Panhard motor-car with my own eyes that would not make me any more inclined to assume that the same thing would happen again. I should not invest largely

in pumpkins with an eye to the motor trade. Cinderella got a ball
dress from the fairy; but I do not suppose that she looked after her
own clothes any the less after it.

SEPTEMBER 18

I do not pray that You should take them out of the world,
but that You should keep them from the evil one. They are
not of the world, just as I am not of the world. Sanctify
them by Your truth. Your word is truth. As You sent Me
into the world, I also have sent them into the world.
— JOHN 17:15–18 NKJV

Now shutting out things is all very well, but it has one simple
corollary: that from everything we shut out, we are ourselves
shut out.

A PASSAGE FROM *CHARLES DICKENS: A CRITICAL STUDY* (1906)

If we are to look for lessons, here at least is the last and deepest
lesson of Dickens. It is in our own daily life that we are to look for
the portents and the prodigies. This is the truth, not merely of the
fixed figures of our life; the wife, the husband, the fool that fills
the sky. It is true of the whole stream and substance of our daily
experience.

SEPTEMBER 19

> *When men are cast down, then thou shalt say, There is*
> *lifting up; and he shall save the humble person.*
>
> —JOB 22:29

All men are ordinary men; the extraordinary men are those who know it.

A PASSAGE FROM *CHARLES DICKENS: A CRITICAL STUDY* (1906)

Piety produces intellectual greatness precisely because piety in itself is quite indifferent to intellectual greatness. The strength of Cromwell was that he cared for religion. But the strength of religion was that it did not care for Cromwell; did not care for him, that is, any more than for anybody else . . .

It has often been said, very truly, that religion is the thing that makes the ordinary man feel extraordinary; it is an equally important truth that religion is the thing that makes the extraordinary man feel ordinary.

ON THIS DAY

- In 1930, GKC and his wife, Frances, set sail for North America from Liverpool. The purpose: a series of scheduled lectures at the University of Notre Dame.

SEPTEMBER 20

He restores my soul; He leads me in the paths of
righteousness for His name's sake.

—Psalm 23:3 nkjv

In this world heaven is rebelling against hell. For the orthodox there can always be a revolution; for a revolution is a restoration.

A PASSAGE FROM *THE USES OF DIVERSITY* (1920)

I believe a great part of such poetic pleasure as I have comes from a certain disdainful indifference in actual things. Demeter withered up the cornfields: I like the cornfields because they grow in spite of me. At least, I can lay my hand on my heart and say that no cornfield ever grew with my assistance. Ajax defied the lightning; but I like the lightning because it defies me. I enjoy stars and the sun or trees and the sea, because they exist in spite of me; and I believe the sentiment to be at the root of all that real kind of romance which makes life not a delusion of the night, but an adventure of the morning.

It is, indeed, in the clash of circumstances that men are most alive. When we break a lance with an opponent the whole romance is in the fact that the lance does break. It breaks because it is real: it does not vanish like an elfin spear. And even when there is an element of the marvellous or impossible in true poetry, there is always also this element of resistance, of actuality and shock. The most really poetical impossibility is an irresistible force colliding with an immovable post. When that happens it will be the end of the world.

It is true, of course, that marvels, even marvels of transformation, illustrate the noblest histories and traditions. But we should notice a rather curious difference which the instinct of popular legend has in almost all cases kept. The wonder-working done by good people, saints and friends of man, is almost always represented in the form of restoring things or people to their proper shapes.

SEPTEMBER 21

The heavens declare the glory of God; and the firmament shows His handiwork.

—PSALM 19:1 NKJV

In this world of ours we do not go on and discover small things: rather we go on and discover big things. It is the detail that we see first: it is the design that we only see very slowly and some men die never having seen it at all.

A PASSAGE FROM *THE USES OF DIVERSITY* (1920)

Historians seem to have completely forgotten the two facts—first, that men act from ideas; and second, that it might, therefore, be as well to discover which ideas. The mediaevals did not believe primarily in "chivalry," but in Catholicism, as producing chivalry among other things.

ON THIS DAY

- In 1929, GKC's article "The New Immoral Philosophy" was published in the *Illustrated London News*.

SEPTEMBER 22

And these stones shall be for a memorial.
—JOSHUA 4:7 NKJV

Cathedrals and columns of triumph were meant, not for people more cultured and self-conscious than modern tourists, but for people much rougher and more casual. Those heaps of live stone like frozen fountains, were so placed and poised as to catch the eye of ordinary inconsiderate men going about their daily business; and when they are so seen they are never forgotten.

A PASSAGE FROM *THE USES OF DIVERSITY* (1920)

We shall never make anything of moral and religious movements in history until we begin to look at their theory as well as their practice.

SEPTEMBER 23

For ye are all one in Christ Jesus.
—GALATIANS 3:28

Chaucer's knight rode with a cook quite naturally; because the thing they were all seeking together was as much above knighthood as it was above cookery. Soldiers and swindlers and bullies and outcasts, they were all going to the shrine of a distant saint.

A PASSAGE FROM *CHARLES DICKENS: A CRITICAL STUDY* (1906)

It was [Dickens] who had the things of Chaucer, the love of large jokes and long stories and brown ale and all the white roads of England. Like Chaucer he loved story within story, every man telling a tale. Like Chaucer he saw something openly comic in men's motley trades. Sam Weller [of The Pickwick Papers*] would have been a great gain to the Canterbury Pilgrimage and told an admirable story.*

SEPTEMBER 24

Remember now thy Creator . . .
—ECCLESIASTES 12:1

"But," I reflected, "if the beatification of the world is not a work of nature but a work of art, then it involves an artist." And here again my contemplation was cloven by the ancient voice which said, "I could have told you all this a long time ago."

LITERARY CRITIC JULIUS WEST ON GKC

For a series of books on artists, [Chesterton] wrote two, on William Blake *and* G. F. Watts. *The first is all about mysticism, and so is the second. They are for the layman, not for the artist. They could be read with interest and joy by the colour-blind.*

And, incidentally, they are extremely good criticism. Therein is the triumph of Chesterton. Give him a subject which he can relate with his own view of the universe, and space wherein to accomplish this feat, and he will succeed in presenting his readers with a vividly outlined portrait, tinted, of course, with his own personality, but indisputably true to life.

And he showed me a pure river of water of life, clear as crystal, proceeding from the throne of God and of the Lamb. In the middle of its street, and on either side of the river, was the tree of life, which bore twelve fruits, each tree yielding its fruit every month. The leaves of the tree were for the healing of the nations. And there shall be no more curse, but the throne of God and of the Lamb shall be in it, and His servants shall serve Him.

—REVELATION 22:1–3 NKJV

[Yet again, I heard the ancient voice say:] "If there is any certain progress it can only be my kind of progress, the progress towards a complete city of virtues and dominations where righteousness and peace contrive to kiss each other. An impersonal force might be leading you to a wilderness of perfect flatness or a peak of perfect height. But only a personal God can possibly be leading you . . . to a city with just streets and architectural proportions, a city in which each of you can contribute exactly the right amount of your own colour to the many-coloured coat of Joseph."

GKC, FROM *THE LIVING AGE* MAGAZINE (1914)

I think it was Jefferies who said that all men ought to be idle; and that we should get all the work we wanted done by harnessing to our machinery the tremendous tides of the sea. Something analogous

*has been lately suggested by Mr. Wells; but I disagree with it; I
think it would destroy the [idea of a] holiday . . .*

*Men jaded or dazed with duties wish to look out across that
fruitless field, in which God has sown we know not what seed and
shall raise we know not what harvest. They wish to behold how
enormous is their irresponsibility.*

ON THIS DAY ─────────────────────────────────

- In 1930, GKC and his wife, Frances, arrived in Quebec,
  after taking ship in Liverpool eight days earlier. The trip
  was undertaken so that GKC could give a long-scheduled
  series of lectures at the University of Notre Dame.

SEPTEMBER 26

*Be strong and of good courage; do not be afraid, nor be
dismayed, for the Lord your God is with you wherever
you go.*

—JOSHUA 1:9 NKJV

He has come to the most dreadful conclusion a literary man
can come to, the conclusion that the ordinary view is the right
one. It is only the last and wildest kind of courage that can
stand on a tower before ten thousand people and tell them that
twice two is four.

A PASSAGE FROM *THE USES OF DIVERSITY* (1920)

*[George Wyndham] had that spiritual ambition which is itself
the ascending flame of humility; and which has been wanting
to the English since the squire grew greater than the knight. He*

seemed to await an adventure that never quite came to him on earth; and his life and death were swift, as if he were struck by lightning as with an accolade, or had won spurs that were wings upon the wind.

ON THIS DAY ─────────────────────────────

- In 1931, GKC's article "The Only Rational Wars" was published in the *Illustrated London News*.

───

SEPTEMBER 27

───

Follow after charity.
—1 CORINTHIANS 14:1

Take another case: the complicated question of charity, which some highly uncharitable idealists seem to think quite easy. Charity is a paradox, like modesty and courage. Stated baldly, charity certainly means one of two things—pardoning unpardonable acts, or loving unlovable people.

A PASSAGE FROM *CHARLES DICKENS: A CRITICAL STUDY* (1906)

As long as [Dickens] was dealing with such penury and such festivity his touch was almost invariably sure. But when he came to more difficult cases, to people who for one reason or another could not be cured with one good dinner, he did develop this other evil, this genuinely vulgar optimism of which I speak. And the mark of it is this: that he gave the characters a comfort that had no especial connection with themselves; he threw comfort at them like alms. There are cases at the end of his stories in which his kindness to his characters is a careless and insolent kindness.

- In 1930, GKC's article "My Silver Anniversary with the ILN" was published in the *Illustrated London News*.

SEPTEMBER 28

For this child I prayed; and the Lord hath given me my petition which I asked of him.

—1 SAMUEL 1:27

The whole difference between construction and creation is exactly this: that a thing constructed can only be loved after it is constructed; but a thing created is loved before it exists, as the mother can love the unborn child.

A PASSAGE FROM *THE USES OF DIVERSITY* (1920)

These elementary things, the land, the roof, the family, may seem mean and miserable; and in a cynical civilization very probably will seem mean and miserable. But the things themselves are not mean or miserable; and any reformer who says they are is not only taking hold of the stick by the wrong end, he is cutting off the branch by which he is hanging. The stamp of social failure is not that men have these simple things, but, rather, that they do not have them; or even when they do, do not know that they have them.

- In 1929, GKC's article "The Abolition of Sunday" was published in the *Illustrated London News*.

- And in 1930, GKC gave a lecture entitled "The New Enslavement of Women" in the city of Montreal, Canada. His wife, Frances, wrote that the evening was "a very great success," enthusiastically received, and well attended.

SEPTEMBER 29

Wherefore take unto you the whole armour of God, that ye may be able to withstand in the evil day, and having done all, to stand.

—EPHESIANS 6:13

[Christianity taught that] one could fight all the forces of existence without deserting the flag of existence. One could be at peace with the universe and yet be at war with the world. St. George could still fight the dragon, however big the monster bulked in the cosmos, though he were bigger than the mighty cities or bigger than the everlasting hills.

GKC, AS DESCRIBED BY THE LITERARY CRITIC JULIUS WEST (1916)

As a matter of strict fact [Chesterton] only describes his adventures in Fairyland, which is all the earth. He tells us of his profound astonishment at the consistent recurrence of apples on apple trees, and at the general jolliness of the earth. He describes, very beautifully, some of the sensations of childhood making the all-embracing discovery that things are what they seem, and the even more joyful feeling of pretending that they are not, or that they will cease to be at any moment.

SEPTEMBER 30

... the bringing in of a better hope ... by the which we draw
nigh unto God.

—HEBREWS 7:19

The truth is that the tradition of Christianity (which is still the only coherent ethic of Europe) rests on two or three paradoxes or mysteries which can easily be impugned in argument and as easily justified in life. One of them, for instance, is the paradox of hope or faith—that the more hopeless is the situation the more hopeful must be the man.

A PASSAGE FROM *THE USES OF DIVERSITY* (1920)

Almost every other simple type of our working population had seen a Leprechaun. A fisherman had seen a Leprechaun. A farmer had seen a Leprechaun. Even a postman had probably seen one.

But there was one simple son of the people whose path had never before been crossed by the prodigy. Never until then had a policeman seen a Leprechaun. It was only a question of whether the monster should take the policeman away with him into Elfland (where such a policeman as he would certainly have been fettered by the fatal love of the fairy queen), or whether the policeman should take away the monster to the police-station. The forces of this earth prevailed; the constable captured the elf, instead of the elf capturing the constable. The officer took him to the workhouse, and opened a new epoch in the study of tradition and folk-lore.

What will the modern world do if it finds (as very likely it will) that the wildest fables have had a basis in fact; that there are creatures of the border land, that there are oddities on the fringe of fixed laws, that there are things so unnatural as easily to be called preternatural? I do not know what the modern world will do about these things; I only know what I hope. I hope the modern world will be as sane about these things as the mediaeval world was about them. Because I believe that an ogre can have two heads, that is no reason why I should lose the only head that I have.

OCTOBER 1

Let the fields rejoice, and all that is therein.
—1 CHRONICLES 16:32

I was like one who had advanced into a hostile country to take one high fortress. And when that fort had fallen the whole country surrendered and turned solid behind me. The whole land was lit up, as it were, back to the first fields of my childhood.

A PASSAGE FROM *THE USES OF DIVERSITY* (1920)

As a rule, there is no difference between the critic and ascetic except that the ascetic sorrows with a hope and the critic without a hope.

DURING THIS MONTH

- In 1900, GKC's collection of nonsense verse *Greybeards At Play* was published.
- In 1902, GKC's collection of essays *Twelve Types* was published.
- In 1917, GKC's study *A Short History of England* was published.
- In 1920, GKC's collection of essays *The Uses of Diversity* was published.

- In 1922, GKC's book of poems *The Ballad of St. Barbara* was published.
- In 1923, GKC's study *St. Francis of Assisi* was published.
- And in 1928, GKC's collection of essays *Generally Speaking* was published.

OCTOBER 2

And the peace of God, which surpasses all understanding, will guard your hearts and minds through Christ Jesus.

—PHILIPPIANS 4:7 NKJV

The only kind of hope that is of any use in a battle is a hope that denies arithmetic. Whatever may be the meaning of the contradiction, it is the fact that the only kind of charity which any weak spirit wants, or which any generous spirit feels, is the charity which forgives the sins that are like scarlet. Whatever may be the meaning of faith, it must always mean a certainty about something we cannot prove.

A PASSAGE FROM *CHARLES DICKENS: A CRITICAL STUDY* (1906)

But this is a spiritual certainty, that all men are tragic. And this again, is an equally sublime spiritual certainty, that all men are comic. No special and private sorrow can be so dreadful as the fact of having to die. And no freak or deformity can be so funny as the mere fact of having two legs. Every man is important if he loses his life; and every man is funny if he loses his hat, and has to run after it. And the universal test everywhere of whether a thing is popular, of the people, is whether it employs vigorously these extremes of the tragic and the comic. Shelley, for instance, was an aristocrat, if ever there was one in this world. He was a Republican, but he was not a democrat: in his poetry there is every perfect quality except this pungent and popular stab. For the tragic and the comic you must go, say, to Burns, a poor man. And all over the world, the folk literature, the popular literature, is the same. It consists of very dignified sorrow and very undignified fun. Its sad tales are of broken hearts; its happy tales are of broken heads.

ON THIS DAY ─────────────────────────────────────

- In 1930, GKC and his wife, Frances, arrived in Toronto, Canada, on a scheduled stop prior to the series of lectures he was slated to give at the University of Notre Dame.

OCTOBER 3

For God has not given us a spirit of fear, but of power and of love and of a sound mind. Therefore do not be ashamed of the testimony of our Lord.
> —2 TIMOTHY 1:7–8 NKJV

Christianity is always out of fashion because it is always sane; and all fashions are mild insanities.

A PASSAGE FROM *THE USES OF DIVERSITY* (1920)

It is a common and recurrent mood to regard man as a hopeless Yahoo. But it is not a natural mood to regard man as a hopeful Yahoo, as the Evolutionists did, as a creature changing before one's eyes from bestial to beautiful, a creature whose tail has just dropped off while he is staring at a far-off divine event.

ON THIS DAY

- In 1930, GKC gave a lecture in Toronto, Canada, on "Culture and the Coming Peril." He delivered this address at St. Michael's College, a Catholic school within the University of Toronto. Some 2,500 people were in attendance. It was on this occasion that GKC was asked about his height and weight. He quipped: "About six foot two, but my weight has never been successfully calculated."
- And in 1931, GKC's article "Theorising About Human Society" was published in the *Illustrated London News*.

OCTOBER 4

For I say, through the grace given to me, to everyone who is among you, not to think of himself more highly than he ought to think, but to think soberly.

—ROMANS 12:3 NKJV

But the essential point of it is merely this, that whatever primary and far-reaching moral dangers affect any man, affect all men. All men can be criminals, if tempted; all men can be heroes, if inspired.

And this doctrine does away altogether with Carlyle's pathetic belief (or any one else's pathetic belief) in "the wise few." There are no wise few. Every aristocracy that has ever existed has behaved, in all essential points, exactly like a small mob. Every oligarchy is merely a knot of men in the street—that is to say, it is very jolly, but not infallible.

A PASSAGE FROM ONE OF GKC'S SERMONS AT
ST. PAUL'S CHURCH, COVENT GARDEN (1904)

When you undertake legislation for the poor, try and realise that you are legislating for men, and not for some far removed race of people whom you have never seen. Try and think about the laws which you approve, and the course of action to which you agree, and then think whether you would like it to return suddenly upon you with truncheon and battle-axe! Realise, in a word, the fundamental unity and fraternity of men in all legislation.

ON THIS DAY ─────────────────────────────────

- In 1930, GKC and his wife, Frances, arrived in South Bend, Indiana, home to the University of Notre Dame. They were met at the train station by the university's president, Father Charles O'Donnell. Reporters were also present. GKC told them, tongue planted firmly in cheek, that he had no notion of why Notre Dame would have invited him to come. Nor did he know why they thought him an educator, much less that he was educated. He had, he said, only written a few books.

- During the time GKC spent at Notre Dame, he gave two lecture courses—comprised of 36 lectures in all. One course was on Victorian literature, the other on Victorian history. His audiences during this time averaged 500 in attendance.

OCTOBER 5

> *Then everyone came whose heart was stirred, and everyone*
> *whose spirit was willing . . .*
>
> —EXODUS 35:21 NKJV

Poets will tend towards Christian orthodoxy for a perfectly plain reason: because it is about the simplest and freest thing now left in the world.

GKC, AS DESCRIBED BY THE LITERARY CRITIC JULIUS WEST (1916)

G. K. C. is not a text, praise be, and whether he lives or dies, long may he be spared the hands of an editor or interpreter who is also an irrepressible authority on anapaests and suchlike things. He is a poet, and a considerable poet, not because of his strict attention to the rules of prosody, but because he cannot help himself.

ON THIS DAY

- In 1929, GKC's article "The Family of Bright Young Things" was published in the *Illustrated London News.*

OCTOBER 6

> *Nevertheless I am not ashamed, for I know whom I have*
> *believed and am persuaded that He is able to keep what I*
> *have committed to Him until that Day.*
>
> —2 TIMOTHY 1:12 NKJV

These are the days when the Christian is expected to praise every creed except his own.

A PASSAGE FROM *TREMENDOUS TRIFLES* (1910)

The problem of the fairy tale is—what will a healthy man do with a fantastic world? The problem of the modern novel is—what will a madman do with a dull world? In the fairy tales the cosmos goes mad; but the hero does not go mad. In the modern novels the hero is mad before the book begins, and suffers from the harsh steadiness and cruel sanity of the cosmos.

ON THIS DAY

- In 1930, GKC gave the first of his lectures on Victorian literature at the University of Notre Dame.

OCTOBER 7

Jesus Christ is the same yesterday, today, and forever.
— HEBREWS 13:8 NKJV

An imbecile habit has arisen in modern controversy of saying that such and such a creed can be held in one age but cannot be held in another. Some dogma, we are told, was credible in the twelfth century, but is not credible in the twentieth.

You might as well say that a certain philosophy can be believed on Mondays, but cannot be believed on Tuesdays. You might as well say of a view of the cosmos that it was suitable to half-past three, but not suitable to half-past four. What a man can believe depends upon his philosophy, not upon the clock or the century.

GKC, FROM THE PAGES OF *THE CATHOLIC WORLD* (1923)

Literary criticism is largely a string of labels.

ON THIS DAY ————————————————————

- In 1930, GKC met with Cardinal Hayes, the Archbishop of New York over lunch. Later that afternoon, GKC and his wife, Frances, travelled by train to Chicago, where GKC lectured once again on "The New Enslavement of Women" at the Orchestra Hall. The evening gave rise to another memorable Chestertonian quip. When some in the audience shouted that they could not hear, GKC declared: "Don't worry, you're not missing a thing."

  During the same evening, GKC was asked which of his books he liked best. He said he "hadn't read them all," but admitted that *The Flying Inn* had been "the most fun to write."

OCTOBER 8

Unto him be glory in the church by Christ Jesus throughout all ages, world without end.

—EPHESIANS 3:21

The Church always seems behind the times, when it is really beyond the times; it is waiting till the last fad shall have seen its last summer. It keeps the key of a permanent virtue.

LINES FROM *THE BALLAD OF THE WHITE HORSE* (1911)

O go you onward; where you are
Shall honour and laughter be,
Past purpled forest and pearled foam,
God's winged pavilion free to roam,
Your face, that is a wandering home,
A flying home for me.

A PASSAGE FROM *ALL I SURVEY* (1933)

I learned to like Swift for all the things for which Macaulay and Thackeray disliked him. I liked him for liking Bolingbroke; for despising Marlborough; for showing up the Glorious Hanoverian Succession in Ireland as a very low and dirty job; for treating the wit of the Freethinkers with contempt; for giving the first place to the virtue of Honour, which practically disappeared from politics and financial affairs about this time.

It is doubtless true that he was too bitter and exclusive, but that is no reason why we should be. And the final phase of true philanthropy is not complete until it can love the misanthrope.

OCTOBER 9

Come home with me, and eat bread.
—1 KINGS 13:15

It is a good thing for a man to live in a family in the same sense that it is a beautiful and delightful thing for a man to be snowed up in a street. They all force him to realize that life is not a thing from outside, but a thing from inside. Above all, they all insist upon the fact that life, if it be a truly stimulating and fascinating life, is a thing which, of its nature, exists in spite of ourselves.

LINES FROM *THE BALLAD OF THE WHITE HORSE* (1911)

> *The gates of heaven are lightly locked,*
> *We do not guard our gain,*
> *The heaviest hind may easily*
> *Come silently and suddenly*
> *Upon me in a lane.*
> *And any little maid that walks*
> *In good thoughts apart,*
> *May break the guard of the Three Kings,*
> *And see the dear and dreadful things*
> *I hid within my heart.*
> *The meanest man in grey fields gone*
> *Behind the set of sun,*
> *Heareth between star and other star,*
> *Through the door of the darkness fallen ajar,*
> *The council, eldest of things that are,*
> *The talk of the Three in One.*

OCTOBER 10

> *Vanity of vanities, all is vanity.*
> —ECCLESIASTES 1:2 NKJV

"Many clever men like you have trusted to civilization. Many clever Babylonians, many clever Egyptians, many clever men at the end of Rome. Can you tell me, in a world that is flagrant with the failures of civilisation, what there is particularly immortal about yours?"

LINES FROM *THE BALLAD OF THE WHITE HORSE* (1911)

> *I tell you naught for your comfort,*
> *Yea, naught for your desire,*
> *Save that the sky grows darker yet*
> *And the sea rises higher.*
> *"Night shall be thrice night over you,*
> *And heaven an iron cope.*
> *Do you have joy without a cause,*
> *Yea, faith without a hope?*

OCTOBER 11

Remember and do all My commandments, and be holy for your God.

—NUMBERS 15:40 NKJV

Defy the conventions . . . keep the commandments.

C. S. LEWIS ON GKC'S *BALLAD OF THE WHITE HORSE* (1934)

Don't you like the way Chesterton takes hold of you in that poem, shakes you, and makes you want to cry? . . . Here and there it achieves the heroic, the rarest quality in modern literature.

But how is it possible not to see that what comes through all this is permanent and dateless? Does not the central theme of the Ballad—the highly paradoxical message which Alfred receives from the

Virgin—embody the feeling, and the only possible feeling, with which in any age almost defeated men take up such arms as are left them and win?

ON THIS DAY

- In 1930, GKC's article "The Laziness of the Modern Intellect" was published in the *Illustrated London News*.

OCTOBER 12

Keep the traditions just as I delivered them to you.
—1 CORINTHIANS 11:2 NKJV

He is a very shallow critic who cannot see an eternal rebel in the heart of a conservative.

LINES FROM *THE BALLAD OF THE WHITE HORSE* (1911)

Ride through the silent earthquake lands,
Wide as a waste is wide,
Across these days like deserts, when
Pride and a little scratching pen
Have dried and split the hearts of men,
Heart of the heroes, ride.
Up through an empty house of stars,
Being what heart you are,
Up the inhuman steeps of space
As on a staircase go in grace,
Carrying the firelight on your face
Beyond the loneliest star.

Take these; in memory of the hour
We strayed a space from home
And saw the smoke-hued hamlets, quaint
With Westland king and Westland saint,
And watched the western glory faint
Along the road to Frome.

OCTOBER 13

He has put eternity in their hearts.
—ECCLESIASTES 3:11 NKJV

If Mr. McCabe asks me why I import frivolity into a discussion of the nature of man, I answer, because frivolity is a part of the nature of man. If he asks me why I introduce what he calls paradoxes into a philosophical problem, I answer, because all philosophical problems tend to become paradoxical. If he objects to my treating of life riotously, I reply that life is a riot.

And I say that the Universe as I see it, at any rate, is very much more like the fireworks at the Crystal Palace than it is like his own philosophy [of atheism]. About the whole cosmos there is a tense and secret festivity—like preparations for Guy Fawkes' day.

Eternity is the eve of something. I never look up at the stars without feeling that they are the fires of a schoolboy's rocket, fixed in their everlasting fall.

OCTOBER 14

Ask for the old paths, where the good way is, and walk in it; then you will find rest for your souls.
—JEREMIAH 6:16 NKJV

We often read nowadays of the valour or audacity with which some rebel attacks a hoary tyranny or an antiquated superstition. There is not really any courage at all in attacking hoary or antiquated things, any more than in offering to fight one's grandmother. The really courageous man is he who defies tyrannies young as the morning and superstitions fresh as the first flowers.

A LINE FROM *THE USES OF DIVERSITY* (1920)

... life not a delusion of the night, but an adventure of the morning.

OCTOBER 15

He gives to all life, breath, and all things.
—ACTS 17:25 NKJV

A man cannot be wise enough to be a great artist without being wise enough to wish to be a philosopher. A man cannot have the energy to produce good art without having the energy to wish to pass beyond it. A small artist is content with art; a great artist is content with nothing except everything.

PASSAGES FROM *THE USES OF DIVERSITY* (1920)

Real wisdom may be better than real wit, but there is much more sham wisdom than there is sham wit.

For the wisdom of man alters with every age; his prudence has to fit perpetually shifting shapes of inconvenience or dilemma. But his folly is immortal: a fire stolen from heaven.

OCTOBER 16

Therefore choose life, that both you and your descendants may live.

—DEUTERONOMY 30:19 NKJV

Cynicism denotes that condition of mind in which we hold that life is in its nature mean and arid; that no soul contains genuine goodness, and no state of things genuine reliability.

LINES FROM *THE BATTLE OF THE STORIES* (1915)

Behold, we are men of many lands, in motley seasons set,
From Riga to the rock of Spain, from Orkney to Olivet,
Who stand up in the council in the turning of the year
And, standing, give the judgment on the evil house of fear;
Knowing the End shall write again what we have written
    here.
On the day when God remembers and no man can forget.

OCTOBER 17

> *Let them first learn to show piety at home.*
> —1 TIMOTHY 5:4 NKJV

If we wish to preserve the family, we must revolutionize the nation.

LINES FROM *THE BATTLE OF THE STORIES* (1915)

They came uncounted like the stars that circle or are set,
They circled and they caught us in a sparkling
  casting-net.
We burst it in the mountain gate where all the guns
  began,
When the snow stood up at Christmas on the hills of
  Ardahan.
The guns—and not a bell to tell that God was made a
  man—
But we did all remember, though all the world forget.

ON THIS DAY ─────────────────────────────

- In 1931, GKC's article "The Rebellion Against Yesterday's Rebels" was published in the *Illustrated London News*.

*Eye hath not seen, nor ear heard, neither have entered
into the heart of man, the things which God hath
prepared for them that love him.*

—1 CORINTHIANS 2:9

Let us, then, go upon a long journey and enter on a dreadful
search. Let us, at least, dig and seek till we have discovered our
own opinions. The dogmas we really hold are far more fantastic, and, perhaps, far more beautiful than we think.

GKC, DESCRIBED BY LITERARY CRITIC JULIUS WEST (1916)

*If Chesterton invents a fantastic world, full of fantastic people who
speak Chestertonese, then he is quite entitled to waive any trifling
conventions which hinder the liberty of his subjects . . .*

*None of Chesterton's heroes do, as a matter of fact, become cam-
els, but I would nevertheless strongly advise any young woman about
to marry one of them to take out an insurance policy against unforeseen transformations.*

ON THIS DAY

- In 1930, GKC's article "Wall Street and Christian Science"
  was published in the *Illustrated London News*.

OCTOBER 19

> *Fight the good fight of faith, lay hold on eternal life, to*
> *which you were also called and have confessed.*
> —1 TIMOTHY 6:12 NKJV

Truths turn into dogmas the instant that they are disputed. Thus every man who utters a doubt defines a religion. And the scepticism of our time does not really destroy the beliefs, rather it creates them; gives them their limits and their plain and defiant shape. . . .

We who are Christians never knew the great philosophic common sense which inheres in that mystery until the anti-Christian writers pointed it out to us.

The great march of mental destruction will go on. Everything will be denied. Everything will become a creed. It is a reasonable position to deny the stones in the street; it will be a religious dogma to assert them. It is a rational thesis that we are all in a dream; it will be a mystical sanity to say that we are all awake. Fires will be kindled to testify that two and two make four. Swords will be drawn to prove that leaves are green in summer.

We shall be left defending, not only the incredible virtues and sanities of human life, but something more incredible still, this huge impossible universe which stares us in the face. We shall fight for visible prodigies as if they were invisible. We shall look on the impossible grass and the skies with a strange courage. We shall be of those who have seen and yet have believed.

ON THIS DAY ────────────────────────────────

- In 1929, GKC's article "Mr. Darrow on Divorce" was published in the *Illustrated London News*.
- And in 1930, the Chestertons were once more in Chicago, where GKC took part in a debate with Dr. Bridges, head of the Chicago Ethical Society. The topic: "Is the New Woman Enslaved?"

OCTOBER 20

I will make My justice rest as a light of the peoples.
        —ISAIAH 51:4 NKJV

Reason and justice grip the remotest and loneliest star.

A PASSAGE FROM *WHAT'S WRONG WITH THE WORLD* (1910)

Becket objected to a priest being tried even by the Lord Chief Justice. And his reason was simple: because the Lord Chief Justice was being tried by the priest. The judiciary was itself sub-judice. The kings were themselves in the dock. The idea was to create an invisible kingdom, without armies or prisons, but with complete freedom to condemn publicly all the kingdoms of the earth.

OCTOBER 21

> *That you may become blameless and harmless, children*
> *of God without fault in the midst of a crooked and*
> *perverse generation, among whom you shine as lights in*
> *the world.*
>
> —PHILIPPIANS 2:15 NKJV

One can sometimes do good by being the right person in the wrong place.

ON SIR WALTER SCOTT, A PASSAGE FROM *TWELVE TYPES* (1903)

In truth, one of Scott's most splendid traits is his difficulty, or rather incapacity, for despising any of his characters. He did not scorn the most revolting miscreant as the realist of to-day commonly scorns his own hero. Though his soul may be in rags, every man of Scott can speak like a king.

OCTOBER 22

> *In honour preferring one another . . .*
> —ROMANS 12:10

There is a great man who makes every man feel small. But the real great man is the man who makes every man feel great.

A PASSAGE FROM *ORTHODOXY* (1908)

Progress should mean that we are always walking towards the New Jerusalem. It does mean that the New Jerusalem is always walking away from us. We are not altering the real to suit the ideal. We are altering the ideal: it is easier.

OCTOBER 23

They have erred from the faith, and pierced themselves through with many sorrows.

—1 TIMOTHY 6:10

[The modern man] says, with a conscious laugh, "I suppose I am very heretical," and looks round for applause. The word "heresy" not only means no longer being wrong; it practically means being clear-headed and courageous. The word "orthodoxy" not only no longer means being right; it practically means being wrong. All this can mean one thing, and one thing only. It means that people care less for whether they are philosophically right.

A PASSAGE FROM ONE OF GKC'S SERMONS AT ST. PAUL'S CHURCH, COVENT GARDEN (1904)

That ancient thing which the Old Testament called "idolatry," and which the Middle Ages called "heresy," is one of the most important factors in human life. There are no men who have no idol; there are no men who have no god. They may have a wrong idol, or a wrong god. Idolatry, heresy, believing the wrong thing, admiring the wrong thing—that there is, if you like—but there are no men who do not believe or admire [something].

OCTOBER 24

> *... but of those who believe to the saving of the soul.*
> —HEBREWS 10:39 NKJV

But there are some people, nevertheless—and I am one of them—who think that the most practical and important thing about a man is still his view of the universe.

A PASSAGE FROM *ALL I SURVEY* (1933)

But the evolutionary educator, having never since his birth been in anything but the dark, naturally believes that he is in the daylight. His very notion of daylight is something which is so blank as to be merely blind. There are no depths in it, either of light or darkness. There are no dimensions in it; not only no fourth, but no third, no second, and hardly a first; certainly no dimensions in which the mind can move. Therefore the mind remains fixed, in a posture that is called progressive. It never looks back, even for remembrance; it never looks the other way, even for experiment; it never looks at the other side, even for a paradox; it never winks the other eye. It simply knows all there is; and there does not seem to be much to know.

I have recently been looking through a specimen of this sort of scientific summary of the story of man; and I am relieving my feelings. Those writers sometimes say they are agnostic about God. Would to God they would consent to be agnostics about Man! Would they would leave the love of beauty or mystery as mysterious as they really are.

Every child is born facing some open questions. He finds them open just as he finds his ears or his lungs or his nostrils open; and he knows by instinct that through these open questions he draws in the air and life of the universe. Why dreams are different from daylight, why dead things are different from live things, why he himself is different from others, why beauty makes us restless and even love is a spring of quarrels, why we cannot so fit into our environment as to forget it and ourselves; all these things are felt vaguely by children on long, empty afternoons; or by primitive poets writing the epics and legends of the morning of the world.

OCTOBER 25

Therefore shall a man leave his father and his mother,
and shall cleave unto his wife: and they shall be one flesh.
—GENESIS 2:24

If Browning or Mrs. Browning had not desired any people to know that they were fond of each other, they would not have written and published "One Word More" or "The Sonnets from the Portuguese." Nay, they would not have been married in a public church, for every one who is married in a church does make a confession of love of absolutely national publicity, and tacitly, therefore, repudiates any idea that such confessions are too sacred for the world to know.

The ridiculous theory that men should have no noble passions or sentiments in public may have been designed to make private life holy and undefiled, but it has had very little actual effect except to make public life cynical and preposterously unmeaning. But the words of a poem or the words of the English Marriage Service, which are as fine as many poems, is a language dignified and deliberately intended to be understood by all.

ON THIS DAY

- In 1930, GKC's article "The Ideal Detective Story" was published in the *Illustrated London News*.

OCTOBER 26

Righteousness exalts a nation, but sin is a reproach to any people.

—Proverbs 14:34 NKJV

Now, in our time, philosophy or religion, our theory, that is, about ultimate things, has been driven out, more or less simultaneously, from two fields which it used to occupy. General ideals used to dominate literature. They have been driven out by the cry of "art for art's sake."

General ideals used to dominate politics. They have been driven out by the cry of "efficiency," which may roughly be translated as "politics for politics' sake." Persistently for the last twenty years the ideals of order or liberty have dwindled in our books; the ambitions of wit and eloquence have dwindled in our parliaments. Literature has purposely become less political; politics have purposely become less literary. General theories of the relation of things have thus been extruded from both; and we are in a position to ask, "What have we gained or lost by this extrusion? Is literature better, is politics better, for having discarded the moralist and the philosopher?"

When everything about a people is for the time growing weak and ineffective, it begins to talk about efficiency. So it is that when a man's body is a wreck he begins, for the first time, to talk about health.

- In 1929, GKC's article "Dr. Freud and Ancient Myth" was published in the *Illustrated London News*.

OCTOBER 27

But where can wisdom be found? And where is the place of understanding?

—Job 28:12 NKJV

Our affairs are hopelessly muddled by strong, silent men. And just as this repudiation of big words and big visions has brought forth a race of small men in politics, so it has brought forth a race of small men in the arts.

Our modern politicians claim the colossal license of Caesar and the Superman, claim that they are too practical to be pure and too patriotic to be moral; but the upshot of it all is that a mediocrity is Chancellor of the Exchequer. Our new artistic philosophers call for the same moral license, for a freedom to wreck heaven and earth with their energy; but the upshot of it all is that a mediocrity is Poet Laureate.

OCTOBER 28

> *Whoso findeth a wife findeth a good thing, and obtaineth*
> *favour of the Lord.*
>
> —PROVERBS 18:22

One of the qualities again which make Browning most charming, is the fact that he felt and expressed so simple and genuine a satisfaction about his own achievements as a lover and husband, particularly in relation to the care of his wife.

"If he is vain of anything," writes Mrs. Browning, "it is of my restored health." Later, she adds with admirable humour and suggestiveness, "and I have to tell him that he really must not go telling everybody how his wife walked here with him, or walked there with him, as if a wife with two feet were a miracle in Nature."

When a lady in Italy said, on an occasion when Browning stayed behind with his wife on the day of a picnic, that he was "the only man who behaved like a Christian to his wife," Browning was elated to an almost infantile degree. But there could scarcely be a better test of the essential manliness and decency of a man than this test of his vanities. Browning boasted of being domesticated; there are half a hundred men everywhere who would be inclined to boast of not being domesticated. Bad men are almost without exception conceited, but they are commonly conceited of their defects.

OCTOBER 29

Why art thou cast down, O my soul? and why art thou
disquieted within me? hope in God: for I shall yet praise
him, who is the health of my countenance, and my God.

—PSALM 43:5

For with any recovery from morbidity there must go a certain
healthy humiliation. There comes a certain point in such conditions when only three things are possible: first a perpetuation
of Satanic pride, secondly tears, and third laughter.

A PASSAGE FROM *ORTHODOXY* (1908)

Humility was largely meant as a restraint upon the arrogance and
infinity of the appetite of man. He was always outstripping his
mercies with his own newly invented needs. His very power of enjoy-
ment destroyed half his joys. By asking for pleasure, he lost the chief
pleasure; for the chief pleasure is surprise.

OCTOBER 30

To receive the instruction of wisdom, justice, and judgment,
and equity...

—PROVERBS 1:3

Politicians are none the worse for a few inconvenient ideals.

A PASSAGE FROM *ALL I SURVEY* (1933)

It often happens that by-products are bigger than big production, and that side-issues are larger than the main issue. Much of the political muddle and squabble comes from people trying to reach what they call a practical agreement. It is a very unpractical thing to trust to practical agreement. Two people may agree to keep a cat; but if they only agree because one is a lover of animals, and the other has a fiendish pleasure in watching cruelty to birds, it is probable that the practical agreement will not last very long. Other occasions will arise, in which it will be found to suffer from the absence of a theoretical agreement. There is at this moment many a parley between two politicians, seeking to find a practical agreement about a Tax on Tobacco or the dumping of Danish bacon, who are, in fact, forbidden for ever to come to any kind of real agreement, for the simple reason that they live in two different worlds; as, for instance, one in the globe that is picked out in red patches of the British Empire, and the other in the great grey orbis terrarum *in which all lands are alike. These men would really have to settle the big question before they settled the small question. But, in what we call practical politics, it is the small question that is called the big question. And the big question would only be permitted as a small parenthesis in the middle of the small question.*

ON THIS DAY ─────────────────────────────────────

- In 1909, George Bernard Shaw wrote to GKC: "I still think that you could write a useful sort of play if you were started . . .

  "In Ireland I sat down and began writing a scenario for you. But before I could finish it I had come back to London; and now it is all up with the scenario: in England I can do nothing but talk. I therefore now send you the thing as far as I scribbled it; and I leave you to invent what escapades you please for the hero, and to devise some sensational means of getting him back to heaven again, unless you prefer to end with the millennium in full swing."

Biographer Maisie Ward notes that Shaw's "scenario" dealt with the return of St. Augustine to the England he remembered converting.

OCTOBER 31

What is man, that thou art mindful of him?
—PSALM 8:4

The author of *The Book of Job* says, "I will show you the relations between man and heaven by a tale of primeval sorrows and the voice of God out of a whirlwind."

Virgil says, "I will show you the relations of man to heaven by the tale of the origin of the greatest people and the founding of the most wonderful city in the world."

Dante says, "I will show you the relations of man to heaven by uncovering the very machinery of the spiritual universe, and letting you hear as I have heard, the roaring of the mills of God."

Milton says, "I will show you the relations of man to heaven by telling you of the very beginning of all things, and the first shaping of the thing that is evil in the first twilight of time."

NOVEMBER 1

> *That I might make thee know the certainty of the words*
> *of truth . . .*
>
> —PROVERBS 22:21

It is a platitude, and none the less true for that, that we need to have an ideal in our minds with which to test all realities. But it is equally true, and less noted, that we need a reality with which to test ideals.

A PASSAGE FROM *ALL I SURVEY* (1933)

One thing [Walter Scott] did find in the past, not yet quite destroyed in the present, and it was his chief inspiration. He knew nothing of the religion of the past, and his notion of Gothic was more barbarous than that of any Goth. But he had extracted from his feudal traditions something on which his spirit truly fed; something without which the modern world is starving. He found the idea of Honour, which is the true energy in all militant eloquence. That a man should defend the dignity of his family, of his farm, of his lawful rank under the King, even of his mere name, of something at least that was larger than himself this was the fire that Scott found still burning out of fourteenth-century feudalism and expressed in eighteenth-century oratory. Of all moral ideals it is the most neglected and misunderstood to-day. It is not strange that the eloquence which sprang from it is misunderstood and neglected also. We see that hollow gaping around us everywhere; in the fact that marriage is discussed as everything except what it is, a vow; or that property is discussed as everything except what it ought to be, an independence. But the modern world is not so happy in its oblivion of honour, or the eloquence that springs from honour, as to force us to believe in the permanent oblivion of Scott.

DURING THIS MONTH ————————————————————

- In 1900, GKC's collection of verse *The Wild Knight* was published.
- In 1910, GKC's study *William Blake* was published, as was his collection of essays *Alarms and Discursions*.
- In 1912, GKC's collection of essays *A Miscellany of Men* was published.
- In 1913, GKC's play *Magic* was published.
- In 1921, GKC's book *Irish Impressions* was published.
- In 1922, GKC's book *The Man Who Knew Too Much* was published.
- In 1925, GKC's study *William Cobbett* was published.
- In 1927, GKC's study *Robert Louis Stevenson* was published.

NOVEMBER 2

And many among them shall stumble, and fall, and be broken.

—ISAIAH 8:15

It is strange that men should see sublime inspiration in the ruins of an old church and see none in the ruins of a man.

A PASSAGE FROM *ORTHODOXY* (1908)

Something certainly must be reared as a barrier, if our race is to avoid ruin. That peril is that the human intellect is free to destroy itself. Just as one generation could prevent the very existence of the next generation, by all entering a monastery or jumping into the sea, so one set of thinkers can in some degree prevent further thinking by teaching the next generation that there is no validity in any human thought.

ON THIS DAY ─────────────────────────

- In 1929, GKC's article "Twilight Sleep and the Breakdown of Reason" was published in the *Illustrated London News*.

NOVEMBER 3

> *Christ hath redeemed us from the curse of the law, being made a curse for us: for it is written, cursed is every one that hangeth on a tree.*
>
> —GALATIANS 3:13

Whatever jest, sentiment or [whim] first set Samuel Johnson touching the wooden posts, he never touched wood with any of the feeling with which he stretched out his hands to the timber of that terrible tree, which was the death of God and the life of man.

A PASSAGE FROM *ORTHODOXY* (1908)

There is the terrible allegory of the "Sleeping Beauty," which tells how the human creature was blessed with all birthday gifts, yet cursed with death; and how death also may perhaps be softened to a sleep.

But I am not concerned with any of the separate statutes of elfland, but with the whole spirit of its law, which I learnt before I could speak, and shall retain when I cannot write. I am concerned with a certain way of looking at life, which was created in me by the fairy tales, but has since been meekly ratified by the mere facts.

It might be stated this way. There are certain sequences or developments (cases of one thing following another), which are, in the true sense of the word, reasonable. They are, in the true sense of the word, necessary. Such are mathematical and merely logical sequences. We in fairyland (who are the most reasonable of all creatures) admit that reason and that necessity. For instance, if the Ugly Sisters are older than Cinderella, it is (in an iron and awful sense) necessary that Cinderella is younger than the Ugly Sisters. There is no getting out of it. Haeckel may talk as much fatalism about that fact as he pleases: it really must be. If Jack is the son of a miller, a miller is the father of Jack. Cold reason decrees it from her awful throne: and we in fairyland submit. If the three brothers all ride horses, there are six animals and eighteen legs involved: that is true rationalism, and fairyland is full of it.

NOVEMBER 4

> *The Son of man must be delivered into the hands of sinful men, and be crucified, and the third day rise again.*
> —LUKE 24:7 NKJV

The cross [is] something more than a historical memory; it does convey, almost as by a mathematical diagram, the truth about the real point at issue; the idea of a conflict stretching outwards into eternity. It is true, and even tautological, to say that the cross is the crux of the whole matter.

A PASSAGE FROM *ALARMS AND DISCURSIONS* (1911)

[Man's] central sanctities, his true possessions, should be Christian and simple. And just as a child would cherish most a wooden horse or a sword that is a mere cross of wood, so man, the great child, must cherish most the old plain things of poetry and piety; that

horse of wood that was the epic end of Ilium, or that cross of wood that redeemed and conquered the world.

NOVEMBER 5

> *For thou hast been a shelter for me.*
> —PSALM 61:3

Guy Fawkes' Day is not only in some rude sense a festival, and in some rude sense a religious festival; it is also, what is supremely symbolic and important, a winter religious festival. Here the 5th of November, which celebrates a paltry Christian quarrel, has a touch of the splendour of the 25th of December, which celebrates Christianity itself.

Dickens and all the jolly English giants who write of the red firelight are grossly misunderstood in this matter. Prigs call them coarse and materialistic because they write about the punch and plum pudding of winter festivals. The prigs do not see that if these writers were really coarse and materialistic they would not write about winter feasts at all. Mere materialists would write about summer and the sun.

The whole point of winter pleasure is that it is a defiant pleasure, a pleasure armed and at bay. The whole point is in the fierce contrast between the fire and wine within and the roaring rains outside. And some part of the sacredness of firelight we may allow to fireworks.

ON THIS DAY —————————————————————————

- In 1930, GKC was awarded an honorary doctorate by the University of Notre Dame. After this honour was conferred, GKC stated that he felt unworthy of it as he was only a journalist. Still, he said, he hoped he had proved it was possible to be an honest journalist.

NOVEMBER 6

Justice standeth afar off: for truth is fallen in the street.
—ISAIAH 59:14

We do not need to get good laws to restrain bad people. We need to get good people to restrain bad laws.

[There is a] habit in the governing class of talking about legislation as if it were something which did not affect them at all. We always talk of what laws we shall make, of the laws we shall have instituted. It is very seldom indeed we talk of what laws we shall obey.

A PASSAGE FROM *ORTHODOXY* (1908)

But as I put my head over the hedge of the elves and began to take notice of the natural world, I observed an extraordinary thing. I observed that learned men in spectacles were talking of the actual things that happened—dawn and death and so on—as if they were rational and inevitable. They talked as if the fact that trees bear fruit were just as necessary as the fact that two and one trees make three.

But it is not. There is an enormous difference by the test of fairyland; which is the test of the imagination. You cannot imagine two and one not making three. But you can easily imagine trees not growing fruit; you can imagine them growing golden candlesticks or tigers hanging on by the tail.

These men in spectacles spoke much of a man named Newton,

who was hit by an apple, and who discovered a law. But they could not be got to see the distinction between a true law, a law of reason, and the mere fact of apples falling. If the apple hit Newton's nose, Newton's nose hit the apple. That is a true necessity: because we cannot conceive the one occurring without the other. But we can quite well conceive the apple not falling on his nose; we can fancy it flying ardently through the air to hit some other nose, of which it had a more definite dislike.

NOVEMBER 7

> *By faith he sojourned in the land of promise, as in a strange country.*
>
> —HEBREWS 11:9

But life is a vale. Never forget at any moment of your existence to regard it in the light of a vale.

A PASSAGE FROM *TWELVE TYPES* (1903)

But certainly antithesis is not artificial. An element of paradox runs through the whole of existence itself. It begins in the realm of ultimate physics and metaphysics, in the two facts that we cannot imagine a space that is infinite, and that we cannot imagine a space that is finite.

It runs through the inmost complications of divinity, in that we cannot conceive that Christ in the wilderness was truly pure, unless we also conceive that he desired to sin. It runs, in the same manner, through all the minor matters of morals, so that we cannot imagine courage existing except in conjunction with fear, or magnanimity existing except in conjunction with some temptation to meanness.

And at the ninth hour Jesus cried with a loud voice, saying,
Eloi, Eloi, lama sabachthani? which is, being interpreted,
my God, my God, why hast thou forsaken me?

—MARK 15:34

When the world shook and the sun was wiped out of heaven, it was not at the crucifixion, but at the cry from the cross: the cry which confessed that God was forsaken of God.

A PASSAGE FROM *ORTHODOXY* (1908)

And this fairy-tale sentiment also sank into me and became my sentiment towards the whole world. I felt and feel that life itself is as bright as the diamond, but as brittle as the window-pane; and when the heavens were compared to the terrible crystal I can remember a shudder. I was afraid that God would drop the cosmos with a crash.

Remember, however, that to be breakable is not the same as to be perishable. Strike a glass, and it will not endure an instant; simply do not strike it, and it will endure a thousand years. Such, it seemed, was the joy of man, either in elfland or on earth; the happiness depended on not doing something which you could at any moment do and which, very often, it was not obvious why you should not do.

ON THIS DAY

- In 1930, GKC's article "Travellers' Tales and the Truth" was published in the *Illustrated London News*.

NOVEMBER 9

Serve him in truth with all your heart.
—1 SAMUEL 12:24

You can only find truth with logic if you have already found truth without it.

A PASSAGE FROM *ORTHODOXY* (1908)

Now it is the charge against the main deductions of the materialist that, right or wrong, they gradually destroy his humanity; I do not mean only kindness. I mean hope, courage, poetry, initiative, all that is human. For instance, when materialism leads men to complete fatalism (as it generally does), it is quite idle to pretend that it is in any sense a liberating force. It is absurd to say that you are especially advancing freedom when you only use free thought to destroy free will.

ON THIS DAY ─────────────────

- In 1929, GKC's article "The Modern Recoil from the Modern" was published in the *Illustrated London News*.

NOVEMBER 10

Many waters cannot quench love, neither can the floods drown it.
—SONG OF SOLOMON 8:7

The truth which the Brontës came to tell us is the truth that many waters cannot quench love.

A PASSAGE FROM *THE BALL AND THE CROSS* (1909)

"Oh, I have heard all that!" said Turnbull with genial contempt. "I have heard that Christianity keeps the key of virtue, and that if you read Tom Paine you will cut your throat at Monte Carlo. It is such rubbish that I am not even angry at it. You say that Christianity is the prop of morals; but what more do you do? When a doctor attends you and could poison you with a pinch of salt, do you ask whether he is a Christian? You ask whether he is a gentleman, whether he is an M.D.—anything but that. When a soldier enlists to die for his country or disgrace it, do you ask whether he is a Christian? You are more likely to ask whether he is Oxford or Cambridge at the Boat Race. If you think your creed essential to morals why do you not make it a test for these things?"

"We once did make it a test for these things," said MacIan smiling, "and then you told us that we were imposing by force a faith unsupported by argument. It seems rather hard that having first been told that our creed must be false because we did use tests, we should now be told that it must be false because we don't. But I notice that most anti-Christian arguments are in the same inconsistent style."

"That is all very well as a debating-club answer," replied Turnbull good-humouredly, "but the question still remains: Why don't you confine yourself more to Christians if Christians are the only really good men?"

"Who talked of such folly?" asked MacIan disdainfully. "Do you suppose that the Catholic Church ever held that Christians were the only good men? Why, the Catholics of the Catholic Middle Ages talked about the virtues of all the virtuous Pagans until humanity was sick of the subject. No, if you really want to know what we mean when we say that Christianity has a special power of virtue, I will tell you. The Church is the only thing on earth that can perpetuate a type of virtue and make it something more than a fashion."

NOVEMBER 11

> *Narrow is the way, which leadeth unto life.*
> —MATTHEW 7:14

Thus there was George Macdonald, a Scot of genius as genuine as Carlyle's; he could write fairy-tales that made all experience a fairy-tale. He could give the real sense that every one had the end of an elfin thread that must at last lead them into Paradise.

A PASSAGE FROM *THE BALL AND THE CROSS* (1909)

[McIan] felt he had been hurled into some new incarnation: into the midst of new relations, wrongs and rights, with towering responsibilities and almost tragic joys which he had as yet had no time to examine. Heaven had not merely sent him a message; Heaven itself had opened around him and given him an hour of its own ancient and star-shattering energy.

NOVEMBER 12

> *Ye have in heaven a better and an enduring substance.*
> —HEBREWS 10:34

Since I first read [*The Princess and the Goblin*] some five alternative philosophies of the universe have come to our colleges out of Germany, blowing through the world like the east wind. But for me that castle is still standing in the mountains and the light in its tower is not put out. All George MacDonald's other stories, interesting and suggestive in their several ways, seem to be illustrations and even disguises of that one.

A PASSAGE FROM *THE BALL AND THE CROSS* (1909)

For faith by its very nature is fierce, and as it were at once doubtful and defiant.

NOVEMBER 13

All the earth shall be filled with the glory of the Lord.
—NUMBERS 14:21 NKJV

There was only one who really represented what Scottish religion should have been, if it had continued the colour of the Scottish mediaeval poetry. In his particular type of literary work [George Macdonald] did indeed realize the apparent paradox of a St. Francis of Aberdeen, seeing the same sort of halo round every flower and bird.

It is not the same thing as any poet's appreciation of the beauty of the flower or bird. A heathen can feel that and remain heathen, or in other words remain sad. It is a certain special sense of significance, which the tradition that most values it calls sacramental. To have got back to it, or forward to it, at one bound of boyhood, out of the black Sabbath of a Calvinist town, was a miracle of imagination.

A PASSAGE FROM *THE BALL AND THE CROSS* (1909)

"France!" asserted Turnbull with a sort of rollicking self-exaggeration, very unusual with him, "France, which is one torrent of splendid scepticism from Abelard to Anatole France."

"France," said MacIan, "which is one cataract of clear faith from St. Louis to Our Lady of Lourdes."

NOVEMBER 14

> *The fool hath said in his heart, There is no God.*
> —PSALM 14:1

The secularists have not wrecked divine things; but the secularists have wrecked secular things, if that is any comfort to them. The Titans did not scale heaven; but they laid waste the world.

A PASSAGE FROM *THE BALL AND THE CROSS* (1909)

They had a dreary walk across wastes of grey shingle in the grey dawn before they began to come within hail of human fields or roads; nor had they any notion of what fields or roads they would be. Their boots were beginning to break up and the confusion of stones tried them severely, so that they were glad to lean on their swords, as if they were the staves of pilgrims. MacIan thought vaguely of a weird ballad of his own country which describes the soul in Purgatory as walking on a plain full of sharp stones, and only saved by its own charities upon earth.

ON THIS DAY

- In 1931, GKC's article "The Scottish War Memorial" was published in the *Illustrated London News*.

NOVEMBER 15

Christ Jesus came into the world to save sinners; of whom
I am chief.

—1 TIMOTHY 1:15

In so far as I am Man I am the chief of creatures. In so far as I am
a man I am the chief of sinners.

PASSAGES FROM *A MISCELLANY OF MEN* (1912)

I can't play the piano, but I can play the fool.

I would sooner call myself a journalist than an author; because a
journalist is a journeyman.

ON THIS DAY

- In 1930, GKC and his wife, Frances, departed the University
  of Notre Dame, deeply grateful for the many kindnesses
  they'd been shown. They hadn't left, however, before GKC
  had caused something of a stir. It seems that three or four
  days before his last lecture, he had rather rashly invited
  students to bring copies of his books by his temporary residence for signing. They took him at this word, and he ended
  up having to autograph some 600 or 700 books.

NOVEMBER 16

My soul waiteth for the Lord more than they that watch
for the morning: I say, more than they that watch for the
morning.

—PSALM 130:6

If any frightened curate still says that it will be awful if the
darkness of free thought should spread, we can only answer
him in the high and powerful words of Mr. Belloc, "Do not, I
beseech you, be troubled about the increase of forces already
in dissolution. You have mistaken the hour of the night: it is
already morning."

We have no more questions left to ask. We have looked for
questions in the darkest corners and on the wildest peaks. We
have found all the questions that can be found. It is time we
gave up looking for questions and began looking for answers.

PASSAGES FROM *A MISCELLANY OF MEN* (1912)

People who sniff at amateurs in private life still manage to venerate
absolute duffers in public life.

Comfortable valleys accept us with open arms and warm words,
like comfortable innkeepers.

ON THIS DAY ───────────────────────────

- In 1929, GKC's article "The New Woman" was published in
  the *Illustrated London News.*

NOVEMBER 17

Thou madest him a little lower than the angels; thou
crownedst him with glory and honour, and didst set him
over the works of thy hands.

—HEBREWS 2:7

It is the simple truth that man does differ from the brutes in kind and not in degree; and the proof of it is here; that it sounds like a truism to say that the most primitive man drew a picture of a monkey and that it sounds like a joke to say that the most intelligent monkey drew a picture of a man. Something of division and disproportion has appeared; and it is unique. Art is the signature of man.

NOVEMBER 18

Bow thy heavens, O Lord, and come down: touch the
mountains, and they shall smoke.

—PSALM 144:5

I felt in my bones, first, that this world does not explain itself. It may be a miracle with a supernatural explanation; it may be a conjuring trick, with a natural explanation. But the explanation of the conjuring trick, if it is to satisfy me, will have to be better than the natural explanations I have heard. The thing is magic, true or false.

Second, I came to feel as if magic must have a meaning, and meaning must have some one to mean it. There was something personal in the world, as in a work of art; [and] whatever it meant it meant violently.

A PASSAGE FROM *THE BALL AND THE CROSS* (1909)

No, the great Freethinker, with his genuine ability and honesty, does not in practice destroy Christianity. What he does destroy is the Freethinker who went before. Freethought may be suggestive, it may be inspiriting, it may have as much as you please of the merits that come from vivacity and variety.

But there is one thing Freethought can never be by any possibility— Freethought can never be progressive. It can never be progressive because it will accept nothing from the past; it begins every time again from the beginning; and it goes every time in a different direction. All the rational philosophers have gone along different roads, so it is impossible to say which has gone furthest. Who can discuss whether Emerson was a better optimist than Schopenhauer was pessimist?

NOVEMBER 19

I will instruct thee and teach thee in the way which thou shalt go: I will guide thee with mine eye.

—PSALM 32:8

When I was a boy there were two curious men running about who were called the optimist and the pessimist. I constantly used the words myself, but I cheerfully confess that I never had any very special idea of what they meant. The only thing which might be considered evident was that they could not mean what they said; for the ordinary verbal explanation was that the optimist thought this world as good as it could be, while the pessimist thought it as bad as it could be.

Both these statements being obviously raving nonsense, one had to cast about for other explanations. An optimist could not mean a man who thought everything right and nothing wrong. For that is meaningless; it is like calling everything right and nothing left.

Upon the whole, I came to the conclusion that the optimist thought everything good except the pessimist, and that the pessimist thought everything bad, except himself.

It would be unfair to omit altogether from the list the mysterious but suggestive definition said to have been given by a little girl, "An optimist is a man who looks after your eyes, and a pessimist is a man who looks after your feet."

I am not sure that this is not the best definition of all. There is even a sort of allegorical truth in it. For there might, perhaps, be a profitable distinction drawn between that more dreary thinker who thinks merely of our contact with the earth from moment to moment, and that happier thinker who considers rather our primary power of vision and of choice of road.

NOVEMBER 20

For there is none other name under heaven given among men, whereby we must be saved.

—ACTS 4:12

The remarkable thing about Christianity was that it was the first to preach Christianity. Its peculiarity was that it was peculiar, and simplicity and sincerity are not peculiar, but obvious ideals for all mankind. Christianity was the answer to a riddle, not the last truism uttered after a long talk.

A PASSAGE FROM *THE USES OF DIVERSITY* (1920)

A modern "thinker" will find it easier to make up a hundred problems than to make up one riddle. For in the case of the riddle, he has to make up the answer.

NOVEMBER 21

> *These be the names of the mighty men whom David had . . .*
> —2 SAMUEL 23:8

The fire faded, and the slow, strong stars came out. And the seven strange men were left alone, like seven stone statues on their chairs of stone. Not one of them had spoken a word.

They seemed in no haste to do so, but heard in silence the hum of insects and the distant song of one bird. Then Sunday spoke, but so dreamily that he might have been continuing a conversation rather than beginning one.

"We will eat and drink later," he said. "Let us remain together a little, we who have loved each other so sadly, and have fought so long. I seem to remember only centuries of heroic war, in which you were always heroes—epic on epic, iliad on iliad, and you always brothers in arms."

ON THIS DAY —————————————————————————

- In 1931, GKC's article "The Wit of Charles II" was published in the *Illustrated London News*.

NOVEMBER 22

Whoso findeth a wife findeth a good thing, and obtaineth favour of the Lord.

—PROVERBS 18:22

The principle expressed in the Prayer Book in the words "for better, for worse" . . . is the principle that all noble things have to be paid for, even if you only pay for them with a promise.

LINES FROM *THE BALLAD OF THE WHITE HORSE* (1911)

> *Therefore I bring these rhymes to you,*
> *Who brought the cross to me,*
> *Since on you flaming without flaw*
> *I saw the sign that Guthrum saw*
> *When he let break his ships of awe,*
> *And laid peace on the sea.*

ON THIS DAY

- In 1930, GKC's article "Browning and the American Optimists" was published in the *Illustrated London News*.

NOVEMBER 23

Even as ye are called in one hope of your calling [there is]
one Lord, one faith, one baptism, one God and Father of
all, who is above all, and through all, and in you all.
                                        —EPHESIANS 4:4–6

If snowflakes fell in the shape, say, of the heart of Midlothian, it
might be an accident. But if snowflakes fell in the exact shape of
the maze at Hampton Court, I think one might call it a miracle.

It is exactly as of such a miracle that I have since come to
feel of the philosophy of Christianity. The complication of our
modern world proves the truth of the creed more perfectly than
any of the plain problems of the ages of faith.

A PASSAGE FROM *ALARMS AND DISCURSIONS* (1911)

Perhaps you do not know where Ethandune is. Nor do I; nor does any-
body. That is where the somewhat sombre fun begins. I cannot even
tell you for certain whether it is the name of a forest or a town or a hill. I
can only say that in any case it is of the kind that floats and is unfixed.
If it is a forest, it is one of those forests that march with a million legs,
like the walking trees that were the doom of Macbeth. If it is a town, it
is one of those towns that vanish, like a city of tents. If it is a hill, it is a
flying hill, like the mountain to which faith lends wings.

ON THIS DAY ─────────────────────────────

- In 1929, GKC's article "Inspiration by the Muse" was
  published in the *Illustrated London News*.

NOVEMBER 24

I know that thou canst do every thing.
—JOB 42:2

A man is not really convinced of a philosophic theory when he finds that something proves it. He is only really convinced when he finds that everything proves it.

A PASSAGE FROM *G. F. WATTS* (1904)

Men talk of philosophy and theology as if they were something specialistic and arid and academic. But philosophy and theology are not only the only democratic things. They are democratic to the point of being vulgar, to the point, I was going to say, of being rowdy. They alone admit all matters: they alone lie open to all attacks. All other sciences may while studying their own, laugh at the rag-tag and bobtail of the sciences . . .

There is no detail from buttons to Kangaroos that does not enter into the [happy] confusion of philosophy. There is no fact of life from the death of a donkey to the general Post-office, which has not its place to dance and sing in, in the glorious carnival of theology.

NOVEMBER 25

When I consider thy heavens, the work of thy fingers, the moon and the stars, which thou hast ordained . . .
—PSALM 8:3

The Christian is quite free to believe that there's a considerable amount of settled order and an inevitable development in the universe. But the materialist is not allowed to admit into his spotless machine the slightest speck of spiritualism or miracle.

A PASSAGE FROM *ORTHODOXY* (1908)

Any one who likes, therefore, may call my belief in God merely mystical; the phrase is not worth fighting about. But my belief that miracles have happened in human history is not a mystical belief at all; I believe in them upon human evidences as I do in the discovery of America.

Upon this point there is a simple logical fact that only requires to be stated and cleared up. Somehow or other an extraordinary idea has arisen that the disbelievers in miracles consider them coldly and fairly, while believers in miracles accept them only in connection with some dogma. The fact is quite the other way. The believers in miracles accept them (rightly or wrongly) because they have evidence for them. The disbelievers in miracles deny them (rightly or wrongly) because they have a doctrine against them.

NOVEMBER 26

But we have the mind of Christ.
—1 CORINTHIANS 2:16 NKJV

If we want to uproot inherent cruelties or lift up lost populations we cannot do it with the scientific theory that matter precedes mind; we can do it with the supernatural theory that mind precedes matter.

A PASSAGE FROM *TREMENDOUS TRIFLES* (1910)

But the true result of all experience and the true foundation of all religion is this. That the four or five things that it is most practically essential that a man should know, are all of them what people call paradoxes. That is to say, that though we all find them in life to be mere plain truths, yet we cannot easily state them in words without being guilty of seeming verbal contradictions. One of them, for instance, is the unimpeachable platitude that the man who finds most pleasure for himself is often the man who least hunts for it. Another is a paradox of courage; the fact that the way to avoid death is not to have too much aversion to it. Whoever is careless enough of his bones to climb some hopeless cliff above the tide may save his bones by that carelessness. Whoever will lose his life, the same shall save it; an entirely practical and prosaic statement.

NOVEMBER 27

I have considered the days of old, the years of ancient times.
—PSALM 77:5 NKJV

Now in history there is no Revolution that is not a Restoration. Among the many things that leave me doubtful about the modern habit of fixing eyes on the future, none is stronger than this: that all the men in history who have really done anything with the future have had their eyes fixed upon the past.

I need not mention the Renaissance, the very word proves my case. The originality of Michael Angelo and Shakespeare began with the digging up of old vases and manuscripts.

ON THIS DAY

- In 1926, Chesterton spoke of his friend Jack Phillimore in *G. K.'s Weekly*. Phillimore had been at one time Professor of Greek, at another of Latin, at Glasgow University. In tribute to his friend, GKC said: "He looked much more like a sailor than a professor; his dark square face and clear eyes and compact figure were of a type often seen among sailors; and in whatever academic enclave he stood, he always seemed to have walked in from outside, bringing with him some of the winds of the world, and some light from the ends of the earth."

NOVEMBER 28

*O taste and see that the Lord is good: blessed is the man
that trusteth in him.*

—PSALM 34:8

In the modern world we are primarily confronted with the extraordinary spectacle of people turning to new ideals because they have not tried the old. Men have not got tired of Christianity; they have never found enough Christianity to get tired of. Men have never wearied of political justice; they have wearied of waiting for it.

A PASSAGE FROM *ALL THINGS CONSIDERED* (1908)

The editors of the magazines bring out their Christmas numbers so long before the time that the reader is more likely to be still lamenting for the turkey of last year than to have seriously settled down to a solid anticipation of the turkey which is to come. Christmas numbers of magazines ought to be tied up in brown paper and kept for Christmas Day. On consideration, I should favour the editors being tied up in brown paper. Whether the leg or arm of an editor should ever be allowed to protrude I leave to individual choice.

- In 1901, Rudyard Kipling wrote to publisher Brimley Johnson, praising GKC's book of poems *The Wild Knight*.
- In 1931, GKC's article "On Dependence and Independence" was published in the *Illustrated London News*.

NOVEMBER 29

Holy, holy, holy, is the Lord of hosts: the whole earth is full of his glory.

—ISAIAH 6:3

But the world is more full of glory
Than you can understand.

A PASSAGE FROM *ALARMS AND DISCURSIONS* (1911)

Lastly, there is this value about the colour that men call colourless; that it suggests in some way the mixed and troubled average of existence, especially in its quality of strife and expectation and promise. Grey is a colour that always seems on the eve of changing to some other colour; of brightening into blue or blanching into white or bursting into green and gold. So we may be perpetually reminded of the indefinite hope that is in doubt itself; and when there is grey weather in our hills or grey hairs in our heads, perhaps they may still remind us of the morning.

ON THIS DAY

- In 1930, GKC's article "The Worship of the Practical" was published in the *Illustrated London News*.

NOVEMBER 30

And she brought forth her firstborn son, and wrapped
him in swaddling clothes, and laid him in a manger;
because there was no room for them in the inn.

—LUKE 2:7

> *And at night we win to the ancient inn*
> *Where the child in the frost is furled,*
> *We follow the feet where all souls meet*
> *At the inn at the end of the world.*

ON THIS DAY

- In 1929, GKC's article "The Isolation of the Englishman" was published in the *Illustrated London News*.

DECEMBER 1

Therefore the Lord himself shall give you a sign.

—ISAIAH 7:14

The wise man will follow a star, low and large and fierce in the heavens; but the nearer he comes to it the smaller and smaller it will grow, till he finds it the humble lantern over some little inn or stable. Not till we know the high things shall we know how lowly they are.

A PASSAGE FROM *THE EVERLASTING MAN* (1925)

But above all, it is true of the most tremendous issue; of that tragedy which has created the divine comedy of our creed. Nothing short of the extreme and strong and startling doctrine of the divinity of Christ will give that particular effect that can truly stir the popular sense like a trumpet; the idea of the king himself serving in the ranks like a common soldier.

DURING THIS MONTH

- In 1900, GKC's collection of essays *The Defendant* was published.

DECEMBER 2

Behold, a virgin shall conceive, and bear a son.
—ISAIAH 7:14

> *The Christ-child lay on Mary's lap,*
> *His hair was like a light.*
> *(O weary, weary were the world,*
> *But here is all aright.)*
> *The Christ-child lay on Mary's heart,*
> *His hair was like a fire.*
> *(O weary, weary is the world,*
> *But here the world's desire.)*

A PASSAGE FROM *THE EVERLASTING MAN* (1925)

This is the trinity of truths symbolised here by the three types in the old Christmas story; the shepherds and the kings and that other king who warred upon the children. It is simply not true to say that other religions and philosophies are in this respect its rivals. It is not true to say that any one of them combines these characters; it is not true to say that any one of them pretends to combine them . . .

No other story, no pagan legend or philosophical anecdote or historical event, does in fact affect any of us with that peculiar and even poignant impression produced on us by the word Bethlehem. No other birth of a god or childhood of a sage seems to us to be Christmas, or anything like Christmas.

DECEMBER 3

And, lo, the star, which they saw in the east, went before them.

—MATTHEW 2:9

Go humbly; humble are the skies,
And low and large and fierce the Star;
So very near the Manger lies
That we may travel far.

A PASSAGE FROM *THE EVERLASTING MAN* (1925)

Herod had his place, therefore, in the miracle play of Bethlehem, because he is the menace to the Church Militant, and shows it from the first as under persecution and fighting for its life. For those who think this a discord, it is a discord that sounds simultaneously with the Christmas bells.

DECEMBER 4

Hide me under the shadow of thy wings.
—PSALM 17:8

Any one thinking of the Holy Child as born in December would mean by it exactly what we mean by it; that Christ is not merely a summer sun of the prosperous but a winter fire for the unfortunate.

A PASSAGE FROM *THE EVERLASTING MAN* (1925)

Christmas for us in Christendom has become one thing, and in one sense even a simple thing. But like all the truths of that tradition, it is in another sense a very complex thing . . .

There is something defiant in it also; something that makes the abrupt bells at midnight sound like the great guns of a battle that has just been won. All this indescribable thing that we call the Christmas atmosphere only hangs in the air as something like a lingering fragrance or fading vapour from the exultant explosion of that one hour in the Judean hills nearly two thousand years ago. But the savour is still unmistakable, and it is something too subtle or too solitary to be covered by our use of the word peace.

DECEMBER 5

> *Let us now go even unto Bethlehem, and see this thing*
> *which is come to pass, which the Lord hath made known*
> *unto us.*
>
> —LUKE 2:15

The place that the shepherds found was not an academy or an
abstract republic; it was not a place of myths . . . explained or
explained away. It was a place of dreams come true.

A PASSAGE FROM *THE EVERLASTING MAN* (1925)

The popular presentation of this popular story, in so many miracle
plays and carols, has given to the shepherds the costumes, the lan-
guage, and the landscape of the separate English and European
countrysides. We all know that one shepherd will talk in a Somerset
dialect or another talk of driving his sheep from Conway towards
Clyde. Most of us know by this time how true is that error, how
wise, how artistic, how intensely Christian and Catholic is that
anachronism.

ON THIS DAY ───────────────────────────────

- In 1930, GKC's article "On Abraham Lincoln and America"
  was published in the *Illustrated London News*.

Now when Jesus was born in Bethlehem of Judaea in
the days of Herod the king, behold, there came wise men
from the east to Jerusalem.

—MATTHEW 2:1

The more we are proud that the Bethlehem story is plain enough to be understood by the shepherds, and almost by the sheep, the more do we let ourselves go, in dark and gorgeous imaginative frescoes or pageants about the mystery and majesty of the Three Magian Kings.

A PASSAGE FROM *THE WISDOM OF FATHER BROWN* (1914)

It was one of those chilly and empty afternoons in early winter, when the daylight is silver rather than gold and pewter rather than silver. If it was dreary in a hundred bleak offices and yawning drawing rooms, it was drearier still along the edges of the flat Essex coast, where the monotony was the more inhuman for being broken at very long intervals by a lamp-post that looked less civilised than a tree, or a tree that looked more ugly than a lamp-post. A light fall of snow had half-melted into a few strips, also looking leaden rather than silver, when it had been fixed again by the seal of frost; no fresh snow had fallen, but a ribbon of the old snow ran along the very margin of the coast, so as to parallel the pale ribbon of the foam.

The line of the sea looked frozen in the very vividness of its violet-blue . . . For miles and miles, forward and back, there was no breathing soul, save two pedestrians, walking at a brisk pace, though one had much longer legs and took much longer strides than the other.

It did not seem a very appropriate place or time for a holiday, but Father Brown had few holidays, and had to take them when he could, and he always preferred, if possible, to take them in company with his old friend Flambeau, ex-criminal and ex-detective. The priest had had a fancy for visiting his old parish at Cobhole, and was going north-eastward along the coast.

DECEMBER 7

Behold, I bring you good tidings of great joy, which shall be to all people. For unto you is born this day in the city of David a Saviour, which is Christ the Lord.

—LUKE 2:10–11

SELECTIONS FROM "THE TRUCE OF CHRISTMAS"

Passionate peace is in the sky—
And in the snow in silver sealed
The beasts are perfect in the field . . .
The idle humble hill and wood
Are bowed upon the sacred birth,
And for one little hour the earth
Is lazy with the love of good—
Hunger is hard and time is tough,
But bless the beggars and kiss the kings,
For hope has broken the heart of things . . .
Only till Christmastide go by
Passionate peace is in the sky.

DECEMBER 8

And the desire of all nations shall come: and I will fill this
house with glory.

—HAGGAI 2:7

All the old customs surrounding the celebration of the birth
of Christ are made by human instinct so as to insist and re-
insist upon this crucial quality. Everything is so arranged that
the whole household may feel, if possible, as a household does
when a child is actually being born in it.

The thing is a vigil and a vigil with a definite limit. People sit
up at night until they hear the bells ring. Or they try to sleep at
night in order to see their presents the next morning. Everywhere
there is a limitation, a restraint; at one moment the door is shut,
at the moment after it is opened. The hour has come.

A PASSAGE FROM *CHARLES DICKENS: A CRITICAL STUDY* (1906)

But the power of hoping through everything, the knowledge that
the soul survives its adventures, that great inspiration comes to the
middle-aged; God has kept that good wine until now . . .

There is nothing that so much mystifies the young as the consis-
tent frivolity of the old. They have discovered their indestructibility.
They are in their second and clearer childhood, and there is a mean-
ing in the merriment of their eyes.

DECEMBER 9

> *If thou canst believe, all things are possible to him that believeth.*
>
> —MARK 9:23

All Dickens' books are Christmas books. But this is still truest of his two or three famous Yuletide tales—*The Christmas Carol* and *The Chimes* and *The Cricket on the Hearth*. Of these *The Christmas Carol* is beyond comparison the best as well as the most popular . . .

The Christmas Carol is a happy story first, because it describes an abrupt and dramatic change. It is not only the story of a conversion, but of a sudden conversion; as sudden as the conversion of a man at a Salvation Army meeting.

DECEMBER 10

> *And the Lord . . . will preserve me unto his heavenly kingdom.*
>
> —2 TIMOTHY 4:18

One of the things that strike root is Christmas: and another is middle-age. The other great pillar of private life besides property is marriage; but I will not deal with it here.

Suppose a man has neither wife nor child: suppose he has only a good servant, or only a small garden, or only a small house, or only a small dog. He will still find he has struck unintentional root. He realizes there is something in his own garden that was not even in the Garden of Eden; and therefore is not (I kiss my hand to the Socialists) in Kew Gardens or in Kensington Gardens. He realizes, what Peter Pan could not be made to realize, that a plain human house of one's own, standing in one's own backyard, is really quite as romantic as a rather cloudy house at the top of a tree or a highly conspiratorial house underneath the roots of it.

But this is because he has explored his own house, which Peter Pan and such discontented children seldom do. All the same, the children ought to think of the Never-Never Land—the world that is outside. But we ought to think of the Ever-Ever Land—the world which is inside, and the world which will last. And that is why, wicked as we are, we know most about Christmas.

ON THIS DAY

- In 1933, H. G. Wells wrote to Chesterton saying, "An *Illustrated London News* Xmas cutting comes like the season's greetings. If after all my Atheology turns out wrong and your Theology right I feel I shall always be able to pass into Heaven (if I want to) as a friend of G. K. C.'s. Bless you."

DECEMBER 11

And your heart shall rejoice, and your joy no man taketh from you.

—JOHN 16:22

So long as the Christmas feast had some kind of assumed and admitted meaning, it was praised, and praised sympathetically, by the great men whom we should call most unsympathetic with it. That Shakespeare and Dickens and Walter Scott should write of it seems quite natural. They were people who would be as welcome at Christmas as Santa Claus. But I do not think many people have ever wished they could ask Milton to eat the Christmas pudding.

Nevertheless, it is quite certain that his Christmas ode is not only one of the richest but one of the most human of his master-pieces. I do not think that anyone specially wanting a rollicking article on Christmas would desire, by mere instinct, the literary style of Addison. Yet it is quite certain that the somewhat diffi-cult task of really liking Addison is rendered easier by his account of the Coverley Christmas than by anything else he wrote.

I even go so far as to doubt whether one of the little Cratchits (who stuffed their spoons in their mouths lest they should scream for goose) would have removed the spoon to say, "Oh, that Tennyson were here!" Yet certainly Tennyson's spirits do seem to revive in a more or less real way at the ringing of the Christmas bells in the most melancholy part of *In Memoriam*.

These great men were not trying to be merry: some of them, indeed, were trying to be miserable. But the day itself was too strong for them; the time was more than their temperaments; the tradition was alive. The festival was roaring in the streets, so that [they] were honestly carried off their feet.

DECEMBER 12

And thou shalt have joy and gladness; and many shall rejoice at his birth.

—Luke 1:14

In such a sacred cloud the tale called *The Christmas Carol* begins, the first and most typical of all [Dickens's] Christmas tales . . .

It has the same kind of artistic unity that belongs to a dream. A dream may begin with the end of the world and end with a tea-party; but either the end of the world will seem as trivial as a tea-party or that tea-party will be as terrible as the day of doom.

The incidents change wildly; the story scarcely changes at all: *The Christmas Carol* is a kind of philanthropic dream, an enjoyable nightmare, in which the scenes shift bewilderingly and seem as miscellaneous as the pictures in a scrap-book, but in which there is one constant state of the soul, a state of rowdy benediction and a hunger for human faces.

A PASSAGE FROM *THE WILD KNIGHT* (1900)

> *... is it not time*
> *Some of Love's chosen broke the girth,*
> *And told the good all men have known,*
> *Since the first morning of the earth?*

ON THIS DAY

- In 1931, GKC's article "Hazy Language About the Creed" was published in the *Illustrated London News*.

DECEMBER 13

> *Be glad in the Lord, and rejoice, ye righteous: and shout for joy.*
>
> —PSALM 32:11

One of the carols has for a sort of rowdy refrain the more or less meaningless halloo of "Ut hoy!"

Even reading it on a printed page after five hundred years, it is impossible not to have a sort of illusion that we are hearing the loud but distant hail of some hearty shepherd far away upon the hills. If it is ever sung, that chorus can hardly be sung too loud.

I will not attempt to inquire here why the mediæval carol, as distinct from the modern hymn, could manage to achieve the resounding reality of that shout. I should be inclined to suggest that some part of it may have been due to men really believing that there was something to shout about.

But certainly the spirit of Christmas is in these songs more than in any other literature that has since been produced; and if I am forbidden by good taste to express myself in theological terms, I will confine myself to saying in a loud voice, "Ut hoy!"

A PASSAGE FROM *THE WILD KNIGHT* (1900)

> *That though the jest be old as night,*
> *Still shaketh sun and sphere,*
> *An everlasting laughter,*
> *Too loud for us to hear.*

ON THIS DAY

- In 1930, GKC's article "On Progress, and Overthrowing Progress" was published in the *Illustrated London News.*

DECEMBER 14

> *He hath shewed thee, O man, what is good.*
> —MICAH 6:8

Christmas is . . . not a moveable feast. Many excessive schools of lunatics have tried in vain to move it, and even to move it away. In spite of all sorts of intellectual irritations and pedantic explaining away, human beings will almost certainly go on observing this winter feast in some fashion.

If it is for them only a winter feast, they will be found celebrating it with winter sports. If it is for them only a heathen feast, they will keep it as the heathens do. But the great majority of them will go on observing forms that cannot be so explained; they will keep Christmas day with Christmas gifts and Christmas benedictions; they will continue to do it; and some day suddenly they will wake up and discover why.

A PASSAGE FROM *THE WILD KNIGHT* (1900)

> *The dolls have crowns and aureoles,*
> *Helmets and horns and wings,*
> *For they are the saints and seraphim,*
> *The prophets and the kings.*

ON THIS DAY

- In 1929, GKC's article "The Age of America" was published in the *Illustrated London News*.

DECEMBER 15

Blessed are you poor, for yours is the kingdom of God.
Blessed are you who hunger now, for you shall be filled.
—LUKE 6:20–21 NKJV

I have never read anything at all adequate about the very beautiful and profound tradition of the "soul-cake" or "souling cake" connected with the ceremony of All Soul's Eve. The passage about it in this book [on *Funeral Customs*] is necessarily brief but very compact and contains some valuable information. It also contains a version which I had not seen of that very touching appeal in which there is all the tender irony of the Christian idea. The last two lines are given here thus:

> *If you ain't got a penny, a ha'penny will do,*
> *If you ain't got a ha'penny, then God bless you.*

I have always thought there was something very moving in that last gesture, admitting the man addressed into the brotherhood of the poor.

CHRISTMASTIME AS GKC SAW IT

On this day . . . children go door to door singing songs and asking for soul cakes.

A BIT OF WHIMSY

> *Behold the simple sum of things*
> *Where, in one splendour spun,*
> *The stars go round the Mulberry Bush,*
> *The Burning Bush, the Sun.*

DECEMBER 16

Behold, a virgin shall be with child, and shall bring forth
a son, and they shall call his name Emmanuel, which
being interpreted is, God with us.

—MATTHEW 1:23

Hark! Laughter like a lion wakes
To roar to the resounding plain,
And the whole heaven shouts and shakes,
For God Himself is born again.

In his book, The Wild Knight of Battersea, *literary scholar F.A.*
Lea wrote of Chesterton's unique gift for describing the way that joy
touches life and literature. He had the ability, Lea said, to write of
"the love that is laughter." This ability was much in evidence when
Chesterton penned this brief, enigmatic, but very profound reflection
in his classic text, Orthodoxy. *"Perhaps," he wrote, "we sit in a starry*
chamber of silence, while the laughter of the heavens is too loud for us
to hear." This is a thought that Chesterton also rendered in verse:

Never we know but in sleet and snow
The place where the great fires are,
That the midst of earth is a raging mirth,
And the heart of the earth a star.

DECEMBER 17

> *And ye shall find rest unto your souls.*
> —MATTHEW 11:29

The beauty and the real blessing of the story do not lie in the mechanical plot of it, the repentance of Scrooge, probable or improbable; they lie in the great furnace of real happiness that glows through Scrooge and everything round him; that great furnace, the heart of Dickens.

Whether the Christmas visions would or would not convert Scrooge, they convert us. Whether or no the visions were evoked by real Spirits of the Past, Present, and Future, they were evoked by that truly exalted order of angels who are correctly called High Spirits. They are impelled and sustained by a quality which our contemporary artists ignore or almost deny, but which in a life decently lived is as normal and attainable as sleep, positive, passionate, conscious joy. The story sings from end to end like a happy man going home.

A PASSAGE FROM *CHARLES DICKENS: A CRITICAL STUDY* (1906)

Comfort, especially this vision of Christmas comfort, is the reverse of a gross or material thing. It is far more poetical, properly speaking, than the Garden of Epicurus. It is far more artistic than the Palace of Art. It is more artistic because it is based upon a contrast, a contrast between the fire and wine within the house and the winter and the roaring rains without. It is far more poetical, because there is in it a note of defence, almost of war; a note of being besieged by the snow and hail; of making merry in the belly of a fort. The man who said that an Englishman's house is his castle said much more than he meant.

A PASSAGE FROM *THE WILD KNIGHT* (1900)

This is the town of thine own home,
And thou hast looked on it at last.

DECEMBER 18

Blessed are the eyes which see the things that ye see.
—LUKE 10:23 NKJV

The greatest tribute to Christianity in the modern world is Tennyson's "Ulysses." The poet reads into the story of Ulysses the conception of an incurable desire to wander.

But the real Ulysses does not desire to wander at all. He desires to get home. He displays his heroic and unconquerable qualities in resisting the misfortunes which baulk him; but that is all. There is no love of adventure for its own sake; that is a Christian product. There is no love of Penelope for her own sake; that is a Christian product. Everything in that old world would appear to have been clean and obvious. A good man was a good man; a bad man was a bad man.

For this reason they had no charity; for charity is a reverent agnosticism towards the complexity of the soul. For this reason they had no such thing as the art of fiction, the novel; for the novel is a creation of the mystical idea of charity. For them a pleasant landscape was pleasant, and an unpleasant landscape unpleasant. Hence they had no idea of romance; for romance consists in thinking a thing more delightful because it is dangerous; it is a Christian idea.

A BIT OF WHIMSY

I had a rather funny dream,
Intense, that is, and mystic;
I dreamed that, with one leap and yell,
The world became artistic.

DECEMBER 19

Happy shalt thou be, and it shall be well with thee.
—Psalm 128:2

The Christmas Carol owes much of its hilarity to [a] second source—the fact of its being a tale of winter and of a very wintry winter. There is much about comfort in the story; yet the comfort is never enervating: it is saved from that by a tingle of something bitter and bracing in the weather.

Lastly, the story exemplifies throughout the power of the third principle—the kinship between gaiety and the grotesque. Everybody is happy because nobody is dignified. We have a feeling somehow that Scrooge looked even uglier when he was kind than he had looked when he was cruel. The turkey that Scrooge bought was so fat, says Dickens, that it could never have stood upright. That top-heavy and monstrous bird is a good symbol of the top-heavy happiness of the stories.

FROM *GREYBEARDS AT PLAY* (1900)

We aged ones play solemn parts—
Sire—guardian—uncle—king.
Affection is the salt of life,
Kindness a noble thing.

ON THIS DAY

• In 1931, GKC's article "The Cult of Success" was published in the *Illustrated London News*.

DECEMBER 20

I went with them to the house of God, with the voice of
joy and praise, with a multitude that kept holyday.
—PSALM 42:4

Dickens might seem a strange champion for so historical and poetical a tradition [as Christmas]. He wrote no poetry; he knew no history. For the historical book which he wrote for children has not half so much right to be called history as Sam Weller's cheerful song beginning "Bold Turpin vunce" has to be called poetry. He saved Christmas not because it was historic, but because it was human.

A PASSAGE FROM *TREMENDOUS TRIFLES* (1909)

[This novel] describes two innocent children gradually growing at once omniscient and half-witted under the influence of the foul ghosts of a groom and a governess. As I say, I doubt whether Mr. Henry James ought to have published it . . . but I will give that truly great man a

chance. I will approve the thing, as well as admire it, if he will write another tale just as powerful about two children and Santa Claus.

A BIT OF WHIMSY

I am, I think I have remarked,
Terrifically old,
(The second Ice-age was a farce,
The first was rather cold.)

DECEMBER 21

Let us draw near with a true heart.
—HEBREWS 10:22 NKJV

The popular paradox of *A Christmas Carol* is very well symbolised in its title. Everybody has heard Christmas carols; and certainly everybody has heard of Christmas.

Yet these things are only popular because they are traditional; and the tradition has often been in need of defence, as Dickens here defended it.

If a little more success had crowned the Puritan movement of the seventeenth century, or the Utilitarian movement of the nineteenth century, these things would, humanly speaking, have become merely details of the neglected past, a part of history or even of archaeology.

ON THIS DAY ────────────────────────────

- In 1929, GKC's article "The Psychological Theory of History" was published in the *Illustrated London News*.

DECEMBER 22

*The whole land is made desolate, because no man layeth
it to heart.*

—Jeremiah 12:11

The historical and moral importance [of *A Christmas Carol*] is
really even greater than the literary importance. In this respect
it bears some resemblance to another of his works, which might
seem superficially its very contrary. *A Christmas Carol* is perhaps the most genial and fanciful of all his stories. *Hard Times*
is perhaps the most grim and realistic.

But in both cases the moral beauty is perhaps greater than
the artistic beauty; and both stand higher in any study of the
man than of the writer. And although one represents the first
skirmish in defence of the old traditions, and the second the
final pitched battle against the new theories, in both cases the
author is fighting for the same cause. He is fighting an old miser
named Scrooge, and a new miser named Gradgrind; but it is
not only true that the new miser has the old avarice, it is also
true that the old miser has the new arguments.

Scrooge is a utilitarian and an individualist; that is, he is a
miser in theory as well as in practise. He utters all the sophistries
by which the age of machinery has tried to turn the virtue of charity into a vice. Indeed this is something of an understatement.
Scrooge is not only as modern as Gradgrind but more modern
than Gradgrind. He belongs not only to the hard times of the
middle of the nineteenth century, but to the harder times of the
beginning of the twentieth century; the yet harder times in which
we live.

DECEMBER 23

> *Verily I say unto you, inasmuch as ye have done it unto*
> *one of the least of these my brethren, ye have done it*
> *unto me.*
>
> —MATTHEW 25:40

Dickens gives the right reply; and that with a deadly directness worthy of a much older and more subtle controversionalist. The answer to anyone who talks about the surplus population is to ask him whether he is the surplus population; or if he is not, how he knows he is not.

That is the answer which the Spirit of Christmas gives to Scrooge; and there is more than one fine element of irony involved in it. . . . We have all met professors, of stunted figure and the most startling ugliness, who explain that all save the strong and beautiful should be painlessly extinguished in the interests of the race.

A PASSAGE FROM *ALL THINGS CONSIDERED* (1908)

But I say that whatever the day is that is to you festive or symbolic, it is essential that there should be a quite clear black line between it and the time going before. And all the old wholesome customs in connection with Christmas were to the effect that one should not touch or see or know or speak of something before the actual coming of Christmas Day. Thus, for instance, children were never given their presents until the actual coming of the appointed hour.

A BIT OF WHIMSY

Come snow! where fly, by some strange law,
Hard snowballs—without noise—
Through streets untenanted, except
By good unconscious boys.

DECEMBER 24

Our heart is enlarged.
—2 CORINTHIANS 6:11

Before we come to the question of what Dickens did for Christmas we must consider the question of what Christmas did for Dickens. How did it happen that this bustling, nineteenth-century man, full of the . . . utilitarian and liberal epoch, came to associate his name chiefly in literary history with [this] festival.

A PASSAGE FROM *THE USES OF DIVERSITY* (1920)

It is exactly because Christmas is not only a feast of children, but in some sense a feast of fools, that Dickens is in touch with its mystery.

FROM *GREYBEARDS AT PLAY* (1900)

There is a shout among the stars,
"To-night a child is born."

DECEMBER 25

THE HOUSE OF CHRISTMAS

There fared a mother driven forth
Out of an inn to roam;
In the place where she was homeless
All men are at home.
The crazy stable close at hand,
With shaking timber and shifting sand,
Grew a stronger thing to abide and stand
Than the square stones of Rome.

For men are homesick in their homes,
And strangers under the sun,
And they lay their heads in a foreign land
Whenever the day is done.
Here we have battle and blazing eyes,
And chance and honour and high surprise,
But our homes are under miraculous skies
Where the yule tale was begun.

A Child in a foul stable,
Where the beasts feed and foam;
Only where He was homeless
Are you and I at home;
We have hands that fashion and heads that know,
But our hearts we lost—how long ago!
In a place no chart nor ship can show
Under the sky's dome.

This world is wild as an old wives' tale,
And strange the plain things are,
The earth is enough and the air is enough
For our wonder and our war;

But our rest is as far as the fire-drake swings
And our peace is put in impossible things
Where clashed and thundered unthinkable wings
Round an incredible star.
To an open house in the evening
Home shall men come,
To an older place than Eden
And a taller town than Rome.
To the end of the way of the wandering star,
To the things that cannot be and that are,
To the place where God was homeless
And all men are at home.

DECEMBER 26

Return unto thy rest, O my soul; for the Lord hath dealt
bountifully with thee.

—PSALM 116:7

There are two ways of getting home; and one of them is to stay there.
The other is to walk around the whole world till we come back to the
same place; and I have tried to trace such a journey.

PASSAGES FROM *THE INNOCENCE OF FATHER BROWN* (1911)

"*The most beautiful crime I ever committed,*" Flambeau would say
in his highly moral old age, "*was also, by a singular coincidence, my
last. It was committed at Christmas.*"

"*. . . [it was] a cheery, cosy, English middle-class crime; a crime
of Charles Dickens. I did it in a good old middleclass house near
Putney, a house with a crescent of carriage drive, a house with a*

stable by the side of it, a house with the name on the two outer gates, a house with a monkey tree. Enough, you know the species. I really think my imitation of Dickens's style was dexterous and literary. It seems almost a pity I repented the same evening."

Crook looked at him with an eye of interest and even respect. "Does one want to own soot?" he asked.

"One might," answered Brown, with speculation in his eye. "I've heard that gardeners use it. And I once made six children happy at Christmas when the conjuror didn't come, entirely with soot— applied externally."

"Oh, splendid," cried Ruby. "Oh, I wish you'd do it to this company."

ON THIS DAY

• In 1931, GKC's article "Chaucer and Christmas" was published in the *Illustrated London News*.

DECEMBER 27

Thou art my Son, this day have I begotten thee.
—Acts 13:33

The sketch of the human story began in a cave; the cave which popular science associates with the cave-man and in which practical discovery has really found archaic drawings of animals. The second half of human history, which was like a new creation of the world, also begins in a cave. There is even a shadow of such a fancy in the fact that animals were again present; for it was a cave used as a stable . . .

It was here that a homeless couple had crept underground with the cattle when the doors of the caravanserai [roadside inn] had been shut in their faces; and it was here beneath the very feet of the passers-by, in a cellar under the very floor of the world, that Jesus Christ was born.

ON THIS DAY ————————————————————————

- In 1930, GKC's article "The Return of Old Things" was published in the *Illustrated London News*.

DECEMBER 28

The revelation of the mystery, which was kept secret since the world began . . .

—ROMANS 16:25

A mass of legend and literature has repeated and rung the changes on that single paradox; that the hands that had made the sun and stars were too small to reach the huge heads of the cattle. Upon this paradox, we might almost say upon this jest, all the literature of our faith is founded.

It is at least like a jest in this, that it is something which the scientific critic cannot see. He laboriously explains the difficulty which we have always defiantly and almost derisively exaggerated; and mildly condemns as improbable something that we have almost madly exalted as incredible; as something that would be much too good to be true, except that it is true.

When that contrast between the cosmic creation and the little local infancy has been repeated, reiterated, underlined, emphasised, exulted in, sung, shouted, roared, not to say howled, in a hundred thousand hymns, carols, rhymes, rituals, pictures, poems, and popular sermons, it may be suggested that we hardly need a higher critic to draw our attention to something a little odd about it; especially one of the sort that seems to take a long time to see a joke, even his own joke.

ON THIS DAY ———————————————————————

• In 1929, GKC's article "The Age of Macaulay and Religion" was published in the *Illustrated London News*.

DECEMBER 29

> *But when the fulness of the time was come, God sent forth his Son.*
>
> —GALATIANS 4:4

And the thing [the shepherds] found was of a kind with the things they sought. The populace had been wrong in many things; but they had not been wrong in believing that holy things could have a habitation and that divinity need not disdain the limits of time and space.

ON THIS DAY ———————————————————————

• In 1919, GKC and his wife, Frances, set out for France, the first leg of a journey that would eventually take them to the Holy Land.

DECEMBER 30

*Grace be unto you, and peace, from him which is, and
which was, and which is to come.*

—REVELATION 1:4

. . . under the fulness and the sonorous sanity of Christian
bells.

A PASSAGE FROM *WHAT'S WRONG WITH THE WORLD* (1910)

*Religion, the immortal maiden, has been a maid-of-all-work as
well as a servant of mankind. She provided men at once with the
theoretic laws of an unalterable cosmos; and also with the practical
rules of the rapid and thrilling game of morality. She taught logic
to the student and taught fairy tales to the children; it was her business to confront the nameless gods whose fear is on all flesh, and
also to see that the streets were spotted with silver and scarlet, that
there was a day for wearing ribbons or an hour for ringing bells.*

DECEMBER 31

*Be thou exalted, O God, above the heavens: let thy glory
be above all the earth.*

—PSALM 57:11

*There is but one thing
Which is both work and wage,
Both wound and healing,
Both journey and inn,*

> *Both motive and method,*
> *Both master and servant,*
> *Both giving and receiving,*
> *Both law and freedom,*
> *Both antiquity and novelty,*
> *Both tradition and revolution,*
> *Both mystery and familiarity,*
> *Both innocence and knowledge,*
> *Both germ and consummation,*
> *Both child and ancient,*
> *Both origin and aim.*

ON THIS DAY

- In 1919, GKC and his wife, Frances, arrived in Rome, part of a journey that would eventually take them to the Holy Land.

Supplemental Readings

The Main Festival Days of the Church

ASH WEDNESDAY

> *For the vision is yet for an appointed time, but at the end*
> *it shall speak, and not lie: though it tarry, wait for it;*
> *because it will surely come, it will not tarry.*
>
> —HABAKKUK 2:3

Religion is revelation. In other words it is a vision, and a vision received by faith; but it is a vision of reality. The faith consists in a conviction of its reality.

A PASSAGE FROM *THE EVERLASTING MAN* (1925)

And this is why [religion] had to be a revelation or vision given from above. Any one who will think of the theory of stories or pictures will easily see the point. The true story of the world must be told by somebody to somebody else. By the very nature of a story it cannot be left to occur to anybody. A story has proportions, variations, surprises, particular dispositions, which cannot be worked out by rule in the abstract, like a sum . . .

A man might perhaps work out a proposition of Euclid without having heard of Euclid; but he would not work out the precise legend of Eurydice without having heard of Eurydice. At any rate he would not be certain how the story would end and whether Orpheus was ultimately defeated. Still less could he guess the end of our story; or the legend of our Orpheus rising, not defeated from, the dead.

A WORD OF THE DAY

A civilisation that had religion would have a little more reason.

GOOD FRIDAY

Who by him do believe in God, that raised him up from the dead, and gave him glory; that your faith and hope might be in God.

—I PETER 1:21

[The faith] has endured for nearly two thousand years; and the world within it has been more lucid, more level-headed, more reasonable in its hopes, more healthy in its instincts, more humorous and cheerful in the face of fate and death, than all the world outside. For it was the soul of Christendom that came forth from the incredible Christ.

A PASSAGE FROM *THE EVERLASTING MAN* (1925)

Right in the middle of all these things stands up an enormous exception. It is quite unlike anything else. It is a thing final like the trump of doom, though it is also a piece of good news; or news that seems too good to be true. It is nothing less than the loud assertion that this mysterious maker of the world has visited his world in person.

In Christendom hope has never been absent; rather it has been errant, extravagant, excessively fixed upon fugitive chances.

EASTER DAY

> For I delivered unto you first of all that which I also
> received, how that Christ died for our sins according to
> the scriptures; and that he was buried, and that he rose
> again the third day.
>
> —1 CORINTHIANS 15:3–4

A PASSAGE FROM *AS I WAS SAYING* (1936)

The historical case for the Resurrection is that everybody else,
except the Apostles, had every possible motive to declare what they
had done with the body, if anything had been done with it. The
Apostles might have hidden it in order to announce a sham miracle,
but it is very difficult to imagine men being tortured and killed for
the truth of a miracle which they knew to be a sham.

A PASSAGE FROM *ALL I SURVEY* (1933)

I believe that, again and again, man was at the cross-roads and
might have taken another road. Nobody can prove or disprove it
metaphysically; but I am the more content with a philosophy which
permits of occasional miracles, because the alternative philosophy
does not even permit of alternatives. It forbids a man even to dream
of anything so natural as the Ifs of History.

ASCENSION DAY

And while they looked stedfastly toward heaven as
he went up, behold, two men stood by them in white
apparel; which also said, Ye men of Galilee, why stand ye
gazing up into heaven? this same Jesus, which is taken up
from you into heaven, shall so come in like manner as ye
have seen him go into heaven.

—ACTS 1:10–11

PASSAGES FROM *THE NEW JERUSALEM* (1921)

Then I looked up and saw in the long jagged lines of road and rock and cleft something of the swiftness of such a thunderbolt. What I saw seemed not so much a scene as an act; as when abruptly Michael barred the passage of the Lord of Pride. Below me all the empire of evil was splashed and scattered upon the plain, like a wine-cup shattered into a star. Sodom lay like Satan, flat upon the floor of the world. And far away and aloft, faint with height and distance, small but still visible, stood up the spire of the Ascension like the sword of the Archangel, lifted in salute after a stroke.

We went in a little rocking Ford car down steep and jagged roads among ribbed and columned cliffs; but the roads below soon failed us altogether; and the car had to tumble like a tank over rocky banks and into empty river-beds, long before it came to the sinister and discoloured landscapes of the Dead Sea. And the distance looks far enough on the map, and seems long enough in the motor journey, to make a man feel he has come to another part of the world; yet so much is it all a single fall of land that even when he gets out beyond Jordan in the wild country of the Shereef he can still look back and see, small and faint as if in the clouds, the spire of the Russian church (I fancy) upon the hill of the Ascension.

THE DAY OF PENTECOST

> And when the day of Pentecost was fully come, they were
> all with one accord in one place. And suddenly there
> came a sound from heaven as of a rushing mighty wind,
> and it filled all the house where they were sitting. And
> there appeared unto them cloven tongues like as of fire,
> and it sat upon each of them. And they were all filled
> with the Holy Ghost.
>
> —ACTS 2:1–4

A PASSAGE FROM *ORTHODOXY* (1908)

*Last and most important, it is exactly this which explains what is so
inexplicable to all the modern critics of the history of Christianity. I
mean the monstrous wars about small points of theology, the earth-
quakes of emotion about a gesture or a word.*

*It was only a matter of an inch; but an inch is everything when
you are balancing. The Church could not afford to swerve a hair's
breadth on some things if she was to continue her great and daring
experiment of the irregular equilibrium. Once let one idea become
less powerful and some other idea would become too powerful. It
was no flock of sheep the Christian shepherd was leading, but a
herd of bulls and tigers, of terrible ideals and devouring doctrines,
each one of them strong enough to turn to a false religion and lay
waste the world. Remember that the Church went in specifically for
dangerous ideas; she was a lion tamer.*

*The idea of birth through a Holy Spirit, of the death of a divine
being, of the forgiveness of sins, or the fulfilment of prophecies, are
ideas which, any one can see, need but a touch to turn them into
something blasphemous or ferocious . . .*

Of these theological equalisations I have to speak afterwards.

Here it is enough to notice that if some small mistake were made in doctrine, huge blunders might be made in human happiness. A sentence phrased wrong about the nature of symbolism would have broken all the best statues in Europe. A slip in the definitions might stop all the dances; might wither all the Christmas trees or break all the Easter eggs. Doctrines had to be defined within strict limits, even in order that man might enjoy general human liberties. The Church had to be careful, if only that the world might be careless.

This is the thrilling romance of Orthodoxy. People have fallen into a foolish habit of speaking of orthodoxy as something heavy, humdrum, and safe. There never was anything so perilous or so exciting as orthodoxy.

TRINITY SUNDAY

And Jesus, when he was baptized, went up straightway out of the water: and, lo, the heavens were opened unto him, and he saw the Spirit of God descending like a dove, and lighting upon him. And lo a voice from heaven, saying, This is my beloved Son, in whom I am well pleased.
— MATTHEW 3:16–17

A PASSAGE FROM *THE THING: WHY I AM A CATHOLIC* (1930)

A thinking man can think himself deeper and deeper into Catholicism . . . the great mysteries like the Blessed Trinity or the Blessed Sacrament are the starting-point for trains of thought . . .

To accept the Logos as a truth is to be in the atmosphere of the absolute, not only with St. John the Evangelist, but with Plato and all the great mystics of the world . . . To exalt the Mass is to enter into a magnificent world of metaphysical ideas, illuminating all the

*relations of matter and mind, of flesh and spirit, of the most imper-
sonal abstractions as well as the most personal affections . . .*

*Even what are called the fine doctrinal distinctions are not dull.
They are like the finest operations of surgery; separating nerve from
nerve but giving life.*

HOLY CROSS DAY, SEPTEMBER 14

*For to this end Christ both died, and rose, and revived,
that he might be Lord both of the dead and living.*

—ROMANS 14:9

I picked up the rather remarkable book called *Who Moved the
Stone?* under the impression that it was a detective story . . . and
so it was, and a good one. It was a mystery story, though in the
higher sense of dealing with the mysteries of religion, [specifi-
cally] the evidence for the Resurrection . . .

The author, Mr. Frank Morrison, writes with a dry detachment worthy of the school of scepticism. Strangely enough, the
writer himself set out from that school; for he began as a sceptic
and . . . became sceptical of scepticism.

A PASSAGE FROM *A MISCELLANY OF MEN* (1912)

*And when I look across the sun-struck fields, I know in my inmost
bones that my joy is not solely in the spring; for spring alone, being
always returning, would always be sad. There is something or somebody walking there, to be crowned with flowers; and my pleasure
is in some promise yet possible, and in the resurrection of the dead.*

ALL SAINTS' DAY, NOVEMBER 1

Others were tortured, not accepting deliverance; that
they might obtain a better resurrection: and others had
trial of cruel mockings and scourgings, yea, moreover of
bonds and imprisonment: they were stoned, they were
sawn asunder, were tempted, were slain with the sword:
they wandered about in sheepskins and goatskins; being
destitute, afflicted, tormented; (of whom the world was
not worthy:) they wandered in deserts, and in mountains,
and in dens and caves of the earth.

—HEBREWS 11:35–38

GKC's hymn "O God of Earth and Altar" was first performed in 1913, and is traditionally sung to an English melody arranged by Ralph Vaughan Williams.

> *O God of earth and altar,*
> *Bow down and hear our cry,*
> *Our earthly rulers falter,*
> *Our people drift and die;*
> *The walls of gold entomb us,*
> *The swords of scorn divide,*
> *Take not thy thunder from us,*
> *But take away our pride.*
> *From all that terror teaches,*
> *From lies of tongue and pen,*
> *From all the easy speeches*
> *That comfort cruel men,*
> *From sale and profanation*
> *Of honour and the sword,*
> *From sleep and from damnation,*

> *Deliver us, good Lord.*
> *Tie in a living tether*
> *The priest and prince and thrall,*
> *Bind all our lives together,*
> *Smite us and save us all;*
> *In ire and exultation*
> *Aflame with faith, and free,*
> *Lift up a living nation,*
> *A single sword to Thee.*

THE VISIT OF THE VIRGIN MARY TO ELISABETH, MAY 31

> *And whence is this to me, that the mother of my Lord*
> *should come to me?*
>
> —LUKE 1:43

In any case, I can never recapture in words the waves of sympathy with strange things that went through me in that twilight of the tall pillars, like giants robed in purple, standing still and looking down into that dark hole in the ground.

Here halted that imperial civilization, when it had marched in triumph through the whole world; here in the evening of its days it came trailing in all its panoply in the pathway of the three kings. For it came following not only a falling but a fallen star and one that dived before them into a birthplace darker than a grave.

And the lord of the laurels, clad in his sombre crimson, looked down into that darkness, and then looked up, and saw that all the stars in his own sky were dead. They were deities no longer but only a brilliant dust, scattered down the vain void of Lucretius.

The stars were as stale as they were strong; they would never die for they had never lived; they were cursed with an incurable immortality that was but the extension of mortality; they were chained in the chains of causation and unchangeable as the dead. There are not many men in the modern world who do not know that mood, though it was not discovered by the moderns; it was the final and seemingly fixed mood of nearly all the ancients. Only above the black hole of Bethlehem they had seen a star wandering like a lost spark; and it had done what the eternal suns and planets could not do.

CHRISTMAS DAY, DECEMBER 25

And they came with haste, and found Mary, and Joseph, and the babe lying in a manger.

—LUKE 2:16

LINES FROM "THE WISE MEN"

The Child that was ere worlds begun
(. . . We need but walk a little way . . .
We need but see a latch undone . . .)
The Child that played with moon and sun
Is playing with a little hay.

FROM MAISIE WARD'S BIOGRAPHY, *GILBERT KEITH CHESTERTON* (1943)

I should like to collect all the essays and poems on Christmas; he wrote several every year, yet each is different, each goes to the heart of his thought.

As Christopher Morley says: "One of the simple greatnesses of

G. K. C. shows in this, that we think of him instinctively toward Christmas time."

Some men, it may be, are best moved to reform by hate, but Chesterton was best moved by love—and nowhere does that love shine more clearly than in all he wrote about Christmas. It will be for this philosophy, this charity, this poetry, that men will turn over the pages of G. K.'s Weekly a century hence.

THE EPIPHANY, JANUARY 6

> And the angel answered and said unto her, The Holy Ghost shall come upon thee, and the power of the Highest shall overshadow thee: therefore also that holy thing which shall be born of thee shall be called the Son of God.
>
> —LUKE 1:35

After one moment when I bowed my head
And the whole world turned over and came upright,
And I came out where the old road shone white,
I walked the ways and heard what all men said.
Step softly, under snow or rain,
To find the place where men can pray;
The way is all so very plain,
That we may lose the way.
Oh, we have learnt to peer and pore
On tortured puzzles from our youth.
We know all labyrinthine lore,
We are the three Wise Men of yore,
And we know all things but the truth.
Go humbly . . . it has hailed and snowed

With voices low and lanterns lit,
So very simple is the road,
That we may stray from it.

GEORGE, MARTYR, PATRON OF ENGLAND, APRIL 23

Who hath delivered us from the power of darkness, and
hath translated us into the kingdom of his dear Son.
—COLOSSIANS 1:13

Lydda or Ludd has already been noted as the legendary birthplace of St. George, and as the camp on the edge of the desert from which, as it happened, I caught the first glimpse of the coloured fields of Palestine that looked like the fields of Paradise. Being an encampment of soldiers, it seems an appropriate place for St. George; and indeed it may be said that all that red and empty land has resounded with his name like a shield of copper or of bronze . . .

Whatever we think of St. George, most people would see a mere fairy-tale in St. George and the Dragon. I dare say they are right; and I only use it here as a figure for the sake of argument . . .

St. George is but a servant and the Dragon is but a symbol, but [this story] is precisely about the central reality, the mystery of Christ and His mastery of the powers of darkness.

A PASSAGE FROM *TREMENDOUS TRIFLES* (1909)

Fairy tales, then, are not responsible for producing in children fear, or any of the shapes of fear; fairy tales do not give the child the idea of the evil or the ugly; that is in the child already, because it is in the world already. *Fairy tales do not give the child his first idea of bogey. What fairy tales give the child is his first clear idea of the possible defeat of bogey. The baby has known the dragon intimately ever since he had an imagination. What the fairy tale provides for him is a St. George to kill the dragon.*

Exactly what the fairy tale does is this: it accustoms him for a series of clear pictures to the idea that these limitless terrors had a limit, that these shapeless enemies have enemies in the knights of God, that there is something in the universe more mystical than darkness, and stronger than strong fear.

PETER AND PAUL, APOSTLES, JUNE 29

And when it was day, he called unto him his disciples: and of them he chose twelve, whom also he named apostles.

—LUKE 6:13

But if there really be anything of the nature of progress, it must mean, above all things, the careful study and assumption of the whole of the past. I accuse Mr. Lowes Dickinson and his school of reaction in the only real sense. If he likes, let him ignore these great historic mysteries—the mystery of charity, the mystery of chivalry, the mystery of faith. If he likes, let him ignore the plough or the printing-press. But if we do revive and pursue the pagan ideal of a simple and rational self-completion we shall end—where Paganism ended. I do not mean that we shall end in destruction. I mean that we shall end in Christianity.

A PASSAGE FROM *ALL I SURVEY* (1933)

I believe that, again and again, man was at the cross-roads and might have taken another road. Nobody can prove or disprove it metaphysically; but I am the more content with a philosophy which permits of occasional miracles, because the alternative philosophy does not even permit of alternatives. It forbids a man even to dream of anything so natural as the Ifs of History.

The Secularist says that Christianity has been a gloomy and ascetic thing, and points to the procession of austere or ferocious saints who have given up home and happiness . . . But it never seems to occur to him that the very oddity and completeness of these men's surrender make it look very much as if there were really something actual and solid in the thing for which they sold themselves.

MARY MAGDALENE, JULY 22

Ye are all the children of light, and the children of the day: we are not of the night, nor of darkness.

—I Thessalonians 5:5

They took the body down from the cross and one of the few rich men among the first Christians obtained permission to bury it in a rock tomb in his garden; the Romans setting a military guard lest there should be some riot and attempt to recover the body. There was once more a natural symbolism in these natural proceedings; it was well that the tomb should be sealed with all the secrecy of ancient eastern sepulture and guarded by the authority of the Caesars. For in that second cavern the whole of that great and glorious humanity which we call antiquity was gathered up and covered over; and in that place it was buried. It was the end of a very great thing called human history; the history that was merely human. The mythologies and the philosophies were buried there, the gods and the heroes and the sages. In the great Roman phrase, they had lived. But as they could only live, so they could only die; and they were dead.

On the third day the friends of Christ coming at daybreak to the place found the grave empty and the stone rolled away. In varying ways they realised the new wonder; but even they hardly realised that the world had died in the night. What they were looking at was the first day of a new creation, with a new heaven and a new earth; and in a semblance of the gardener God walked again in the garden, in the cool not of the evening but the dawn.

ACKNOWLEDGMENTS

In a book of this kind, expressions of gratitude must necessarily be brief. But they are no less heartfelt for all that. I here wish to acknowledge my debt to many Chestertonians—friends who have shown me and my books much kindness. So to Joseph Pearce, Malcolm Guite, Dale Ahlquist, and Nancy Brown—my sincere thanks. I have benefitted greatly from your knowledge of GKC, and your reflections on his life and legacy.

To Os Guinness, here's another book to say thank you for all that your books have meant to me. To Lady Davson, in whose home the Chestertons, Gilbert and Frances, stayed over one hundred years ago—a small tribute of thanks for so graciously hosting my wife, Kelly, our little son, Sam, and me. Mermaid Street, Number 4, is a place where the gift of friendship was everywhere in evidence during our stay. I think of Rye, as I do so often of Chesterton, with much gratitude. Thank you, Kate.

And to Kelly and Sam themselves, bless you both for being my family, each day is a gift. I shall always remember Christmas (a time Chesterton loved and celebrated in his writings) as a time when a rare first British edition of *The Ball and the Cross* was given to me as a present—along with another first of GKC's literary biography *Robert Louis Stevenson*. Both have become treasured companions for my journey. But best of all, by far, is that I get to share my journey with you.

BIBLIOGRAPHY

Review of *All Things Considered*, by G. K. Chesterton. *The Spectator*, November 7, 1908: 710.

Belloc, Hilaire. *Verses*. New York: Laurence Gomme, 1916.

Berdan, J. M. *Modern Essays*. Edited by J. M. Berdan, J. R. Schultz, et al. New York: Macmillan, 1915.

Chesterton, G. K. *Alarms and Discursions*. London: Methuen and Co., Ltd., 1910.

———. *All I Survey*. London: Methuen and Co., 1934.

———. *All Things Considered*. New York: John Lane Company, 1913.

———. *Appreciations and Criticisms of Charles Dickens*. London: J. M. Dent and Sons, Ltd., 1911.

———. *Autobiography*. London: Hutchinson and Co., 1936.

———. *Avowals and Denials*. New York: Dodd, Mead and Company, 1935.

———. *The Ball and the Cross*. New York: John Lane Company, 1909.

———. *The Ballad of St. Barbara and Other Verses*. London: Cecil Palmer, 1922.

———. *The Ballad of the White Horse*. London: Methuen and Co., 1911.

———. Introduction to *The Book of Job*. London: Cecil Palmer and Hayward, 1916.

———. Quoted in *The Catholic World* 116, no. 696.

———. *Charles Dickens: A Critical Study*. New York: Dodd, Mead and Company, 1906.

———. Quoted in "Chesterton Asks Amity." *New York Times*, April 10, 1921.

———. Quoted in "Chesterton Cites Shakespeare's Slip." *New York Times*, January 17, 1921.

———. *Chesterton Day by Day: Selections from the Writings in Prose and Verse of G. K. Chesterton, with an Extract for Every Day of the Year and for Each of the Moveable Feasts*, 2nd edition. London: Kegan, Paul, Trench, Trübner & Co. Ltd., 1912. Originally published in *The Daily News*.

———. Quoted in "Chesterton Here for Lecture Tour." *New York Times*, January 11, 1921.

———. Quoted in "Chesterton Talks on 'Health Perils.'" *New York Times*, January 24, 1921.

———. Introduction to *A Christmas Carol*, by Charles Dickens, vii–xi. London: Cecil Palmer, 1922.

———. *Christendom in Dublin*. London: Sheed and Ward, 1932.

———. Preface to *Christiana and Her Children: A Mystery Play*, by Lilian Ann Duncan Pearce. Longmans, Green and Company, 1914.

———. *The Collected Works of G. K. Chesterton: The Illustrated London News, 1929–1931*, vol. 35: 283–284. San Francisco: Ignatius Press, 1991.

———. Quoted in *Collier's* 44, February 19, 1910.

———. *The Crimes of England*. New York: John Lane Company, 1916.

———. Quoted in *The Daily News*, February 25, 1905.

———. *The Defendant*. New York: Dodd, Mead and Co., 1902.

———. From a review of *The Defendant*, by G. K. Chesterteron. *The Outlook* 72, no. 3, 1902.

———. *Divorce versus Democracy*. London: The Society of SS Peter and Paul—Publishers to the Church of England, 1916.

———. "The Eclipse of Sentiment." *The Outlook*, December 2, 1905.

———. Quoted in "Epic of 'Paradox Lost' is Chesterton's Hopes." *New York Times*, February 7, 1921.

———. Introduction to *Essays Literary and Critical*, by Matthew Arnold. London: J. M. Dent and Sons, Ltd., 1914.

———. *The Everlasting Man*. New York: Dodd, Mead and Company, 1925.

———. Introduction *Famous Paintings*. London: Cassell and Company, Limited, 1913.

———. *Fancies Versus Fads*. London: Methuen and Co., Ltd., 1923.

———. *The Flying Inn*. New York: John Lane Company, 1914.

———. "From the Notebooks of G. K. C." *The Tablet*, April 4, 1953.

———. *Generally Speaking*. New York: Dodd, Mead and Company, 1929. Originally published as "Defending Our English Institutions." *Illustrated London News*, June 11, 1927.

———. *Generally Speaking*. New York: Dodd, Mead and Company, 1929. Originally published as "The Falling Value of Words." *Illustrated London News*, May 21, 1927.

———. *Generally Speaking*. New York: Dodd, Mead and Company, 1929. Originally published as "On Being Impartial." *Illustrated London News*, March 22, 1924.

———. *Generally Speaking*. New York: Dodd, Mead and Company, 1929. Originally published as "On Sentimentalism." *Illustrated London News*, August 20, 1927.

———. *Generally Speaking*. New York: Dodd, Mead and Company, 1929. Originally published as "The Romance of the Past and the Romance of the Future." *Illustrated London News*, 1922.

———. *George Bernard Shaw*. New York: John Lane Company, 1909.

———. Introduction to *George MacDonald and His Wife*, by Greville MacDonald. London: George Allen and Unwin, 1924.

———. *G. F. Watts*. London: Ducksworth and Co., 1914.

———. *The G. K. C. Calendar: A Quotation from the Works of G. K. Chesterton for Every Day in the Year*, 2nd Edition. London: Cecil Palmer, 1921.

———. *Greybeards at Play*. London: R. Brimley Johnson, 1900.

———. *Heretics*. New York: John Lane Company, 1909.

———. *The Home Book of Verse*. New York: Henry Holt and Company, 1918.

———. Quoted in *The Homiletic Review* 71, no. 3 (March 1916).

———. Quoted in "'Inevitable? Bah!' says Chesterton." *New York Times*, January 22, 1921.

———. *The Innocence of Father Brown*. New York: John Lane Company, 1911.

———. *Irish Impressions*. Macmillan and Co., Ltd., 1904.

———. *Is It a New World?* London: Hodder and Stoughton, Ltd., 1920.

———. Preface to *The Little Wings: Poems and Essays*, by Vivienne Dayrell. Oxford: Basil Blackwell, 1921.

———. *The Living Age* 7, vol. 26. January, February, March 1905. Boston: The Living Age Company.

———. *The Living Age* 7, vol. 44, July, August, September 1909. Boston: The Living Age Company.

———. *The Man Who Was Thursday*. New York: Dodd, Mead and Company, 1910.

———. *A Miscellany of Men*. New York: Dodd, Mead and Company, 1912.

———. "Mr. Blatchford and My Neighbour." *The Daily News*, November 14, 1906.

———. *The Napoleon of Notting Hill*. London: John Lane Company, 1904.

———. *The New Jerusalem*. New York: George H. Doran, 1921.

———. *On Lying in Bed*. Edited by Alberto Manguel. Calgary, Canada: Bayeux Arts, 2000.

———. *On Running After One's Hat*. Edited by E. V. Knox. New York: Dodd, Mead and Company, 1933.

———. *Orthodoxy*. New York: John Lane Company, 1909.

———. Introduction to *The Pilgrim's Progress*, by John Bunyan. London: Cassell and Company, Ltd., 1904.

———. *Poems*. New York: Dodd, Mead and Company, 1922.

———. Quoted in *The Readers' Classics* 1. Edited by G. K. Chesterton, Holbrook Jackson, et al. Bath, England: Cedric Chivers, Ltd., 1919.

———. "The Riddle of Love." *The Collected Works of G. K. Chesterton* 10, 219. San Francisco: Ignatius Press, 2008.

———. *Robert Browning*. New York: The MacMillan Company, 1903.

———. "A Sally at Preventive Medicine." *Modern Medicine* 3, no. 2 (February 1921).

———. Introduction to *Samuel Johnson*, edited by Alice Meynell, vii–xx. London: Herbert and Daniel, 1911.

———. *A Shilling for My Thoughts: Being a Selection from the Essays, Stories, and Other Writings of G. K. Chesterton*, 3rd edition. London: Methuen and Co., Ltd., 1921.

———. Introduction to *The Song of Roland*, translated by Charles Scott Moncrieff, ix–xii. London: Chapman and Hall, Ltd., 1919.

———. *St. Francis of Assisi.* London: Hodder and Stoughton, Ltd., 1923.

———. *Stevenson.* New York: Dodd, Mead and Company, 1928.

———. *The Thing: Why I Am A Catholic.* New York: Dodd, Mead and Co., 1930.

———. *Tremendous Trifles.* New York: Dodd, Mead and Company, 1920.

———. *Twelve Types.* London: Arthur L. Humphreys, 1906.

———. *The Uses of Diversity.* London: Methuen and Co., Ltd., 1920.

———. *Varied Types.* New York: Dodd, Mead and Company, 1903.

———. *The Victorian Age in Literature.* New York: Henry Holt and Company, 1913.

———. Quoted in "What G. K. C. Thinks of Us." *New York Times,* March 27, 1921.

———. *What I Saw in America.* New York: Dodd, Mead and Company, 1922.

———. *What's Wrong with the World.* New York: Dodd, Mead and Company, 1910.

———. *The Wild Knight.* London: J. M. Dent and Sons, Ltd., 1914.

———. *William Blake.* London: Duckworth and Co., 1910.

———. *The Wisdom of Father Brown.* New York: John Lane Company, 1914.

———. *The Wit and Wisdom of G. K. Chesterton.* New York: Dodd, Mead and Company, 1911.

———. "Fallacies of the Futurists and New Thinking." *Writing of Today: Models of Journalistic Prose.* Edited by J. W. Cunliffe and G. R. Lomer. New York: The Century Co., 1920.

———. et al. *Leo Tolstoy.* London: Hodder and Stoughton, 1903.

"Chesterton—Angels' Advocate." *The Outlook,* February 26, 1921.

"Chesterton Arrives." *Publishers' Weekly,* January 15, 1921.

Francis, C. M. Review of *Manalive,* by Chesterton. *The Bookman* 35, no. 5 (July 1912).

Halford, E. W. "Culled from the Day's Reading." *Association Men* magazine, 46, no. 11 (July 1921).

Hamilton, Clayton. "The Function of Dramatic Criticism," *The Bookman* 35. New York: Dodd, Mead and Company, 1912.

Haw, George, ed. *The Religious Doubts of Democracy.* New York: The MacMillan Company, 1904.

Hill, Murray. "Murray Hill Sees Mr. Chesterton." *The Bookman* 53, no. 1, March 1921.

H. T. B. Quoted in *Life* magazine 77, no. 1999, February 24, 1921.

Hunt, W. H. *Preachers from the Pew: Lectures Delivered at St. Paul's Church, Covent Garden, Under the Auspices of the London Branch of the Christian Social Union.* London: W. H. Lord and Co., 1906.

Ker, Ian. *Chesterton.* Oxford: Oxford University Press, 2011.

Lea, F. L. *The Wild Knight of Battersea.* James Clarke and Co., Ltd., 1945.

Lewis, C. S. *On Stories and Other Essays on Literature.* Edited by Walter Hooper. New York: Harcourt Books, 1982.

Lewis, C. S. *Yours, Jack: Spiritual Direction from C. S. Lewis.* New York: HarperCollins, 2008.

Masterman, C. F. G. "G. K. Chesterton: An Appreciation." *The Bookman* 16. New York: Dodd, Mead and Company, 1903.

Maynard, Theodore. Introduction to *Poems*, by G. K. Chesterton, ix–xii. Toronto: McClelland and Stewart, Ltd., 1919.

Morris, George Perry. "Gilbert Keith Chesterton." *The Outlook*, November 25, 1905.

Pearce, Joseph. *Wisdom and Innocence: A Life of G. K. Chesterton*. London: Hodder and Stoughton, 1996.

R. B. P. Review of *The New Jerusalem*, by Chesterton. *Atlantic Monthly*, April 1921.

Sayer, George. *Jack: C. S. Lewis and His Times*. London: Macmillan, 1988.

Thomas, Rowland. "Stop Thief!" Review of *George Bernard Shaw*, by G. K. Chesterton. *Collier's* 44, November 27, 1909.

Ward, Maisie. *Gilbert Keith Chesterton*. New York: Sheed and Ward, 1943.

———. *Return to Chesterton*. New York: Sheed and Ward, 1952.

West, Julius. *G. K. Chesterton: A Critical Study*. New York: Dodd, Mead and Company, 1916.

Willing, Ernest J. "Gilbert Keith Chesterton, Christian Idealist." *The Homiletic Review*, 71, no. 3, March 1916.

Zacharias, Ravi. *Recapture the Wonder*. Nashville: Thomas Nelson, 2003.

ABOUT THE AUTHOR

An award-winning author, Kevin Belmonte lives in a seaside village in Maine. For six years, he was the lead script and historical consultant for the motion picture *Amazing Grace*, working closely with Oscar-nominated screenwriter Stephen Knight. For five years, his biography of Wilberforce has been required reading for a course on leadership and character formation at Harvard's Kennedy School of Government. He is also the author of a critically acclaimed literary biography of G. K. Chesterton, *Defiant Joy*. In 2011, he was a featured speaker at the twenty-fifth anniversary Oxbridge Summer Institute. In that setting, he taught seminars at Keble College, Oxford University, and Robinson College, Cambridge University.